D1391796

Penny Pepper is a writer, poet and well-known rights activist. She writes regularly for the *Guardian* and has appeared on *Newsnight*, Sky News, BBC Radio 5 Live and Radio 4's *Today* programme.

Her explicit, taboo-breaking book about sex and disabled people, *Desires Reborn*, was published in 2012, and in 2013 she won a Creative Future Literary Award. In 2014 her one-woman show, *Lost in Spaces*, premiered at the Soho Theatre before going on a successful UK tour. She has also performed in Oxford, Edinburgh and New York.

She is currently finishing work on a novel and her first collection of poetry. She lives in London.

With special thanks to Kevin and James Towner

FIRST
IN THE
WORLD
SOMEWHERE

THE TRUE ADVENTURES OF A
SCRIBBLER, SIREN, SAUCEPOT
AND PIONEER

PENNY
PEPPER

Unbound

This edition first published in 2017

Unbound
6th Floor Mutual House, 70 Conduit Street, London W1S 2GF

www.unbound.com

Text Design by Ellipsis

A CIP record for this book is available from the British Library

ISBN 978-1-78352-347-4 (trade hbk)
ISBN 978-1-78352-348-1 (ebook)
ISBN 978-1-78352-349-8 (limited edition)

Printed in Great Britain by Clays Ltd, St Ives Plc

1 3 5 7 9 8 6 4 2

To Tamsin with love because together we soared

Dear Reader,

The book you are holding came about in a rather different way to most others. It was funded directly by readers through a new website: Unbound. Unbound is the creation of three writers. We started the company because we believed there had to be a better deal for both writers and readers. On the Unbound website, authors share the ideas for the books they want to write directly with readers. If enough of you support the book by pledging for it in advance, we produce a beautifully bound special subscribers' edition and distribute a regular edition and e-book wherever books are sold, in shops and online.

This new way of publishing is actually a very old idea (Samuel Johnson funded his dictionary this way). We're just using the internet to build each writer a network of patrons. At the back of this book, you'll find the names of all the people who made it happen.

Publishing in this way means readers are no longer just passive consumers of the books they buy, and authors are free to write the books they really want. They get a much fairer return too – half the profits their books generate, rather than a tiny percentage of the cover price.

If you're not yet a subscriber, we hope that you'll want to join our publishing revolution and have your name listed in one of our books in the future. To get you started, here is a £5 discount on your first pledge. Just visit unbound.com, make your pledge and type **penny5** in the promo code box when you check out.

Thank you for your support,

Dan, Justin and John
Founders, Unbound

FIRST
IN THE
WORLD
SOMEWHERE

CHAPTER 1

*Book of Words. Daddy told me how fish breathe underwater.
They have things called gills.*

I'm flying, my legs in the air. Daddy pushes the swing. I go higher
and higher, and I start to sing 'Yellow Submarine'.

'A washing-up machine,' Daddy sings.

'A tub of margarine,' Mummy follows on, and Ant makes noises.

The sun is on my face, and my eyes shut tight as I lift in the air
like a bird. 'Custard gone all green.'

Everyone laughs. I float higher.

'Not my custard, Penny,' Mummy says.

Daddy's hands are warm and firm on my back as he swings
me again.

'What do fish breathe with, Penny?' Daddy says on the
next push.

I keep my eyes closed as I think. It's in my blue Book of Words,
a G word.

'She don't know, Daddy, she's silly.'

I open my eyes and see Ant. He jumps up and down, clapping.

'I do, I do!' I say. 'Push me higher, Daddy, please.'

Mummy is on the bench by the swings. Her hair is big today –
perfect.

'Careful with her, Michael,' she says to my dad. 'She had a lot
of pain last night.'

'Girdles!' I say suddenly, staring at my baby brother.

'Girdles?' Daddy repeats with a laugh.

Mummy joins in. 'Do fish wear girdles?'

1

Ant starts clapping again – but I let him off as he's only four.

'Girdles,' I say, as Daddy pushes the swing.

'Does that mean Mummy wears gills, Penny?' he says.

'Yes, fish wear girdles,' I say as I swing into the air shrieking, high enough to see over our holiday chalet, which I know is in Dawlish Warren. Daddy showed me on his map. I can smell the sea and high up here, on the swing, I feel like the seagulls.

'Time for dinner soon,' Mummy says, and on the next swing down Daddy catches me gently and I'm back on earth.

Simon comes running out of his chalet, which is next door to ours. He's five months, six days and eleven hours older than me.

As I get off the swing, he holds out his hand.

'I saved you a flying saucer,' he says and drops the sweet into my fingers.

I glance at Mummy. 'Go on, you can have it this time,' she says. 'But you'd better eat all your dinner.'

I slip the saucer under my tongue, enjoying the fizz as the paper melts.

Simon's mummy and daddy come over to the bench. My daddy sits down and pulls me onto his lap. I'm suddenly very tired.

'How is she today?'

Simon's mummy is called Joyce and his daddy is called Peter. I don't like it when they talk about me as if I'm not there.

Simon gets out his collection of shells and lays them on the ground, the biggest to the smallest. He's talking about the best place to find them, but I can't help listening to Joyce talk to my mummy and daddy.

'She's not too bad,' Mummy says. 'She had a bit of pain in her knees last night.'

Peter, who has thick yellow hair, narrows his eyes. 'What's wrong with her again?'

He is asking my daddy and I feel Daddy tense.

'Still's disease,' he says. 'Juvenile rheumatoid arthritis.'

I'm trying to listen to Simon. I like the shell with pink lines that curl round and round, but I can't help listening to what the grown-ups are saying.

'Does it affect everything?' says Joyce.

'All her joints. Maybe her kidneys,' Mummy says. Her voice sounds funny. 'She's already been in hospital quite a lot and they keep trying her on new tablets.'

I roll my face into Daddy's shirt. I don't want to think about hospitals where they hurt you, tell you it's for your own good and don't let you see your mummy and daddy.

'It's very rare in children,' Daddy says, and I can tell he doesn't want to talk to her while I listen.

'My gran had arthritis. It completely crippled her,' says Joyce.

Daddy stands up abruptly, holding me tight.

Simon collects his shells. 'Are we going for dinner now?'

'I'm hungry,' Ant says, grabbing Mummy's hand.

Peter and Joyce take a step back.

'You're fine, aren't you, Pen?' says Daddy, and I rest my head on his shoulder, never wanting to leave.

'Yes, Daddy,' I say.

In my head I'm thinking that I must ask Daddy about putting the word 'crippled' in my Book of Words on the C page.

We get moved to a different house, when Daddy goes. It's white at the front with a great big window. It's the first thing I look for when the school bus pulls up in front of my new home in Little Chalfont. Sometimes Mummy will be sitting by it, waving to me. But not today.

The radio on the school bus is never tuned in properly. But I can just about make out that it's 'Jennifer Juniper' by Donovan. Mummy bought the single for me, the first one I've ever owned myself.

Mags smells of cigarettes and she's always rough. She undoes my seat belt, takes my left elbow – my sore elbow – and pulls me to my feet.

'Your ruddy mother should come out and carry you down the steps,' she says, smoky breath over my face. 'Or you'll have to use a wheelchair like the others so we can get you on the lift.'

I don't say anything as she stomps down to the pavement, grabs me savagely under the arms to drag me. It hurts, but I won't let her know.

Walking through the front garden, my knees are on fire from being bent up on the long journey. Ant is sitting on the step, a metal aeroplane in his hand.

'Mummy said I must stay here,' he says solemnly. 'I can't go indoors.'

'Why not? Isn't he in?'

'I don't know,' whispers Ant.

I don't feel very warm in my turquoise miniskirt and my favourite pink blouse with the sailor-style collar. Mum hates it anyway and says I'm only ten, miniskirts aren't right.

I really need to go to the toilet. I press against the front door nervously and it swings open.

'Don't walk on the carpet!' a voice yells from upstairs.

It's Jake.

'I need to use the toilet,' I say, stepping inside.

'I've just cleaned the fucking carpet, so you can fucking wait.'

My chest tightens and I sway from one leg to the other to try and take the pressure off my knees. I don't know what to do. I never know what to do when Jake starts shouting and swearing. I wish Mummy would come back.

'I need to go,' I say again.

Jake comes to the top of the stairs and glares down at me.

'I'm telling you to wait,' he says, then disappears back into Mummy's bedroom.

I'm shaking, stuck on the spot. My knees hurt and I'm scared I'll wet myself. I wait for a few seconds then, holding in my breath, I edge along the wall, through the lounge and the kitchen, to the downstairs toilet.

When I've finished I open the door. Jake is there. I freeze.

'You little bitch,' he snarls and grabs my arm, the same arm that Mags grabbed. There's a deep, liquid pain right inside my elbow.

'I know your fucking father spoilt you, but you're not getting any of that with me.'

He grips me and I feel like a ragdoll. His huge hand whacks hard across my knees and I scream as the fire erupts.

'I told you no and I meant no.'

He hits me one more time then lets me go. I fall to the floor, crying, hating the pain, but hating more that I don't understand and I can't fight him back.

I stay still till he's upstairs, and then go outside slowly to sit next to Ant on the doorstep. I manage to take off the patent purple handbag I have around my neck. A present from Jake, like Ant's aeroplane.

'Don't cry, Pen,' says Ant.

I pick up his aeroplane. 'Do you like this?' I ask him.

'I don't know,' he says, gazing at me with big eyes.

'I don't like my bag. I'm going to get rid of it.'

'Put my aeroplane in it,' Ant whispers.

I hold his hand as we go down the road, towards the woods at the top of Money Hill. We throw the things into some bushes and laugh. Jake might beat us for losing them, but we don't care. We'll never care.

We walk home slowly, hoping Mummy is back.

'A year in hospital is a very long time, Penny,' says Nurse Brandy as she tidies my bedside locker. 'But you'll be able to go home soon.'

Nurse Brandy is the best nurse ever at Beechwood Special Hospital. She has long ginger hair. I love the moment I catch her letting it fall down, when she finishes her shift; it's like seeing something I'm not meant to.

'Helena Keely has been in for three years,' I say. 'That's got to be a record.'

Nurse Brandy stops folding my bras and looks at me.

'It's different for Helena, you know that. Her parents live too far away. The other side of the world.'

'Like Borneo?'

Dr Daniel keeps teasing me that I look like one of the wild women of Borneo when I haven't brushed my hair, but I don't even know where Borneo is.

'New Zealand, Penny.'

'She doesn't say much. Doesn't talk about her family,' I say. 'How are we supposed to know anything?'

Nurse Brandy stares at me, holding one of my bras – hateful things.

'I've heard the other girls saying stuff.' I feel awkward that she's stopped speaking. I stare at the wall by my bed. I've got pictures of Gary Glitter and Suzi Quatro. But my favourite is Marc Bolan. I love his cheekbones. I managed to save up every sixpence that Nan gives me each week so I could buy 'Ride a White Swan'. Even if I don't have a record player yet.

'I hate to say it, Penny, but your mum needs to buy you some bigger bras.' Nurse Brandy waves my grey underwear. 'I'm all for the new revolution and burning your bra, but I don't think you'll cope.

My ears are on alert.

'Why can't I burn my bra?' I really, really hate my bras. 'I can be in the revolution.'

Nurse Brandy laughs. 'I'm quite sure you will be, Penny. You'll be right there in the vanguard of Women's Liberation.'

'Vanguard. Liberation,' I repeat, and look for my pen and the little notebook with the pink poodle that Mum sent me in the post.

'I suspect Mrs Marsh will be impressed if you add those words to your vocabulary.' Nurse Brandy nods, still holding the awful shapeless objects. 'But even if you're a rebel, you'll still need some good bras.'

I write the new words slowly into the notebook, avoiding her eyes. I don't want to talk about bras. And I know Mum can't afford anything. My cheeks burn and I think about how to change the subject.

'I get my marks back for the essay this afternoon,' I say as I pretend to write some more. 'It's the one I did about going to the fair.'

Nurse Brandy puts my underwear in the bottom of my locker at last. I can see from the corner of my eye that she's shaking her head.

'Perhaps I'll pop a little letter to your mum about it.' Her voice becomes serious. 'Your breasts are growing, Penny. They need proper support.'

I look up and sigh. 'You know about Helena,' I say. 'Her family have left her, haven't they? Dumped her here because of her arthritis. That's what the older girls say.'

Nurse Brandy's face doesn't change. She smiles her usual smile. It's kind and I've never once been scared of her.

'I'll come back later before I leave to hear about that essay. I'm sure you've done well, Poet of Ward 2.'

I carry on writing in the poodle book. I wonder whether I can write a poem about Helena. I sometimes think I'd like to be dumped on the ward. Jake would be happy but I think it would upset Mum.

Dinner is horrible. I keep meaning to say lunch, like Nurse Brandy tells me. Breakfast lunch dinner. Maybe supper. I'm not sure why it matters and the food is disgusting anyway. We're never quite sure what it is unless it's something obvious like fish fingers, and even those are a funny colour.

I have Mrs Marsh to myself these days because she wants me to work towards doing an O level in English. The lesson after lunch is my favourite because there's no rushing back from physiotherapy.

Today, though, I'm nervous because I did the essay. I worked hard, checked my spelling and managed to find a good pen, which Mrs Marsh says helps my handwriting.

We sit in the small side room at a square table. I don't know how old Mrs Marsh is but I think she's older than Nurse Brandy. She has short hair and talks like no one else I've ever met. I want to ask if she's burnt her bra, but I know I won't.

She puts my essay on the table. I can see there are a few red pen corrections, but at the top she's written A- and the line: 'Penny, this is excellent. One day, you could be a professional writer.'

I tingle. I don't know what to say.

'It's true, Penny,' Mrs Marsh says. 'My husband, he's a journalist and he agrees. Would you like that?'

I still don't know what to say. The thoughts in my head scream YES. I want to show off about the essay to everyone, but I'm scared no one will care. Only Nan, and she doesn't really count.

'Well?' Mrs Marsh pushes the essay closer towards me.

'Yeah, of course I would.'

I know Daddy would let me show off. Daddy would be proud.

I open my mouth, ready to speak.

'Can I be in the vanguard and... write about Women's Liberation?' I say on a rush.

Mrs Marsh laughs and nods.

'Definitely,' she says. 'Most definitely.'

Out at last from Beechwood. This house is a bit better than the others because my bedroom is downstairs and I can stay in it all day, every day, and Mum can manage to bring my wheelchair in.

Under the quilt I lie with my transistor radio close to my ear. 'I Love to Boogie' by T. Rex. It's cold and although it's only early evening, there's no other way to keep warm since the portable heater in my bedroom ran out of gas.

I've got Radio Luxembourg on but I know my batteries are going and there's no chance of new ones. Auntie Mary and Uncle John always give me a bit of pocket money, but I don't know when they'll visit next as Jake doesn't like them. The Social installed a phone in the hall to ring family, but no one's actually allowed to use it, so I can't even call them to come over.

It's dark and the house is quiet. Mum is in the kitchen, across the hall from my bedroom. I stay under the quilt even when I hear Mum's footsteps approach.

'Come on, get up for a bit, Pen,' she says and pulls back the covers.

'I'm too cold, Mum. When can you get some more gas?'

Mum sighs. 'Maybe when Jake's dole money comes in.'

I pick up my radio. 'We haven't got any new batteries, have we?'

Mum shakes her head. 'See if Ant will get you some out of his paper-round money. Or I'll buy them out of next week's Attendance Allowance.'

I can't wait for my birthday because the social worker told me I'll be old enough to get my own little allowance, an invalid's allowance. At least I won't have to feel so guilty asking Mum for everything.

'Come and sit in the lounge and watch telly,' Mum says, bringing my crutches over. 'We've got the paraffin heater on.'

I don't really want to, but I go anyway because I know Mum is worried. She thinks I don't have enough friends and hates that I can't go outside unless she pushes me in my wheelchair. My life is stuck in a rut of trying to keep warm, pleading with Mum to bring me books from the library, the daily struggle to get to the outside toilet, and avoiding Jake.

He's already in the lounge, sitting in his large armchair in the corner, smoking. It makes me want to cough but I manage not to. We don't speak. Mum comes in, helps me sit in my wheelchair then sits on the sofa.

The *Today* programme is on ITV on the telly. I sigh, ready to be bored.

But Bill Grundy is talking to The Sex Pistols. I stare at the screen, at Johnny Rotten's orange hair. At snarling Steve Jones, and amazing, shocking Siouxsie Sioux with her cropped white hair, Bowie make-up and black braces.

I only know a little about The Sex Pistols. I've seen them on the front of Mum's paper. They've been called 'filth' and 'degenerates'.

Ant saw them once in London and he talked about it for days and days, even if he was chucked out of the pub they were playing in for being too young.

Bill Grundy tries to ask them questions, but they don't cooperate. I laugh and look at Mum and Jake, who seem hypnotised.

Jake frowns and Mum looks like a frightened rabbit.

'Horrible,' she says. 'They're horrible.'

Jake lights up a cigarette. 'Probably all fucking poofs.'

The Pistols are winning against Bill.

He tries it on with Siouxsie when she mocks him: 'I've always wanted to meet you.'

'We'll meet afterwards, shall we?' says Bill.

My mouth is dry and I'm tensed up that Jake might turn the TV off in a fit.

'You dirty sod. You dirty old man,' Steve Jones cackles and I'm laughing too.

'Keep going, chief, keep going.' Bill's nasty big tie moves as he speaks. 'You've got another five seconds. Say something outrageous.'

'You dirty bastard!' Steve is in full flow and I think I might pee myself.

Siouxsie, Johnny and the Bromley contingent snigger some more.

'Go on, again,' says Bill.

'You dirty fucker!' Steve responds and we all laugh, them – and me. 'What a fucking rotter!'

The credits come up with the *Today* programme music. I'm breathless and warm and afraid. Afraid like I've taken a favourite drug, like I've swallowed the whole of a mini vodka.

Jake grunts, gets up and turns the telly over. I tell Mum I want to go back to my room, and as I walk slowly on my crutches, I can't help smiling.

After breakfast the next day, I coax Mum to look at my clothes. 'I'll have a sort-out,' I lie. 'Throw things away.'

I look for black. I look for stuff I can cut and shred. I want to chuck out the beige tank tops, the big, pleated skirts, the piles of jumble sale nothing that mean nothing.

Mum looks a bit cross and the clothes go back in the drawer after ten minutes but I know I'm different. The wallpaper looks different. My scabby curtains look different. The air is different. I've got a lot to do and I've got to start somewhere. I get out a notebook and start to write. One poem, two poems, ten poems.

Before I go to bed, I convince Ant to lend me his razor and with a bit of handcream slapped over my eyebrows, I shave them off.

The days are the same. Mum helps me up, to bathe, to get dressed. I sit in my chair. I might read a new book, if the library has it in yet. I eat a lot of cheese on toast because it's vegetarian and cheap. Same, same, same days.

But I'm different. Angry, changed inside, somewhere deep. The pervs, the fuckers, the Grundys of this world. They might think they can win. They might think they can push me around. Fuck that. Fuck that right out down the stupid dirty roads across the shitty estate. I'm getting out. One day, I'll be free.

I've got coloured notebooks in three colours on my small table, and a pad of blue writing paper with lines on it. This is for letters to my two friends, Jackie and Chris, who went to Beechwood Hospital School with me. I owe them both, but it will have to wait till tomorrow because Jake had one of his loony moods, turned off the electricity and it's too dark for anything.

I pick up my red notebook and flinch as a few fireworks go off outside, days early before Bonfire Night. On the cover is the anarchist A and a scratchy biro scrawl – *fascist regime*! In the middle I've written in bold felt-tip:

**IDEAS
BY
KATA KOLBERT**

11

Tonight I'm Kata – a punk in the shadows – and I hate Jake and I hate my nonlife. Now I've got anger on top of all the endless boredom of nothing, day after day. The social worker comes. I don't know what to say to her. She says I might be depressed and need to see a psychiatrist.

If Jake comes in my room, I sit on my notebooks. He threatens me with burning them, even my library books. I'm halfway through *Wide Sargasso Sea*. It's great, really intense. I'm trying to get hold of *Das Kapital* next, although the librarian told Mum it's really heavy.

I go for the orange notebook. I've got a bit of a poem in there about the riots in the summer. The fascist National Front set it all off in Lewisham. Scum. I wish I could have gone, though seeing as I never go anywhere, I know that's stupid.

I put the orange notebook back and pick up the red one, again wondering if I dare light a candle as the house stays horribly quiet. I hope Mum is okay.

I flip to the back page. Squinting and trying to read by the pale street light, I can see a paragraph of handwriting that would have made Mrs Marsh roll her eyes. The beginning of a horror story, doomed love with plenty of gore. I'm not in the mood for it and I flick through until I find a blank page.

I hear a soft thud upstairs and hold my breath. I want to scream, break the silence, shout at how pathetic it all is. But I'm scared, body all clenched. We never know how long we'll be stuck in the dark when Jake has a tantrum.

I strain towards the glimmer of light as I pick up my pen. Romance is the first word that comes from somewhere. I want to turn it inside out, that idea. I want to be liberated and laugh at the idea that romance has anything to say to me. I can hear a dialogue, an argument.

Romance is good, the woman said.
No, romance is bad, I'll shoot off its head.

I laugh to myself – immediately afraid I've made a noise. But a rhyme gets through my head, dances, opens drawers, dusts down the words. I can see the shocked faces already.

I bite the end of the biro. It's cheap and I do yearn for a fountain pen, almost as much as a typewriter. Ant says he'll get me a pen for Christmas. I write the word *dead*, and underline it to build a column of all the words I can think of. Sometimes it stays rolling and rolling on the same line. Sometimes I bend it, maybe *dead* and *dark* will weave all the way through.

The pen will do, while I dream of the typewriter. After a Jake episode I get itchy to write, and the words always come. I put the biro down and smile. I'm a million excited miles away, the nothing-days matter less and less. I'm glad I'm angry and I'm glad I'm different.

The lights come back on and I blink. The sound of the kettle whistling means I can move at last, and when I hear Jake laughing at Benny Hill on the TV in the lounge, I know his shitty mood is over, for now.

Mum makes a noise in the kitchen, a soft cough. It's a relief.

Dr Gillette is the child shrink. She has huge, round glasses and brown-grey hair. It sits on her head like a ragged wig.

I'm at Beechwood, a brief stay for daily physiotherapy. We're in a tiny sliver of a room on the ward. It feels funny, as it's the place where we come to play records in the evenings.

There's an old poster of David Cassidy on the wall, shirt draped open to show his disgusting chest. Some kid has given him a Hitler moustache. It's done in black felt-tip. Someone else has scrawled 'I am the Antichrist' and drawn the Anarchy sign.

Dr Gillette sits below this, smiling.

'I hear that physio is going well, Penny. Can you see any improvements?'

'Not really,' I say and stare at David Cassidy's blobby left nipple. I know she means well.

'How is family life?' she continues.

I shrug and my eyes drop to the floor. There's nothing to say.

'Are you looking forward to going home?' she tries again.

'Of course I am,' I say and scowl.

I don't want to look at her now. I can feel my eyes burning. I hate myself when I cry. And I always do with her. I'm seventeen and shouldn't be seeing a child psychiatrist anyway.

'And the writing is going well?'

I look into her face and try to work out the meaning behind her glasses and her smile.

I smile back. A wide grin, showing all my teeth.

'I write nightmares,' I say. 'Darkness everywhere. And monsters. Maybe with a knife. Maybe a slick, sexy monster who wants to fuck you up the arse with a spiky dildo.'

I'm showing off. I can't help it. It's better than crying.

Dr Gillette nods her head. Unmoved as always.

'There's one about kids drowning in cauldrons of hot blood,' I say. 'Men are lacerated in flesh-eating swamps. Ghosts violate women. Blood spews and guts get shredded.'

'It's good you do this, Penny. I know you excel at it. But maybe you could expand your repertoire? Write something you find really difficult. Set yourself a challenge.'

I'm thinking. Lots and lots of thinking. Everything is a challenge, you prat.

'Do the doctors think I'm crazy? Am I crazy?' I say and hold my breath.

'Of course not.' She smiles, a malevolent Cheshire cat. 'You are just rather sensitive. And you have been a little unhappy at times, haven't you?'

I don't know whether she wants me to answer. We leave the question hanging in the air, caught in David Cassidy's Hitler moustache. I know I can't trust her to understand what's in my head. I told her once, just once, that I had cut myself and they put me on a tablet that made me so sleepy I couldn't write a thing.

'There's really exciting things out there right now. That's why I can't wait to go home. I'm going to make things happen.'

Dr Gillette almost laughs. I want to knock the glasses off her face.

'You'll make something happen, Penny, I've no doubt about that. But softly, softly. No need to rush. Let the nightmares fade a bit.'

I cast my eyes back to David Cassidy and decide later, you – you, ugly-mug, will be ripped right down. While I play my *New Boots and Panties!!* LP.

Somewhere, life is happening. And I am going to be part of it. It's Fate and Destiny.

Home. Bored. Writing. Rejection. Then I'm back in Beechwood again. Nurse Brandy has long since left. I'm on my bed, waiting for the dreaded boss, Dr A. She bellows like a rutting bull, looks like Brezhnev in a dress and scares the shit out of everyone. Including the staff, who are more nervous than we, jumping around like fidgety squaddies whenever she marches into the ward.

I'm in for tests and physio. Again. Again. I wait, jittery, keen to get it over with. I want to put on my cassette player and listen to The Specials but I know I can't.

Dr A laughs. The curtains shake as the deep sound blasts down the corridor. I stretch my legs out as straight as they will go and wonder whether I should have worn my miniskirt after all. It's very short and dripping with vicious zips. I'll be told off if she detects things are worse in my joints, and if I need a longer stay in the hospital. But I don't mind too much because hospital is peaceful compared to home.

She's here, large and loud at my bed, her deep-red hair puffed up.

The whitecoats herd behind her, a lot of flustered shuffling. There are the junior doctors, the sister, the senior physiotherapist, students, researchers – we are all very interesting cases. My mouth turns dry and I don't know where to look.

Dr A has eyes that bore into you like lasers.

'Hello, young lady, here you are again!'

I say nothing and know she expects nothing.

Her lasers switch down and bore into a page of my medical notes.

'Bloods?' she barks at Dr Greenberg. He is red-faced, his thick-rimmed black glasses steaming up.

'Raised ESR,' he mumbles, waving a pen over an invisible pad. 'Inflammation high.'

'And what are you up to these days, Penny?' She says my name with a hint of menace and I know this time she is expecting an answer.

'Writing.' The word falls from my lips like an apology.

Dr A stares.

There is silence. It goes on. And on. I'm frozen but hot all over.

'Well, young lady,' she says, addressing her minions, 'I look at the world today and I don't think a writing career is realistic for someone like you.'

She nods her head. They nod their heads. Some murmur noises of agreement.

'I think we'll follow the usual programme,' she continues, now in a conspiratorial tone to Dr Greenberg. 'She's a classic case and she usually responds well. Oh, set up another visit with Dr Gillette in Psychiatry. We need some sensible plans for your future, don't we, young Penelope? Get you toughened up a bit!'

She flicks the lasers back on me and smiles like a famished bear. 'And work hard on those knees. You can't hide the fixed flexion from me!'

The underlings manage a chortle as Dr A marches on to the next bed.

My eyes blink with tears as I contemplate seeing Dr Gillette.

I suddenly don't know what I want. To stay here or to go home? Either seems a dead end, and since my episode with the pills and razors in April I see the shrink at everyone's whim – never by my choice, because I want to.

I toy with my cassette player, to relax into music as soon as I dare, and almost miss a sudden visitor.

She has chestnutty-brown hair to her shoulders, and she wheels alongside my bed, her legs out on a board. One is in a splint. Around her neck is a serious-looking, white neckbrace.

I notice most of all that she has amazing eye make-up. A soft blur of plum over her lids and eyeliner to the edges.

'Are you a writer?' she asks. 'I heard Dr A having a right go about it. What do you write?'

'Anything. Everything,' I say, amazed. 'It's all I've ever wanted to do.'

'Me too. I'm Tamsin by the way.'

'What do you do?' I wriggle myself to the edge of the bed to get into my wheelchair.

'Mostly poetry. But I'll try anything,' she says. 'Love that bloody skirt. You're pretty brave wearing it in here.'

I giggle. Tamsin giggles.

'When did yours start? I was eight when the sod got hold of me.'

I know what she's talking about and am pleased the dreary subject will be out of the way quickly. We know we're rarities. They keep telling us. But as inmates we have to ask.

'I got ill when I was nearly three,' I say. 'Don't remember much about it, other than being taught to say "Still's disease" or "childhood rumertoid-arthur-ritus" like a parrot when I was very young.'

17

Tamsin laughs. 'Oh bloody big arseholes. It's shit, isn't it? I mean, who cares after all? Only them.'

'I know,' I say. 'Exactly.'

Within ten minutes we're at the dining table and we can't stop talking. We spread out our poems. We talk about CND, the crisis in Afghanistan, as Christmas looms near.

I offer to do her a tarot-card reading. She lends me her tape of Leonard Cohen and I promise to do one of The Specials. I tell her I'm KATA KOLBERT. She comes up fast with K.OSS. We talk about our cats, Ollie and Tooty. We both love *Blake's 7*. Wine, vodka. Proust – at least the bits we got through in *Swann in Love*. And we talk about what next. Start a band. Write a novel. Have sex. Move to London. Till it's dark, over and over again we talk.

Next, it has to be what we want.

CHAPTER 2

10 August 1984: I write this in such a state of elation!! Had many letters this morning, amid them was a brown envelope with my name printed in large spiky letters. Yes!! Here was dearest Morrissey writing me the sweetest, most touching of letters!!

Dr Gillette makes me want to vomit. Tamsin begs me to stop seeing her but I don't really know how to fight this. When I come back from an appointment I feel as if my nerves and my thoughts have been pulled outside my body, and are shrieking in the sharp cold air.

All I can do is listen to *The Smiths* by The Smiths. Morrissey's voice is an enchantment that heals. And as the words of the 12" single 'How Soon is Now' melt into my thoughts, I know he knows.

I've got another notebook, especially for The Smiths.

For Morrissey.

But the nagging of Dr Gillette makes me want to do something else.

I want to put my words in a different place and hope they can do some magic.

I rummage through the pile of paper in front of me, through the scraps, the mail-order catalogue bills, the mounting postcards from Tamsin.

At last I find the pad of blue writing paper. I take a deep breath because this has to be the most perfect handwriting I can manage.

I clasp my best, most precious pen and write 'Dear Morrissey'.

Writing letters gets me somewhere sometimes, and the one to him is the most important ever because I know he'll understand.

I have made a pact to myself and Destiny that I will give up writing unless he replies.

I'm worn out. Loads more Dr Gillettes, beardy shrinks and telling me to be realistic. This was a test.

It takes me three hours and I have to start all over again once. But by the time Mum comes in to draw my curtains and chatter about what's for dinner, the letter is in the envelope, with a decent photo of me, with Tooty the cat.

Addressed to Morrissey, c/o Rough Trade. Signed by Kata Kolbert.

Somehow I get through Easter. I hate Easter. And April. I don't know why, but it always feels like a grey, boring time. Extra boring on top of the other boring, of the endless days of boring incarceration.

Mum comes in with a mid-morning coffee, amiably attacking the weather. I notice there's a wedge of post under her arm.

'You've got a funny letter here, Pen,' she says, putting the post on my desk. 'Bloody weird handwriting.'

I look down at the brown envelope. In jagged capital letters there's my address. There's KATA KOLBERT.

I don't recognise it but as I go to rip the letter my heart is bursting from my dry throat, a bird fluttering for freedom. I'm sure my mouth is open as I look at Mum, then look at the letter.

I can't speak. How can I? I know, without any doubt.

It's from Morrissey.

Using my new gift of a precious fountain pen I prise open the corner slowly.

'Shall I do it?' says Mum.

'No!' I gasp and hold it to my body, hating that the sacred moment has been broken. 'It's okay, Mum, I'll do it.'

'Alright, alright,' Mum says, rolling her eyes, grabbing my dirty clothes from the end of my bed. 'But don't forget there's a social worker coming later.'

I don't answer as she leaves the room.

There's always a bloody social worker – and I'm not willing to let thoughts of them pollute this hallowed moment.

I finally defeat the envelope and pull out a postcard of Morrissey and Sandie Shaw. The light of illumination blasts through my senses. Rocks my world to its foundations. In black spiky writing it says:

Dear Kata,
You write delightfully, a priceless gift. And yes I accept the compliments! Believe me, I need them – please send more! The photo shall be cherished.

Be lucky, be happy.
Love Morrissey

My breath quickens. What do I do? Call Tamsin? Write in my journal?

No. Morrissey needs more compliments. So he shall have them.

I will use my priceless gift.

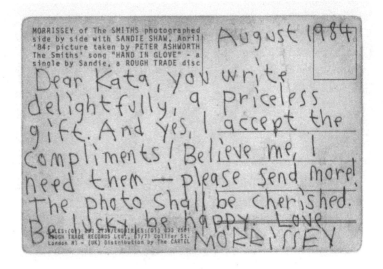

MORRISSEY of The SMITHS photographed side by side with SANDIE SHAW, April '84; picture taken by PETER ASHWORTH The Smiths' song "HAND IN GLOVE" - a single by Sandie, a ROUGH TRADE disc

August 1984

Dear Kata, you write delightfully, a priceless gift. And yes, I accept the compliments! Believe me, I need them — please send more! The photo shall be cherished. Be lucky, be happy. Love MORRISSEY

SALES:(01) 992 5100/ENQUIRIES:(01) 833 2501 ROUGH TRADE RECORDS Ltd., 61/71 Collier St., London N1 - (UK) Distribution by The CARTEL

The 'e' key on my new, secondhand typewriter is dodgy. I smack it with a pencil as the key lifts up. The letter to *Jamming!* magazine must be perfect.

I've got a thin blanket over my legs because the portable gas heater has run out again — and Mum says there's no money to get a new bottle. I pull the blanket higher and start to type. My little tinny cassette player does its best to push out 'Atmosphere' by Joy Division.

The magazine is beside me. 'Breaking down the barriers', it says along the top on the cover. I bite my pencil as the wind howls on and on.

I type a few words, staring at the latest photo from Morrissey on my desk. It's a big one in black and white, that he sent to me personally, and it says, 'Ever and Ever Morrissey'.

I attack the bastard typewriter and ignore the stupid 'e'.

I yearn for friends, people like me who know they are different, who rage, who want things to change. Not just disabled people — though I'm certain there's more than just Tamsin and me out there who feel the same, who want change.

I type 'there are real barriers for some of us' – then delete it.

I take a swig from a tall glass – Ant slipped some vodka in it earlier – and the burn into my guts makes me feel better.

The 'e' key bounces as I lose myself in a flurry for several minutes. Only Tooty interrupts me as he comes in with a small cat-chirrup and jumps on the bed.

Another few lines and another glug of secret vodka.

When I notice it's 2 a.m., I stop and pull the paper from the typewriter, wincing at the faint 'e' imprints. It takes another half an hour to fill them in, in my best handwriting, and I'm so tired I don't know if I can get into bed on my own.

Someone creeps downstairs and there's a soft thud outside my door. I'm not surprised when Ant leans his head around it.

'What you up to, sis? Late to bed again?'

'You can talk,' I say, poking my tongue out. 'I'm writing a letter to *Jamming!* So there.'

Ant comes into the room and flops onto my bed in the corner. 'That's all you bloody do. Write, write, write.'

He scowls, but I know he's proud of me.

'Piss off, Ant,' I say fondly. 'Remind me. How many gigs have you been to this year?'

'Loads. Can't really remember,' Ant yawns.

'And could I have managed at any of them?'

'Not really. It gets crazy, Pen, everyone starts moshing and pogoing.'

I fall silent, staring at my letter.

'I wish you could mend the "e" on this typewriter.'

'What you saying in this letter anyway?'

'They've got this thing, right there on the front cover, about breaking down the barriers. And I've been thinking, do these people know about barriers? It's not just about getting into a concert, it's about people having a better attitude.'

Ant rubs his light stubble.

'I've told you I'll take you. We can give it a go. I'd look after you, Pen.'

The wind pushes against the windows and shakes through the shabby house. I look at him and smile.

'I know you would, Ant, but it's more than just me. After the letter from Morrissey, I have to get to see The Smiths. I have to.'

'We managed Wembley after all,' says Ant. 'You dressed up in your Numanoid gear.'

I groan as I remember.

'Yeah, that was great, Ant, but they still managed to put us in a seat that was down ten steps. It hurt to be carried that far,' I sigh. 'Maybe *Jamming!* will love my battle cry.'

He nods his head slowly.

'When I move to London, things will be different,' I say. 'Tamsin and me will make changes, you'll see.'

'You and that bloody flat in London. Is it ever going to happen?'

'Yes. It will. We've got Red Ken on our side.'

'He hasn't done anything though, has he?...'

Ant is getting bored, I can tell, and he likes tormenting me.

I look at him for a few seconds.

'Hasn't he? Don't be so sure,' I say as I ferret around at my small desk till I find an envelope. I take out the letter slowly and hand it to him.

'You can read, can't you?'

'Duh,' he says, jabs his tongue out and grabs it from my hand.

'So it IS going to happen. But don't you dare tell Mum,' I say. 'Not yet. She will get silly.'

He looks up sharply and drops the letter on the desk.

'Oh go on, you read it.' I unfold it like a holy object. Because my Destiny is in it after all.

'Dear Penny, blah blah blah... Do ask your social worker about the housing transfer scheme. I'll pass your letter on to Tony Banks who can also help...'

Ant looks puzzled but less bored.

'Tamsin and me move to a place in Leyton and someone else moves here to the Chalfonts somewhere,' I add, speaking a bit too loud.

'Lucky them,' Ant says. 'Getting to Shithole St Chalfont.'

I realise my eyes are drooping.

'I'm off to bed,' Ant says. 'You want an arm to lean on first?'

I fold the letter as Ant gets up, and shuffle to the bed, holding onto him.

'Can you lend us a fiver, Pen?' he says, as a parting remark. 'And I'll look at that "e" key tomorrow.'

'Oh alright then. But you better give it back on Friday. Don't be a moody prat like last time.'

'I never get moody,' he laughs, not looking at my eyes. 'Night night.'

'Night, Ant.'

The wind rages. I snuggle up with a purring Tooty.

Tomorrow Mum will post the letter.

Tomorrow things will change.

Tamsin and me by the sea with brother Ant.

CHAPTER 3

20 July 1985: We all paraded off to the pub and over a quick drink aired our worries about the aged recording engineer. I knew instinctively that he was wrecking this day that should have been glorious and perfect.

My letter to *Jamming!* is printed. I smile all day and even into the next. And then the responses arrive via the magazine's office. A few at first: Amy an artist, a natural outsider type. Zed, a gentle and enigmatic British Asian who loves jangly indie pop and The Beatles. He recognises my alienation, an echo of his own.

Before long I receive over a hundred replies to my rallying cry to bash down barriers. They arrive in small packets from all over the UK. One letter is from Freddie, four years younger than me. A London music junkie who puts on bands, part of the North London indie punk scene – a rough Do It Yourself realm where everything is possible, even as we all kick against the evil restrictions of Thatcher.

Freddie writes to me every day and I reply, sometimes by hand, sometimes on the typewriter if the 'e' key holds up. We move on to sharing cassette tapes. Freddie sends me intriguing compilations: Nick Drake, The Residents, Vaughan Williams, Hatfield and the North. If my hi-fi system works, I record The Smiths B-sides, Debussy, Bessie Smith, Blind Lemon Jefferson for him. I don't mind that he outdoes me fast as he introduces me to music I've never had the chance to explore. Jazz, classical, prog, folk and roots – besides endless crates of indie.

He tells me that he knows Alan McGee at Creation Records – they've promoted bands together. Freddie's a guitarist too, who's worked with loads of musicians on the post-punk scene, including

The Television Personalities. Ant had their single 'Where's Bill Grundy Now?' and played it over and over until even Mum was singing it. That was before his record player was mysteriously thrown out of the bedroom window.

I watch out for the postman every morning. Freddie's letters and tapes make my day.

**45–53 SINCLAIR ROAD
LONDON W14**

★ ★ ★

Jamming!'s front cover slogan 'Breaking Down The Barriers' is a very rousing, highly laudable one. It is something I seem to live my entire life attempting - ie. breaking down very particular barriers. But the ones I wish to stamp down often seem invunerable, impenetrable. The weight of prejudice against me – using myself 'symbolically' – sees 'me' unemployed (hardly rare I know!), often segregated from humanity, barred from social activities/venues, hindered at every turn when I attempt any creative exploit and my existance quite often overlooked – albeit usually with malicious intent. The explanation for this prejudice? What ever of the more obvious reasons that spring to mind (pathetic bias against colour, creed, homosexuality etc) I would lay bets you do not guess mine . . . The thing is, 'I walk a bit funny, or, I can't walk at all. Maybe I use a stick, a wheelchair . . . there are many things – we are ALL different anyway – but I refuse to sink to the usual words, the pointless LABLES we are given. Unfortunately you see, the majority of humankind (of which we are actually a large part!) will insist on forgetting we are here – or if we are glanced upon it is normally with ridicule, maybe apprehension/curiosity etc. Yes, the 'Elephant Man Syndrome' is still alive and well and in this modern age (and how hypocrits cried over the film?) – though I suppose it's no wonder, seeing as we're ALL being subverted back into a Victorian Queen Thatcher rotting-slop society . . . Tickets to the new freak shows anyone?

Well I have had ENOUGH! Hoping optimistically that Jamming! is an enlightened zine, I felt yours was the place to froth forth my anger for what must be an important issue. Your stirring rallying words '. . . Apathy and complacency should not be allowed to rule . . . get out there . . . Don't let anyone tell you it can't be done . . . Do it now!' had me torn between shrieking, delighted applause and blind near-tear spattered frustration! Look dears, I'M trying! I sit here surging out endless literary gems (maybe when I'm dead they'll say I was a genius!), I've already attempted to produce a fanzine, but most important and dear to my heart is the band I'm kicking and scratching to keep going! Yeah, really – although I'm beginning to think NO ONE Out There is remotely interested in creating fresh alternative music. Time and time again I've tried to find eager, enthusiastic musicians. Every time I detect a faintest suggestion of a new recruit 'IT' gets in the way: Prejudice. Funny, but I didn't realise my shuffly, higgledy walk ('I wobble on the cobbles' - quoting the fab Ian Dury) had any bearing upon my ability to sing and write etc etc. Which apparently it has. One unwise-guy, replying to an ad, insisted I was 'taking the piss' (out of him!) when I yawningly muttered that I walked a bit odd. I mean, what is an ambitious girl supposed to do? I can see my fate now – archeologists unearthing me in thousands of years time, fossilized beneath endless bundles of manuscripts, and mountinous heaps of song-crammed cassettes! The musical beauties that were never born! Oh god – won't anyone leap with me, out of this suffocation??

I'm wondering if there really ARE any people out there who AREN'T chained to complacency (apart from Jamming!'s readers??). It's bloody hard not to assume the rest of the planet isn't actually . . . asleep! Am I really just an insane wierdo living in an allusionary world??

Before I curtail this venting of the spleen, I must just blather-angry on another point. All of you loose 'n' lucky souls able to intoxicate yourselves with what ever LIVE music is your own personal ecstacy, spare a paltry thought for me (us). As I (apparently) do not exist, no one is going to think I might actually like (no, desperately yearn!) to GET IN to see a band, and consequently they won't be very happy when I arrive on their door-step. Besides being turned away once or twice and refused entry at various places, I/we have been met with an amazing array of indifference – from complete ignorance, to unhelpful grumbling, and squeals (excuses normally) that I can't be let in coz . . . I'M A FIRE HAZARD!! And the rate this goes on, I will bloody well start smuggling in fireworks in my handbag to personally position them under the posteriors of the guilty parties . . . if I could get in!

I'm not wallowing – I DO fight. But alone it is very difficult. I've missed some of my favourite thrills this year already, my biggest woe being that I've yet to see The Smiths (NB. – fellow devotees, how would you react if you knew you could never see the charming four-EVER?) I won't give up hope yet, the battle's just begun! But there will be others, among my 'brethren', in worse circumstances – who have NO hope. And it would only take such a little bit of awareness to change so much. Thank God there are a whispering few who ARE open minded, unprejudiced . . .

Let me conclude with this – of course I'm not NORMAL!! I'm proud of my 'uniqueness', wandering around with pink hair (maybe) . . . flowers . . . umm . . a multicoloured walking cane . . jingle bells!?) . . corndollies . . etc etc! Do you catch my drift – what IS 'normal' for Gawd's sake?? As there isn't a great deal else to do, I can only live in HOPE (ah as always) – perhaps this rant has stirred up a few thoughts in people's minds. If Jamming! will allow my cheek, I would like to beg for folks to write with opinions, or for ANY reason (I'm an excessive letter-writer!) . . . and for interested . . umm . dare I try? . . musicians(whisper!) to clench courage, Going Boldly Where All Have Feared to Tread (so far!) and contact me with view musically spiriting up the land! If no one bothers, my very worst suspicions about the feeble-hearted masses will be sadly confirmed . . .

Please . . . Get True, Get Free!
Kata Kolbert

Five days go by. Or is it 5,000? Mum helps me get up, Mum brings me dinner, Mum brings me tea. I do some writing. Finish a letter. Read a paper. Thatcher is smug because the miners' strike is failing. She is such a monster.

I listen to Joy Division, and then at last I phone Tamsin.

'Don't tell me you've had another hundred letters,' she says. 'Or I might have to slap you hard next time we get together, moo cow.'

I laugh, looking out at the spring day through the grey net curtains that Mum never has time to wash.

'Not so many now. I think there will be some regulars. Zed, who's going to send me a cassette of REM next time, and Amy, who's started a picture of Morrissey for me.'

I pause and add: 'And Freddie of course.'

I feel funny when I say his name. I can't talk about him casually, even to Tam.

'Blimey, he's keen. He's written every day, hasn't he?'

'Yeah,' I say, trying to be arch. 'He's interested in my music, and we're meant to be talking on the phone soon.'

I feel nerves prickle on my cheeks as I say it, my tongue tangling already at the thought of it.

'Make sure he rings you. You know that's better for you.'

Tam knows my ways and my mortal fear of making phone calls, and unlike almost everyone else, she's gentle with me.

'What about you? Had any replies to your *NME* advert?'

I look up and notice Mum coming through the gate.

'I've not had as many as you, Penelope Big Show-Off. But a couple of them sound great. I think I've found us a clutch of musical boys. They're very keen to meet us already. Owen and Dan want to be the next Depeche Mode. Shall I set something up for when you're down?'

Mum is bustling about in the kitchen and I know I won't be able to talk for much longer. Mum doesn't mind me using the phone but I can't concentrate as I know Jake is looming.

'Sounds like a good idea,' I say, although anxiety creeps across my skin. 'You can do the talking though.'

'Oh Pen, we're never going to make you a true bohemian at this rate.'

I know she's teasing and I know it will be okay.

Mum comes bouncing into my bedroom, clutching post and a large plastic bag. Tooty, my perfect small black cat, follows her.

'Is that Tam?' says Mum. 'Hello Tam!' Mum raises her voice and lifts the plastic bag. 'I've got you something for the flat.'

Into my ear Tamsin says, 'Oooh, more for our bottom drawer.'

Mum pulls out a tin waste-paper bin with badly drawn depictions of wildlife in all the wrong colours.

'Thanks, Mum,' I say. 'We need all these things.'

The phone is still pressed to my ear.

'It's disgusting, isn't it?' Tam says. I try not to laugh.

'Lots more letters,' Mum says, putting the pile in front of me.

'Another one from Freddie,' I say, gripping the corner with my teeth.

'Freddie, Freddie, Freddie,' says Tamsin into my ear.

Mum looks up.

'Penny's got a boyfriend,' she says, in a sing-song voice.

And I go hot, all over.

'Hello, Kata Kolbert.' Freddie's voice is London, not cockney, not Mayfair, somewhere in between. I hesitate, face flushing, fingers tingling. Outside of speaking to Tam and my auntie, the phone remains a challenge. But I want to talk to Freddie, and have gone through military levels of planning in my letters to get him to ring me at this time, 2.30 p.m., when no one is in.

'Hi, Freddie,' I say, and hope I don't sound breathless.

'I think it's time I heard your own material, dearheart. I loved the Bessie Smith – now let's have some Kata Kolbert.'

'The demos will be a bit rough and ready,' I tell him. Inside I'm cringing. I want to sound cool and keep my sophisticated persona up to scratch.

'Don't worry about that. You should hear some of the stuff I come across. I know yours is going to be special.'

I laugh, nervously.

'How many songs have you got?' he asks.

'About thirty.'

'Thirty? Dearheart, most of the bands I know have barely got one.'

I laugh.

'Well, I'll send you my best five. How's that?'

'Great. And if you can, put the lyrics in?'

'I'll do it as quickly as possible. I have to wait until it's quiet here. I get moaned at for singing.'

'Well, I think you'll sound lovely,' Freddie says, lowering his voice.

I hear the gate opening. The rest are back.

'Have to go,' I say. 'Sorry.'

I put the phone down clumsily and wait for the back door to open. Mum rushes in to put the kettle on, Jake stomping behind her. I blink back tears. So much for sophisticated.

The letters from *Jamming!* tail off, but I don't really mind. I'm left with a gang of great new friends who are all from out there. And then Freddie. We've talked on the phone a few times and I sent him the tape of my five best songs yesterday. I'm using the red notebook to write some new lyrics and I'm up to date with my journal. But I'm twitchy. And spring is in my head as the days warm up.

Tamsin rings me as usual on our daily catch-up. I'm still opening letters from the *Jamming!* regulars and wedge the phone between shoulder and ear as I rip open today's wodge with my teeth.

'I've had an idea,' she says. 'As you're coming to mine next week, why don't we meet the boys one day and you could invite Freddie over the next?'

I hesitate.

'Well,' says Tam, 'don't make me call you Penelope again.'

'Okay, if your mum and dad don't mind. I want you to meet him anyway.'

'I think you really, really should meet. You like him a lot, don't you?'

'I think so, yes, I do. But, you know…'

'Don't be a wally, Pen. We'll have a man feast. Will our hormones take it?'

I don't need to see her to know that she's pulling one of her lewd faces.

'It's just, you know, very real, isn't it,' I say. 'And they have to get around the Lurgy.'

'We're not wanting to marry them and have their babies just yet, and let's leave shagging out of it for now.'

I laugh out loud.

'We'd better leave that out of it, seeing as we're both gagging.'

I manage to open most of my post while talking and I find I have a letter from the social worker. I stare and stare at the badly typed lines.

'Pen, are you still there?' Tam's voice cuts through.

'Tam, shock-horror probe. Bloody hell. Tam. We've got our move date. We actually have a move date.'

Tamsin is quiet for a few beats.

'Definitely shock-horror probe,' she says eventually in a small faraway voice.

I look up, glad that it's warm outside. Mum is in the front room. I can hear the TV. Jake is in the garden. Ant is upstairs and Tooty is lying in a peaceful cat curl on my bed.

I look at the letter again as I say my goodbyes to Tam.

I scurry through papers and books to unbury my cassette player. It's tinny crap, but it does for now. I've got a mixtape in it, starting with Nina Simone: 'My Baby Just Cares For Me'.

The sun isn't trying hard enough, but I know, I know down to my guts, that this is the ending times of the 5,000+ days of incarceration.

I'm at 'Avalon', the nickname I've given to Tamsin's parents' peaceful house in Walthamstow.

Tamsin and me sit at the large round table in the living room, dolled up to the nines. I'm in my black mini with side zips, my black-and-white-striped Bardot top, leather stud bracelets, and heavy purple eye shadow, Siouxsie-style. Tam wears her blue shift dress with the jagged hem, and her red Dr Martens, her latest hair extensions bunched high on her head. Her eyes outlined in perfect black liner are creations I always envy.

Opposite in a flurry of colour and chic, Owen and Dan beam at us, sipping at the tea supplied by Tam's eager mum.

Tamsin is doing most of the talking, making me blush as she yacks about my songs. I can't help staring at Owen's long, orange kimono and linen trousers, completed by a frilly white Duran Duran shirt. Dan is all floppy fringe, lip gloss and David Sylvian eyes, in a cream suit and cravat in splashes of primary colour.

'How did you like the demos, boys?' Tamsin says, and winks at me.

'What?' I say. I had no idea she'd sent them. I blush to the scarlet roots of my newly dyed hair.

'We love them,' says Owen. 'When are we going to jam?'

'Soon, I hope,' I say. 'It's really great that you want to be part of it.'

'We'll sort something out soon,' says Tamsin. 'She is meeting her new manager tomorrow, you know.'

'You've got a manager?' says Dan in his soft Romford accent.

'It's not firmed up yet,' I say. 'But he's great. He's got a lot of experience and knows Alan McGee.'

Tamsin looks at me and I can't stop talking. All about Freddie and Destiny and Things Starting to Happen.

Freddie's hair is long. He's sent me one photo, but now in the flesh, it really strikes me how unusual that is for a punky type. His face is active and lively, ready with comedy poses. He pouts his lips, rolls his eyes, does the voices. 'Oh, no, missus!'

In the gentle summer sun, I'm back at the table opposite Freddie, Tamsin by my side. I feel shy. Here he is, seeming so much more grown up than me, a guy who wants to be my manager!

'Nice shoes, dearheart,' he says, glancing at my two-tone kitten heels.

'Thanks,' I say. I hate that I'm muttering. But Tamsin's dad, John, rescues me by asking Freddie if he would like a beer. Tamsin has wine and I stick to lemonade, determined not to embarrass myself.

'So you know Alan McGee?' Tamsin says, helping me along.

'Yeah. We've put on a few bands together, like The Wire, The Television Personalities. You know he looks after The Jesus and Mary Chain? But while I think of it, I've got something of my own I'm putting on at the Plough in Leytonstone High Road. Proggy punk band. I don't think there's any steps there either.'

'We'll definitely come,' says Tamsin, looking directly at me.

'You liked my tapes?' I splurge it out, gulping on the lemonade.

'What I'm thinking is, we'll work on choosing a few songs over the phone, then I'll set up a session at this studio I know near Tottenham. If we get that done before you move, so much the better.'

I'm overwhelmed. 'Are you sure? What about the cost?'

Freddie glugs his beer, eyeing me. His face is warm and animated. He looks like a young Oscar Wilde.

'No cost. I'll sort it, sweetness.' He smacks his lips. 'You'll meet my friend Tony. Tone, I call him. Smart guy. An absolute cracking bass player. He likes The Smiths almost as much as you.'

I stop myself from laughing like a silly child.

'And there's Goat. Yes. Goat,' Freddie continues. 'A diamond bloke from Manchester. A true anarchist and a top-class drummer.'

I don't know what to say and play with my straw.

'I love your letters.' Freddie's voice is soft. 'And the way you sing. You really are a talent, Pen, and I want to get it out to the world. That's why, yes doll, I do want to be your manager.'

My cheeks burn warm and the happy sun dances across the tablecloth.

'Even with the situation as it is?' I say.

'What situation?' Freddie frowns.

'That I use a wheelchair. That situation.'

Freddie twists his lips in mockery.

'Dearheart, that is irrelevant. You have the talent, the look, and now you have the manager. Let's set some dates to meet up next month and finalise the studio.'

I nod but my mind races into overdrive. There's all the crap about affording the taxi, Jake making a fuss, and whether I can invade Avalon again.

'I have to come and check out the flat in Leytonstone. So I'm sure we can work something out.'

I relax, pleased the words flowed. We chat a little more as the sun goes down and I realise only then that Tamsin has left the table discreetly and is talking quietly with her mum by the telly.

When Freddie leaves, he kisses me on the lips.

The long wait to freedom is magnified by a rush of interfering social workers chopping and changing details. Lorna ('Drippy') says the tenancy can't start because the painting won't be done until mid-August, when our move date is supposed to be the 10th.

There's a lot to do now I've got another meet with Freddie. Mum is pushing me to pack but she's so busy with the family and Ant is always out with his girlfriend.

'Can't this go?' Mum sweeps up a pile of news clippings in my room. On the top is one about the New Age Travellers at Stonehenge. The notorious Battle of the Beanfield, complete with a photo. 'Dirty old hippies!'

'Mum, leave it alone. It's news,' I say and try to snatch it back. 'Tam and me wanted to join them and protest.'

Mum shakes her head and smiles.

'Don't be silly,' she says. 'What for?'

I can't reply as she hands them back to me.

Every now and again I get a posh paper and keep things from it. Usually the *Guardian* or *The Times*. There's the bit about scientists finding a hole in the atmosphere and the oxygen going. Sometimes there's things about The Smiths. And lately, Freddie has started sending me bits too. A clipping about Gary, who runs the Colour Tapes label in Walthamstow. Tam knows him as well, which makes me happy because it's all Destiny and Fate bringing us together.

Freddie also sends me arty nude postcards.

'You won't have enough to get by on,' Mum says, breaking me from my dream. 'I wish I had more to give you, Pen.'

I'm sad, suddenly, and my eyes film over. Mum is my rock. It dawns on me how different life will be without her.

'And how will you manage? Who will help you with a shower?'

I look at her, emotion rising. 'Mum, we're getting a home help. It'll be okay.'

'I'm glad you're going though, Pen. You've been stuck in this bloody room too long. And Tamsin, she's a tough girl, she'll look after you.'

'I'll miss you, Mum,' I say, the words hoarse and almost too hard to speak.

Mum, my beautiful mum, laughs, shakes her head of dark natural curls.

'Don't go all soppy on me. Let's pack some more. Are you taking boxes to Tamsin's next week? We could do with more plates.'

'If Ant will take me. Her mum and dad don't mind. And anyway I'm meeting Freddie about making a record.'

I say it light as I can, but my heart trembles.

'You be careful, Penny.' Mum pretends to be severe. 'Men can't be trusted. Tamsin's going to be with you when you meet him, isn't she?'

'Of course, Mum!' I say, ladling on the scorn as I lie.

I decide to lose my virginity before I meet Freddie again. I'm too old and I know I'll like it. Maybe I won't bleed. I've read the books, you don't always.

I choose Alan who I've met twice. A penpal for a while before that. He's sent me a nude photo, which I hide inside last year's journal.

I got him with my words.

As usual there are plans to make. Lies to tell. I get on the pill. Make more plans. A big bucket of nerves. Tamsin tells me to read lots of *Delta of Venus* before I do the sex bit. To get me horny and ready.

We are in his mum and dad's house when no one is in. The Lurgy is behaving itself, although I have concerns that my knees may cause problems.

Alan is strong and I like that. He gets me up the two steps without a problem. I've not drunk anything on purpose so I don't need the toilet.

We snog for a while on the sofa and I'm hot and ready for more. His hands push under my black lace top and tweak my nipples.

I yelp in surprise and pleasure.

He tries to pull my top over my head but my arms won't lift that high.

'Head first,' I say, breathless, excited, embarrassed. But off it goes.

Alan is kissing my neck, down to my breasts. And the thrill through my body is electric down to my clit when he sucks my nipple.

He starts to push his thigh between my legs.

'Don't ask me to kneel,' I say in a rush, as he pauses and whips his jeans off.

'It's okay, darlin' – don't worry.' He sits beside me. Strokes my cropped red hair then all the way down. Right down to my knickers. Right into my knickers.

I gasp when his fingers get to me right there. I know this is it. I want him.

Alan takes his underpants off and displays his dick. I'm still not used to it, torn between fascination and a hint of distaste. It's always poking up, pushing towards me. And suddenly, I can't imagine how it will fit into me.

I wonder whether to offer to suck it, but Alan holds me in his big arms, swoops me down, and hovers on top of me.

I think of all the people I have read. Anaïs, *The Women's Room*, *Fear of Flying*. Didn't I dream of the 'zipless fuck' like Erica Jong's Isadora Wing?

Alan lifts my legs into the air and nestles himself between them.

'My knees!' I exclaim, as Alan moves his hands away to lean forward. Somehow we both manage to laugh.

He rests my legs back down.

I sit up, fighting baby tears. I'm a failure. I will never be a real woman. The words crowd in my head, mocking me.

Alan stands up and lights a cigarette, smiling at me.

'We've just got to work it out, Pen.'

I gesture to take a drag on his cigarette, because it's easier than speaking when I feel so shy. I think of *The Joy of Sex* with the hairy man.

I don't smoke and I'm starting to feel sick. I look at Alan, who comes from Slough and likes my poems. Who has lovely eyes, a sexy smile and a great arse.

I take in a deep, deep breath.

'Maybe if you kneel on the edge of the bed with my legs along the length of your body, it might work?' I say. Nervous and hot. But still wanting him.

'It'll be fun trying,' Alan says gently as he swivels me into position.

He strokes me, kisses me. Opens me up like an eager flower. I'm on fire and I know I want him, I need him. Right now.

It hurts me for a second – and then there is pleasure and heat and our breaths in time together. He's inside me, I like it. I like it a lot. I begin to moan softly, moving with his rhythm.

The delicious storm shakes me.

I'm at the Rising Sun, on Woodford New Road. It's 2 p.m. I've come from Avalon. And I wince as usual at the terrible cost of the cab all the way from the Chalfonts to east London. But at least it's summer.

And it's always worth it. Time to talk business and finalise the plans for the studio. The pub is manageable if you use a wheelchair. If I need the loo, I can get in, there's no big step. I'm wearing my short, black slash dress, which I hope turns me into a Morticia with spiky crimson hair, little purple boots on my feet.

Freddie is waiting for me in the pub garden, by a wooden bench.

'Hey Pen. Loving that dress. Must get some photos of you in that for PR, and maybe my private collection.' He winks and I smile shyly.

Once I manage to swing my legs over the seat, Freddie sits down next to me. Right next to me so that our thighs touch.

I grab a small breath.

'I've got you a vodka and Coke,' he says, turning to look into my face. 'You're not too cold, are you? It's much quieter out here and very private.'

'I suppose it is,' I say, aware of his leg against mine. 'Everything is definitely set up then for the studio session?'

'Yes, dearheart – six weeks' time. Tone and Goat are booked and it's all systems go.'

'Will you play the tracks to Alan McGee?' I almost whisper. The Jesus and Mary Chain single 'Upside Down' has been high in the indie charts for months and months. It feels like I'm creeping closer to a god.

Freddie looks at me intently. 'Whatever way we do it, it'll happen, Pen. It'll all happen.'

I look into my glass and hear a loud burst of birdsong in the scrap of Epping Forest behind us.

Freddie puts his hand on my face.

'Hey,' he says, and then he kisses me, beer ripe on his tongue. His other hand creeps under the hem of my short dress to the top of my thigh.

He pulls away and smiles.

'It's about time we did that, Pen – isn't it?'

'Yes,' I say, grinning. 'So let's do it again.'

The grimy taxi chugs along the grey roads of Tottenham. I feel a hint overexposed in my miniskirt and thin black top. But I know I look okay and that's all that matters. Tamsin sits beside me and we chitchat with the taxi driver Abe, a jolly Nigerian who bursts into song, his favourite tune being 'I Just Called to Say I Love You'.

We arrive at the studio. It's down a filthy side road past metal bins and bags full of rubbish, but we're both relieved that at least it's accessible. Freddie bounds out to meet us. He unloads the keyboard, drum machine and Tamsin's wheelchair. I take his arm, tentative on my black and white stilettos, and make my way inside.

The studio is dark, and smells of sick. There are wires that twist on the scuzzy khaki carpet, mapped with dubious stains. The whole place is crammed with musicians' paraphernalia – guitar stands, keyboard stands, mic stands, headphones hanging in tangles off of them all. Amps crowd the floor space and there's a drum kit at the back. Directly opposite is a greasy window, cobwebbed at the edges, where the mixing desk looks out on all of this mess.

I love it, every tiny disgusting detail.

'You ready and eager, dearheart?' Freddie asks and pats my bum before he helps me sit down.

Tone comes in wearing a long black coat, bass guitar in its case. He's very different to Freddie. I fancy him but I would never, ever, tell him. Tamsin and me exchange sly glances, knowing that he's high up on our Orgy List.

Freddie sets up the keyboard for Tam to play, and Tone starts strumming. Goat, the drummer, appears, bringing some Mancunian warmth to the place. He takes off his shabby donkey jacket, sits behind the drum kit, and starts banging away.

'Let's do it then! Become Kata Kolbert. You're the boss,' Goat says, and gives me a drum roll.

'Remember we've only got time to do about three tracks,' Freddie says. 'So we need to get the best stuff laid down.'

My cheeks blush. Freddie has paid for this session, or done a deal, or worked something out. I don't know the details, but I'm consumed with gratitude.

'Okay, let's do "The Deed is Done",' Tone says, laughing. 'I'll give you my review, *NME*-style. Kata Kolbert's jaunty indie-pop tune about a young girl throwing herself away with easy sex and minuscule ambition is sure to be a massive hit.'

'God, love it, Tone, love it,' I say, ignoring the shiver of nerves.

The engineer, Bob, has a Jack Russell, Frodo, who is quiet, but he is one of those dogs that wants to smell everything, including us. Freddie laughs when he sniffs Goat's notorious feet.

We do a couple of run-throughs. It sounds good and my voice is cooperating.

At one point, Tamsin turns to me from the keyboard.

'I love it when you really let go, your voice is like a gorgeous bell.'

I say nothing, not used to compliments.

Tone strums a melody on the bass, which gives the song a meaty groove. Goat joins in, doing fancy drum lines. I want to laugh, as I prepare myself to launch into the first line of 'The Deed is Done'. Freddie picks out notes on the guitar, fuzzing it up to the max. The first word of the song is out of my mouth when, through the glass partition, the sound engineer lifts his hand to stop us. There's a click in my headphones. 'Guys, the balance is all wrong. Too heavy on the bass, man.'

We all look towards him, his Charles Bronson tash fixed round a sneer.

Freddie is cross. Tone stands up, throws his bass down, and, without a word, flies out of the studio. There are a few seconds of silence as we all look at each other.

'He's in a strop,' says Goat, as he taps out a rhythm on the snare drum, rolling his eye in the direction of Bob. 'You know what Tone's like.'

I don't really know, and I'm not sure how to react.

Goat leaps up. 'It's okay, I'll go and find him.'

He leaves the studio before anyone utters a word.

'I think I'll make a dash to the loo then,' I say, looking at Freddie.

Tamsin purses her lips: 'Yeah, well, I'm sure you must.'

As Freddie helps me walk through to the back, he narrows his eyes. 'What did that mean?'

'She knows me too well,' I respond, tugging at his T-shirt, black and too tight on his large frame. 'Give me a kiss.'

He responds by sitting down on a handy chair and scooping me onto his lap and when he knows I'm safe, his hands fly under my skirt with no preamble. I'm lost to him, and arch my body towards his. He gets busy quickly, his fingers dancing.

The abrupt appearance of a yapping Frodo breaks the spell, and I freeze.

'The dog knows what we're up to,' says Freddie, not removing his hand, but attempting with a gentle shove of his leg, to see the dog off.

I feel Freddie's cock underneath me. But Bob is suddenly close and we return to Tamsin, patiently waiting at the keyboard.

'I'll pop to the bog too,' she says, 'but I doubt I'll have as much fun.'

I squirm. Tamsin laughs and wheels away.

Thirty minutes pass. No Goat, no Tone.

'I better go and find them,' Freddie sighs and he's off out the door, leaving me and Tamsin alone with Creepy Bob, who has reappeared with a bottle of milk and a packet of fags.

If Tamsin wasn't with me, I would be frightened. Time drags, and drags some more.

'They coming back or what?' grunts Bob as he lights up.

'Yes,' Tamsin says, underlining it with a stare. 'Most definitely.'

'Someone's gotta pay,' mutters Bob, glancing at my breasts before he wanders off back to his cubbyhole, leaving Frodo to lick at a thick stain on the carpet.

'Fuck off, divvy,' Tamsin mouths at his back, as Freddie returns, bottles clanking.

'Where have you been?' I wail, clutching him as he kisses me. 'We were really worried.'

'Change of plan, dearheart, that's all. We're meeting the others in Finsbury Park. They've gone on ahead and I've come back to get you two.'

'I take it we're having liquid refreshment,' says Tamsin.

'I bloody well hope so,' I sigh. 'I need a drink after this morning.'

Bob and Frodo appear from the back room.

'You know the deal, man,' says Bob, screwing up his mean little eyes. 'You pay me now?'

Turning his back on him, Freddie winks at me. 'I'll just get these lovely ladies into the taxi and come straight back.'

Outside, our favourite taxi driver Abe has opened the car door in readiness. Tamsin is helped into the front seat, her chair quickly packed. I shuffle into the back, expecting Freddie to return to the studio, but he jumps in beside me and, with a big laugh, tells Abe to step on it.

I squeal with pleasure as Freddie cracks open a can of cheap cider. Abe puts his foot down and we head off towards Finsbury Park.

CHAPTER 4

16 August 1985: And so our evening began. I started my drinking, determined to inebriate my mood, to be happy and reckless. I feel full of lecherous curiosity after having nothing but unwanted suppression for my best teenage years. I intend to make up for this.

Ant strides into my room carrying three empty boxes picked up from the farm where he works. August is trying to be sunny and my birthday is looming, but all I can think about as I play a rough tape-recording of Kraftwerk's 'Autobahn' is the move.

'What junk do you want to put in these, Pen?' says Ant, as he puts the boxes on my bed. 'You've got so much crap after all.'

'Cassettes, records and books,' I say, ignoring his mockery. 'At least I'm cultured and manage to read.'

Ant looks at me.

'Like Dad,' he says softly.

I look back at him, interrupted by Jake who is suddenly standing in the doorway. He fills the space with his height, hands on the frame, fingers clenching.

'You're never going to do it in time.' It's a statement not an opening to a conversation.

'I'm helping her,' says Ant. 'She'll get there.'

I say nothing but pretend I'm immersed in organising a pile of 7-inch singles.

'Don't forget to pack that little shit,' Jake continues, gesturing towards Tooty, on the bed, sleeping peacefully. 'It won't last a week in London.'

Ant and me remain silent. He hands me another batch of singles. The first one I see is 'Shipbuilding' by Robert Wyatt.

'I'll strip the walls off the day after you've gone,' says Jake, glancing around the room. 'Might shut your mother up, having this room back at last.'

Ant is turned away from Jake and moves his lips in mimicry. I'm trying not to laugh. Jake disappears noisily and begins to whistle. A sign that he's calm.

'Pen, can you lend me a fiver until I'm paid on Friday?' I look up at Ant, my bruv, with his short dark curly hair and heavy eyebrows showing the line of Mum's family.

'Who's going to lend you fivers when I'm gone? Will it be the new girlfriend?'

I feel myself tense as my eyes film over.

'You won't get rid of me,' he says. 'It's not the other side of the planet. I'll bring Lucy down to meet you. Better than her coming here after all.'

He jerks his head in the direction of the whistling Jake.

'Good,' I say. 'You'd better.'

I look back at my singles. 'The Eton Rifles' by The Jam.

'Put this on,' I say. 'Really loud.'

Ant loves The Jam but Jake can't stand them. He hates anything we like. Ant and me join in the chorus together, Ant pogoing like Sid Vicious on speed.

August wakes up and the sun comes out.

We're at the Tom Allen Centre, Stratford East, across the road from the grimy shopping centre, at a table in the Wimpy with Freddie. The Boys are here too, from the desolate wastes of suburban Essex, our connection sealing fast over shared cassette tapes, making music and an imminent, handy London crash pad.

Sipping lager hidden in a cola bottle, Owen is all legs and arms, stripes and white linen. Some eyeliner, blond hair harshly swept back, in bright cerise trousers, a genius on the synthesiser.

He is twenty-one years old and Tamsin wants to screw him. Have a quickie. Then get over it, and concentrate on languishing loverboy Mike, her boyfriend who never appears from his remote Cornish town.

For now, Owen's skill with sound and keyboard is what we want in support of our first public gig. Pretty Dan next to him will help too, with his New Romantic fringe, buckle boots and gentle smile. And they've brought along Craig. Adorable, dressed to the silver-skirt tranny gills with ripped fishnets, pointy shoes, black biker cap. A lush entourage, gorgeous to look at, and offering Tam and me unexpected assistance.

Next to me is Freddie in a black dress that comes past his knees. Barefoot in red lippy, only I know he's naked underneath, a thought that sends ripples of desire through my skin.

Tamsin and me exchange disbelieving looks. We're not quite sure how we came to be here. Especially me, always shivering inside my shyness.

The Ugly Pygmies – born out of boredom one evening during the 5,000 days of incarceration. Simple fun songs rustled up in an hour or two on my ancient Yamaha keyboard and endless phone chats to Tamsin: 'Jack the Back', 'Please Don't Eat My Mother', 'Shove It with Sin', 'Burn, Burn, Nazi Flag'... Freddie convinced me it would be a great way to break myself in to performing. He sensed how nervous I was and what I'd need to do before I could take Kata Kolbert out of her bedroom and ready to gig.

'The reporter will be here any minute,' Freddie says, shifting in his dress. 'We're looking good. Tamsin, do the famous scowl. Pen, do the pout.'

'Will he want us to get out of our wheelchairs?' I ask.

'Hopefully not. After all, that's part of the point, isn't it?' says Freddie.

'Yes,' Tamsin nods, practising her scowl. 'We'll just say no.'

The reporter is Nick and his music column in the local paper is a good start for us – and for me. He lopes in, chunky camera round his neck, long straggly hair and faded, flared jeans.

'Wow, cool look!' he enthuses, his eyes everywhere from Tamsin's hard stare and massive dreadlocks, to the cleavage of my severe, ripped dress – with cursory nods to Freddie in his dress, and The Boys fluttering behind us.

'Where do you want us then? We don't want to mess about.' Freddie takes charge, which is always a relief.

Nick is enthusiastic. 'Yeah, yeah man, great. Outside by the brick wall. Nice and grimy.'

'In our chairs,' says Tamsin, eyeballing him without a smile so he knows this is not up for negotiation.

Craig gets to his feet, totters to Tamsin, grabs the handles on her wheelchair and shoots her forward while Freddie takes charge of me.

'So what's the aim for the band, guys?'

The Boys, and Freddie, dramatically turn their backs to him, facing away.

'There is no plan,' says Tamsin.

'It's existential,' I add, 'you can't have aims under the boot of Führer Thatcher. We just do what we do, by the day. By the hour. Making meaning for ourselves.'

'Yeah, that's just the way it is,' Tamsin confirms. 'Thatcher wants to crush the working classes. So you can't plan. Plan is a bourgeois word.'

'Plans are about control. Especially if you're… a cripple,' I growl, for effect.

Nick tenses at the word cripple.

'Cripple has been the label of our oppression for too long,' says Tamsin. 'We have to reclaim it, like "queer". Make the word ours.'

Nick nods solemnly as he continues to snap photos. We know he hasn't got a clue.

'And why The Ugly Pygmies?' he asks.

Tamsin looks at me with a half smile.

I look back at Nick.

'Because that's what we are,' I say.

Throughout the shoot, Freddie hands out the vodka, revving me away from my shyness. He passes Nick a beer.

'Thanks, Nick. Look forward to seeing it in *The Gazette*.' Freddie gestures towards him: 'It's time to go-go-go. You coming in for their gig?'

'Of course, man, of course.' Nick's hair flies with excitement. 'You go. Good luck, girls.'

Wheeled back inside, Freddie and Craig help with the set-up on stage. We gaze out at the stacked seating, filling with an array of spike-haired punks, New Wave posers and peacock New Romantics.

Fear boils through my blood.

At the keyboard, I notice my face is numb and my fingers burn. I feebly prod a key, and look at Tamsin. She smiles and hits the button of her Dr Rhythm drum machine.

Freddie stomps to life with a dance, bare-footed, dolled up with smeared red lipstick and splattered-on eyeliner like Robert Smith of The Cure. He blows me a kiss. I attempt a tune on the keyboard as the audience settles down.

A noise thumps into the air. I open my mouth and sing:

'Hey Jack, get outta the shack, don't crack your back...'

The sound isn't my voice and hits my ears as a vodka-drenched shriek. *You can't sing you can't sing you can't sing* sneers in my head. Tamsin collapses with a half-laugh and the drum machine falls dead on the floor.

The audience cheer – or maybe jeer. Freddie dashes on stage and I start crying. From the corner of my eye, I spot Craig, Dan and Owen, smiling, mouthing words I can't understand. Freddie jerks his head and they rush on.

In a marvellous instant, Owen hits a note on my keyboard, Craig starts dancing and the rescued drum machine shudders into fast-beat action.

Fuck you, I scream inside at the sneer, and I sing at the top of my voice. No one cares what comes out. It doesn't matter that I'm pissed off my face, that my nerves are raw. I can sing, I can write and I know it. I get through 'Jack the Back'. I let Kata Kolbert out to play. And through our friends – and Freddie – our skittish, drunk little skins are saved.

Mum is packing my winter clothes into an old suitcase she picked up for £1 from the Barnardo's shop in the village. I twitch when she rolls up my prized charity-shop dresses. August is hurtling on. Two weeks to go. Two weeks until I'm out of here. To London, where Destiny awaits!

The downstairs room where I've lived for the 5,000+ days is crammed full of boxes, bags and a few ageing suitcases, similar to the one Mum is packing.

Mum ignores my twitchy mood and continues rolling things tightly.

'So you've got one of those new microwave things,' she says. 'Can you cook everything in it? Isn't it dangerous?'

Somehow Lorna (Drippy) got us a charity grant to buy one, and we couldn't wait to play with it.

'I'm still a bit worried how you'll manage, Pen,' Mum's voice is soft as she forces the bulging case shut. 'You can't even make a cup of tea.'

'Yes I can, Mum,' I say, hoping it comes out as reassuring and mature. 'You've seen the kettle-pourer. You know I've had a go on it here.'

The kettle-pourer is a deceptively simple idea. The kettle stands on a raised platform, which can be tipped forward with very slight pressure, strapped in place to avoid any serious overspill. It's ugly and beige and medical-looking, but Tam and me begrudgingly admit it's essential. There's no lifting of kettles or anything for our stiff arthriticky wrists. And a kettle will give us food fallbacks, such as Pot Noodle and Cup-a-Soup.

Mum looks at the curtains in the room. 'You sure you don't want to take them?'

'No thanks, Mum. I think we've got enough.'

I don't want to tell her again that I hate the big orange splodges that repeat over and over on the beige background. They are dull and old-fashioned. In a bad way. Not at all bohemian.

For a moment, Mum looks lost and I feel emotion swelling inside my chest.

'Everyone will miss you down the shops,' she says. 'They're all used to our weekly visits.'

The tightening in my belly won't go away, but I won't cry. I can't cry.

'Still,' says Mum brightly, as she tips my underwear from a drawer onto the bed. 'You've got your birthday first. And at least you're here that morning.'

One week to go until then. I've scarcely had time to think about my birthday as it's all planned for Tam and me to go and sign the tenancy at the flat in the afternoon and then have a drink in the pub near to Avalon in the evening. Mum starts humming an old Spandau Ballet song and I realise again the changes around the corner will be immense.

The Lord Clyde in Capworth Street, E10. Six o'clock. I sit with Freddie on one side, Tone on the other and Tamsin in front of me.

We're waiting for The Boys. Tamsin and me sluice ourselves in drink. Freddie tickles me. I can't stop giggling and Tamsin giggles too. We're on vodka and Cokes, one after the other.

I'm wearing a black corset with lace edged at the waist and the bust line. It's a bit Madonna, especially with the long necklaces and bracelets I've added. Below this, a blue tartan skirt, old style, with a proper safety pin. On my legs, fishnets and my red Victorian whore's boots. My recent hair extensions are multicoloured with slashes of blonde, amid blacks, blues, pinks and purples. I have one gold flower in my hair. Eyelashes painted on and a splash of fuchsia on my eyelids.

Tamsin is all spots. Cropped spotty trousers with braces, a black-and-white polka-dot cardigan and a chunky neon-purple choker around her thin neck. Her dreadlock extensions piled high in a purple beret. We have matching green nail varnish.

I gaze at Freddie and tease him at how I love his big nose and flying hippy hair. Tone is all charm, sharp cheekbones and swept-back fringe. My birthday present, the three Anaïs Nin journals I haven't got, on the table in front of me.

At last, The Boys slouch in through the heavy smoke. Owen in his billowing kimono tunic. Craig in a de rigueur leather skirt. They make apologies for the absence of Dan before presents shower me: a phallic-shaped loofer and a lurid birthday card, 'Dominatrix' of a she-male with a giant cock.

'Craig looks like that underneath,' Owen smirks, and Craig kicks him, mouth open.

Several drinks on, we are all surprised by the appearance of the chubby landlady holding champagne and glasses, wishing me a happy birthday.

Promptly, the champagne goes down to join the vodka and I notice the many eyes of the older pub regulars swivelling our way.

Freddie helps me totter to the toilet when my bladder finally demands attention after a typically long battle to ignore it.

The cubicles are very small; the toilet is very low. It's a toilet for normals after all. No bars to grab hold of. In some pain I sway in indecision. I know I won't manage it with my unbending knees and I'm loath to ask Freddie.

'Come on, dearheart, I'll help you,' Freddie says, gently holding me around the waist. 'It's deliciously sleazy – in a good way.'

'I'm sorry,' I whisper, burning up with vodka and embarrassment.

'Ssh, silly thing.' Freddie kisses me and, before I know it, his strong hands have whipped down my knickers – fortunately my best pink satin Frenchies – and lowered me to the loo.

I wee for hours and as I'm finishing, Freddie decides we must snog.

We are interrupted by hearing the landlady barging in, hovering outside the cubicle.

'Are you okay in there?' she asks loudly.

'Yes,' I say breathlessly.

As Freddie helps me up we're startled to hear Owen's voice.

'That bloke Mike from the record company has arrived,' he hisses.

The landlady's heels click on the stone floor and she cackles as she leaves, 'They're all having sex in there!'

When I return to my seat, Tamsin leans over to whisper: 'The landlady is enjoying the entertainment, you and Freddie are star turns.'

Another vodka and Coke and I can do little more than struggle to sit upright. Mike, from some obscure indie record label called Foul Flapjack, and his motley entourage, scowl at us from the bar. I watch Freddie's expressive hands as he fences the unfriendly group into a corner to talk business about the launching of Kata Kolbert.

Cheeks numb and bowels churning, I suddenly realise Tamsin has gone off with The Boys. Tone pecks me on the cheek, waves goodbye and Freddie gestures that he's nipping to the toilet.

Laughing for no particular reason, I keel over sideways on the seat, my corset creaking, my breasts popping out the top. A gaggle of old men cheer, waving cigarettes in the air. I laugh back, and try to make myself decent.

On the piano, in the corner, aged Gay Ricky – who's always been Gay Ricky – the regular tinkler, starts to play 'Roll Out the Barrel'.

I try to join in, but I'm laughing too much. Freddie comes back, sits me up and yanks up my corset to recapture my defiant breasts.

'Mike's a twat,' says Freddie over the din of the cockney knees-up. 'A complete knobhead. No way we're dealing with him, doll.'

I look at him, my blood on fire, my mouth open. I want to shag him right now – if I can control the waves of sickness building to a crescendo in my gullet.

'I think it's time to go,' says Freddie. 'I'm not going to get any sense out of you now, am I?'

His grey-blue eyes are bright with humour.

'No, no,' I moan and cling to him like a child to a teddy. 'I want to go home with you.' He laughs and coaxes me to my feet as the world and my belly spins.

'Come on, that's it,' Freddie holds my arm as I wobble outside to where Tamsin's brother-in-law, Ron, waits in the car to ferry me back to Avalon.

With Freddie's help, I plonk onto the seat. The walk from the pub is too much, I'm too hot, the alcohol is bubbling. Sensing the inevitable, I lurch forward and throw up on the pavement. Again and again, tittering between each puke.

'Thank God you've got good aim, Pen,' says Ron, perpetually good-humoured. 'It looks like you had a fun time then?'

Freddie kisses me on the head and quickly on each of my pushed-up breasts.

'No tongues after that display,' he winks. 'And anyway, see you next week, darlin', in London!'

My head thumps, my insides somersault.

It's the best birthday ever.

CHAPTER 5

23 August 1985: My last day at home. So to bed, and my last night in this prison, this hell. A new home – friends, love, sex, literature, art!

I sit in the car, squashed against the window with suitcases and cardboard boxes shoved against me. The car smells of cigarettes and dog vomit.

Jake careens along the A40.

'Fucking slut!' He growls as a young woman with red hair and a miniskirt jumps across at the lights with a grin.

I try and push my earphones back into my ears but I woke up with a shitty wrist this morning and I can't quite manage it. It doesn't help that Tooty is in his basket on my lap.

'Fucking Paki!' Jake grips the steering wheel and hunches forward.

'Not long now, Pen,' Mum says and turns her head to look at me.

We hit the flyover at Paddington and it feels like lift-off. The roads are different and confusing. The buildings change into a clash of styles and heights. Everything crowds together. There are no cows, there are no timid willow trees, there is no green. This is London.

We slow to a standstill by Madame Tussauds. My guts clamp inwards and I gaze at the hordes of tourists.

'Look at all the fucking nig-nogs,' Jake growls. 'You and that cat won't last a month with these fuckers.'

'Jake, don't.' Mum looks at him and I stiffen. He ignores her and I relax a bit.

We jerk on through more lights and stop again on Pentonville Road, as an old woman with a trolley shuffles across.

Jake revs his engine, the car splutters and we lurch forward.

With some effort I manage to get my earplugs back in at last, Tooty crying softly as we move. I know my Walkman batteries won't last long, but for now I can enjoy Billy MacKenzie, his towering vocals making me feel deliciously miserable.

And I know we are getting closer to my new home.

I am happy. I have Morrissey's postcard. To me. In his strange block writing. It's actually the first letter, with him and Sandie Shaw on the front, and it's quite difficult to keep it in the left cup of my bra. But I have to, or I might die.

I dream as always of his fingers touching it as he wrote this personal message, his essence now on my skin.

Under the other bra cup is a soggy piece of paper with a song lyric on it. From Nick Drake's 'Northern Sky'. This is from Freddie, a sort of love letter. When I think about Freddie my skin flutters and my cheeks blush.

And this is the London I've dreamt of for four long years.

London.

After today, my home. A grown-up home. Not with Mum, not with Ant, not with Jake.

But my home with my best-ever friend, my soul sister Tamsin.

The roads to the new home snake and tangle.

'We've got a mile to go if Antony doesn't fuck up the route,' Jake growls.

My brother Ant never fucks up the route. Mum and me say nothing and keep our eyes down as we turn into Leyton High Road.

When we pull up into the cul-de-sac, I don't see the drab 1930s brick and the peeling window frames. I see a golden hall of freedom. Angels sing, hummingbirds flutter, trumpets blare.

Tamsin arrives with her brother-in-law Ron. Her smile echoes mine and we hang back as our scant belongings and third-hand furniture is taken in. I scream at Ant to mind my aged typewriter, the most precious thing I own.

'Tatty old thing,' Ant snorts and pretends to throw it.

I fall for it. 'Don't be a pig! You don't understand – that's my life.'

'Fucking books,' Jake grunts under his breath, grabbing a box. 'Should've burnt 'em.'

We all ignore Jake. He won't show himself up in front of Tamsin's family. I know he is pleased to be rid of me, but not half as pleased as I am to be rid of him.

I watch him huff, then I catch Mum's nervous eyes and look away.

'It's almost all in,' Ant announces, dragging a case of my clothes. 'You two can come and look and I'll hang the curtains up.'

'I'll put the kettle on, shall I?' Mum says. 'And butter Tooty's paws to stop him straying.'

'That fucking cat won't last a week,' Jake says, again.

I say nothing. I am staring at freedom, and Tamsin is wise to Jake's ways.

Inside the flat, we scoot from room to room, tiny as they are.

'We're here!' I squeal at Tamsin.

'Orgies!' she hisses under her breath.

We've read Anaïs Nin. Rimbaud. About the Bloomsbury set, and are determined to be as bohemian as we can.

Ron strides up. 'What you two sniggering about? Do I want to know?'

'No, Ron, you don't.' Tamsin pulls one of her faces. Ron is nice, but I'm shy around him. I'm used to so few men – only to Jake, Ant, doctors and rare family members. But now I have Freddie and The Boys, I'm learning.

Mum scuttles in with a squirming Tooty, paws sticky yellow. Tamsin releases her cat, the imperious Ollie, from her carrier. There is instant hissing and Tooty hauls himself up Mum's body.

'They have to get on though, don't they, eh?' Mum rubs her scratches but doesn't mention them.

'They will, they just need to settle,' Tamsin says.

Tooty scarpers across the sofa, butter patches everywhere. I sigh, thinking thank God all our furniture is mostly stuff rescued from the tip.

We don't have a lot but what we do have is ours. Odd cutlery, random crockery, lurid green-beige curtains in huge head-spinning circles, cast-offs from a Seventies porn movie. The only pair we could afford that would fit. In the lounge, a battered chunky sideboard in dingy stained wood. No cooker, but a Baby Belling, the stupendous microwave and a small fridge.

Living independently just wasn't done by the likes of us, armies of social workers kept telling us from the start, but Tamsin and me knew it would happen. Their foot-dragging, their endless form-filling, slowed us down. But while they dithered we gathered wherever we could, whatever we could. We weren't fussy and we weren't embarrassed with the tat we were forced to collect from jumble sales and charity shops.

One friend I used to visit, Ellen, had been sent to a care home when her parents died. It was another planet to me. Sneering attendants neglected her, patronised her, stole her few wretched possessions.

I think of Ellen as Ant puts up the curtains.

I am a writer, I am a punk and I am passionate. I will never be put into a home.

Unpacking a small box of papers, I come across *Jamming!* fanzine. I turn to the back page and glow for a moment at my letter, there, printed for the world to see. The letter that brought Freddie to me.

The flat slowly starts to look like a home. Jake sits in the car by himself while Mum fusses in the kitchen, leaving us out some food to eat later. Ant is trying to make sure our TV aerial works.

Ron grabs the empty cardboard boxes as he goes to leave. 'You'll be all right then?' He looks at Tamsin. 'I know you'll be fine, Pen. You've got Freddie.'

As he says it, I melt. He's right. I do have Freddie.

Everyone leaves.

I sit next to Tamsin and we clink our wine glasses. In front of us, on the battered sideboard, an aged TV. We don't care.

It's 9.30, an August evening, and the sun has been out late in the day. The cats are still hiding. We haven't eaten dinner but all we can do is smile.

We drink wine and nibble cheesy triangles.

Tamsin picks up a pen, her favourite posh blue pen, and says: 'Okay, the flat-warming-my-birthday-party orgy. How many people do we actually know?'

I laugh, tipsy.

Pleased as pleased could be.

To be home.

Sandra, our home help, enters our flat with a high-pitched 'Cooee!' and we respond with our 'Cooee!' back.

Tamsin and me had been a bit snide about a home help at first, but we love Sandra to bits. A treasure. She is bright, like an eager sparrow, in her late forties with a round friendly face.

Personal care, dressing, and cooking isn't easy. Up until now it was our mums doing what mums do and what mums have always done for their crippled children.

Sandra is here to prepare our evening meal and get us undressed. That's if there's time.

'Dinner first?' Sandra says, looking at us in turn. 'Or a quick strip? You both said on Monday you were feeling really tired.'

I sigh. 'It's only four-thirty, Sandra, I can't bear it. Getting undressed before dinner. We want to escape all that.'

'Almost as bad as being in the Cheshire home,' says Tamsin. 'But we're not moaning at you, Sandra.'

Sandra has an amazing ability to do jobs as she talks.

Occasionally catching my eye, she proceeds to change my bedclothes.

'You're not in an institution – you can do what you want. You know I don't mind stringing it out to the last moment.'

Tamsin and me exchange mournful glances. We're always knackered from the extraordinary complexity of managing stuff:

getting out of bed, using gadgets to drag things over our heads. Swaying to the toilet, wondering whether you can manage a shower. Wondering whether you smell, and whether you can wait another day when Sandra can help. Wondering how to use some precious minutes from the six hours we have with her each week.

'At least we didn't bother to struggle with our tights,' I say. 'After all, Sandra, what's the point when you have no guests?'

'The point might be staying warm,' smiles Sandra. 'It won't be long before the cold sets in.'

She skips to the kitchen as Tamsin and me shrug.

I go back to the typewriter. All day in between party plans, there's been writing and music. The songs have to be polished in time for Freddie's Phase II, and there is also a story collection on the go – the Gothic tales I have to tell.

Today I'm still weary after my doze and Sandra's cheerfulness startles me. The juggling of her six hours' help, the permanent challenge, the choices we have to make.

Tamsin is up already and in the kitchen with Sandra. I slouch out on my self-painted walking stick, all multicolours with bells on the handle.

Sandra asks about dinner with a teasing smile.

'What do you want to eat tonight?'

Tamsin and me look at each other. I'm always stumped. My priorities are nothing to do with food. My hair is a mess. I can't bear Freddie to see me in a dishevelled state the next day.

'Sandwich for me,' I bleat. 'No butter. Cheese and a teaspoon of salad cream please.'

'Nothing hot, Pen?' Sandra flashes keen eyes.

'Oh no missus, madam,' Tamsin says, pulling a face. 'I know what she likes hot.'

We all laugh. Tamsin can never let an innuendo go.

'A sandwich is fine,' I say. 'Then I'll get you to help with washing my hair.'

'Tuna sweetcorn for me,' Tamsin echoes. 'My hair won't take too long either.'

Sandra, sweet caring Sandra, sighs. She will always do as we ask.

We chat as she makes the food and cuts the bread into triangles. Our cats slink into the kitchen, hypnotised by the smell of tuna.

When my hair is finished, my fresh locks crimped into a large Kate Bush mountain of loveliness, I drag a box into the lounge on my lap, wheeling my wheelchair with my feet.

Minutes pass and I'm surrounded by cassette tapes.

My demo tapes. Some go back five years. One contains the first songs Tamsin and I recorded in a studio in Uxbridge. 'Searching for the Crazy Visitor', 'This Romance', and 'Crooked Vamp'.

I find a rare bootleg of Smiths live tracks, pop it on my Walkman and listen as I sort some more. Morrissey growls about mammary glands and I'm enthralled.

I feel sad that I haven't had a letter from him since moving to London. I did get a Christmas card, and a note about 'How Soon is Now' but nothing more. I glance up and on the wall is a photograph he sent to me, now framed in gold. He gazes down in black and white, shirt open, quiff floppy, the rest of the band blurry behind him. In the corner, it reads: To Kata Love Morrissey XXX.

I glow and drift and murmur the lyrics with him. I know I'll forgive him. He's very famous now and I'm sure he's busy.

I find the tape I'm after. The cassette copy of the tape I sent Freddie months earlier, getting ready for the first studio session.

Sandra leans her head around the door, bird eyes sparkling. 'Eat the sandwich,' she says. 'Make sure you line your stomach!'

I nod, swapping The Smiths for my own tape.

Sandra likes to make disapproving noises about our drinking habits. It does make vomiting a little less painful, but otherwise food is an inconvenience.

'Only one vodka tonight,' Tamsin teases as Sandra leaves. 'We promise.'

On the tape I am singing: 'The Deed is Done':

Slender girl goes up the grassy hill
Combs her hair, there's so much time to kill.

I knew it was good. Tamsin knew it was good. Freddie adored it and now I waited. For him to chat up Alan Mc. Or for Gary from Color Tapes or some musical bigwig somewhere to do the magic.

There was only that future.

And of course – a big fat naughty party.

Me and Tamsin, the first night in the flat.

CHAPTER 6

6 October 1985: After the high tea and silly hats we switched on the TV. Shock was total. We gasped at the scenes of the riot. But it was a bit exciting.

Tamsin makes me a cup of tea and I'm grateful. But I don't want to get dressed.

I sit in the kitchen, clenched into silence.

Freddie arrives at lunchtime, bouncy. He kisses me but I lean away.

'Good news and bad news, honeybun,' he says as he puts the kettle on. 'Got that shithead engineer off my back over the dosh for the studio. But...'

He trails off to look at me.

'Bob blanked the only recording we managed of "The Deed is Done", Pen. We don't have anything. I'm so sorry.'

'Oh,' I say and look out through the glass door into the shabby communal garden.

'We'll sort it out though, I've got an idea.'

I say nothing but know I'm about to cry, and hate myself for it.

'Hey, you okay? Still in your nightie? All ready for me, eh?' Freddie laughs.

I can feel the quaver in my voice even before I speak.

'You don't have to worry.' I blink, forcing out a calm, adult voice: 'I'm not your responsibility after all.'

'What? You look upset, Pen. Is it the pervert neighbour next door?'

'I've been thinking,' I whisper, to stop the tremor in my voice. 'I don't think things should carry on as they are. You don't have to do anything for me.'

Freddie sinks to his knees and strokes my hair. 'You know I love you, Pen. What's this about?'

'When you see who I really am, you'll hate me. Even though I love you,' I blurt out in a rush of sobs. 'I'm not this – this person you think I am. It's a joke. I'm ugly, useless, pathetic. On top of this shit.'

I jab a finger towards the wheelchair below me.

'Stop it, Pen. Where's all this sob story come from?' Freddie says gently, looking into my eyes. 'And don't feel obliged to say you love me because I love you.'

I pull away from him.

'Why do you say that? You want me to make it easier for you to dump me, don't you?'

'Pen, fucking hell. I'm not dumping you!' He stands up and stomps to my bedroom. 'Come on. In here.'

'No, Freddie, don't go in—'

There's a horrible heartbeat of silence.

'Penny, come here. Now.'

I flip cold, my tears frozen.

I know what he's seen.

On my crappy old dressing table I've pushed back my make-up to make space and lined up my paracetamols. I stare at them for hours.

'This is shit, Pen. It's really shit. You want to take them? Go on then. I get the message. I'm nothing to you.'

My tears return. I sob so hard I can't talk and shake my head as much as my stiff neck will allow.

His hands move quickly to scoop away the pills and flush them down the toilet.

I'm still crying, in wretched, wracking waves. Freddie picks me up in his strong arms and puts me on the bed, lays beside me, and pulls up the quilt.

'Shhh now, honeybun. We'll sort this out.'

He strokes my head, and starts murmuring a Nick Drake song. I blank into his voice, my weeping dies down and I fall asleep.

I wake up alone to see the sun slanting into the room.

Freddie hears me stir and dashes in from the kitchen.

'Sleepy babe. You with us now?'

'Yes,' I mumble and grin. As always happens, the fear passes and the world is magically back to how it should be.

'Good, because I didn't tell you the best news. I'm getting Tim Gane from Stereolab to come and record your songs on his 4-track.'

'Tim Gane,' I repeat, wide-eyed.

'Yes. And Pen, remember,' Freddie leans over and kisses me. 'I love you.'

I stroke my black leather bondage dress, the crisp chilly autumn light falling on endless buckles, shiny as razors along each side. I had it made: the eight straps fitting my body perfectly; a tight new skin, with wide straps for the shoulders rising from the plunging V-neck. It's punk, it's fetish – though I pang with guilt at the strong leather smell.

'Penny, that's not a dress,' squeals Sandra, tugging a tangle from my hair.

'Ouch, Sand, careful. These extensions were very, very—'

'Expensive,' she butts in over me with a laugh.

'And done at Antenna,' crows Tamsin. '*The* Antenna.'

'In Kensington,' I say, wincing as another knot catches. 'The King's Road. The first extensions I had were ragtails, black and orange.'

Hanging in thick clumps each side of my ears, Mum hated them.

Tamsin and me went to Antenna on impulse. I spent three weeks of benefits on a taxi to Avalon, and then the phone-bill

63

money on the trip to Kensington and my hair. 'And done by Simon Forbes himself,' Tamsin adds, reading my thoughts as always.

'Old Simon, eh? Well I'm glad you haven't got orange and black now. These multicoloured ones are almost pretty.'

Sandra pulls a strand and simultaneously whips out a duster from her apron pocket. 'I do know that young Freddie's eyes will pop out when he sees you in that.'

'*That*, Sandra, is a leather bondage dress,' I say and stroke it again. It's gloriously indecent. 'I'll probably wear it to the party.'

'Freddie's seen it already. She wore it for our gig in Stratford. In public.' Tamsin gives me a wink. 'It was all popping out there, everything on show.'

'Our almost-gig, you mean,' I sigh, shuddering at the memory.

'No, there was a gig. By The Boys at least, and we had a stab at it. The one and only half-appearance by The Ugly Pygmies!' Tamsin laughs and I laugh.

After a struggle, Sandra manages to balance the bondage dress on a hanger and hook it over my bedroom door.

'I better dash to the laundrette,' she says, smiling, unfazed as always.

When I first met Tamsin, I'd not long had my last session with Dr Gillette, who told me to keep a diary. It was around the same time that Tamsin and me were devouring the journals of Anaïs Nin. I started with one journal, now I have three, not including the random dated notes I will scribble on anything.

Dr Gillette told me I had clinical depression. Told me a lot had happened to me for my age, that I shouldn't be surprised I got fed up, but that there was no need to dwell on the past.

One of the first things I wrote in the brown journal was: 'I have clinical depression and I don't know what it means.'

I know I should write in the brown journal now – that I've been feeling bad, that I counted out the paracetamols. But this stuff is always hard to write because I don't know where it comes from.

The shrinks and doctors always think it's about my wheelchair, my juvenile arthritis. I know it's something else, it's because out there. They don't like me trying. They don't want me breaking down the barriers.

I can hear Tamsin talking to her cat in her bedroom, as she combs out Ollie's long black and white fur.

I decide to try a list. Dr Gillette liked lists. 'How are you feeling?' lists, when the fall down comes. Out of nowhere, as if someone's pushed you from a tower block, in the dark, and you fall, down, down, in slow motion. Knowing that everything everyone says inside the dark must be a lie.

I shudder, glad I can hear Tamsin in the other room and Ollie's piteous meowing. My eyes drop back to the brown journal list:

1. Fear – don't know what about.
2. Confusion – feelings a big mess.
3. Disbelief – nothing good ever happens.
4. Something in my chest like a great big spear someone's pulling backwards and forwards. I think they call that love.
5. See blue journal.

From a pile on our shared desk, I grab my blue journal. It's got a picture of Morrissey in one corner, the rest covered with endless doodles of flowers and cats. I flick to the day and, sitting up as best as I can, write:

I am a writer and a singer. I love living in London with my soul sister Tamsin. I love Freddie and he loves me.

I slam the book shut, feeling breathless and elated.

Sandra pops her head around the door.

'Penny, Tamsin, I'm almost finished.'

For someone who's dragged stuff to the laundrette, hiked a week's worth of food back to us, put it away, washed dishes and done my hair in her two-hour slot, she somehow remains as chirpy as a spring robin.

'Tea, girls? I know I need one. And I've got your post, there's loads of it.'

'I'll make one,' Tamsin says and wheels to the kitchen – to the blessed Kettle Pourer.

The bespoke desk – rustled up by Tamsin's amazingly handy dad – is quickly covered with books and forms as we open the packages marked 'Open University'.

'That looks like a lot of stuff,' says Sandra, a duster in her hand.

'Tamsin and me have enrolled to do a BA,' I say solemnly. 'First year is Victorian Culture and Society.'

'We want to give it a go,' Tamsin echoes my tone.

Sandra pauses. 'You never fancied trying it before?'

'There's no stairs this way,' I say, rolling my eyes. 'And we can use our bog at home. Did we tell you about when we tried to go to Beaconsfield Film School?'

Sandra picks up a black cat ornament and wipes its bottom.

'No, don't think so.'

'They laughed. Right in our faces. Said it was a ludicrous idea,' says Tamsin, anger tightening her pale face. 'It was shit. The usual shit.'

I stay silent, staring at the Open Uni study plan in front of me.

'Oh dear,' says Sandra, as she puts the cat back. 'I bet you girls will do well with this though, but where will you find the time? You've got your music and your writing. And your social life.'

'I'd rather have no time than too much,' I say. 'We've spent too long waiting already.'

There's another second of silence. I notice the leaves on the trees along our street drifting to the pavement.

'Make sure you leave time for Freddie,' Sandra says. 'I can tell you're smitten.'

'Smitten, that's one word for it,' teases Tamsin. 'She'll always find time for what she does with Freddie.'

I blush. Freddie is amazing but love is a ride as hectic as the battle to get my words and songs out into the world.

It's 6 October. We get up and go through our usual, Sandra-less Sunday routine.

'At least it's warm enough to leave off some layers,' says Tamsin, munching a fat croissant.

The pile of clothes left on the sofa makes me feel guilty and I wonder where my handystick is, if I'm ever going to get a dress over my head.

'Shall we start making the jellies by one p.m. and the sarnies soon after?'

Tamsin nods. 'Sandra's done a great job covering most of the furniture in the purple tablecloths. That gets me a bit more into the party spirit.'

'I'm amazed the cats haven't shredded them.'

Tamsin nods again, finishing the last remnant of her croissant, a glamorous Sunday treat and something I'd never eaten before I moved to London.

'Let's do the count. Who's first?'

'The Boys, of course,' says Tamsin, purposely licking her lips. 'There's your Freddie, so you're covered on the orgy front. There's Jean.'

'Yeah, she's only in Romford too.'

'Let's not forget Naomi, though I don't think she's the liberated, arty type.'

Naomi has a decent car and some spare time, meaning we've been able to make it as far out to such exotic locations as Victoria Park and Walthamstow Market. We met her through our new social worker Ophelia (Soppy), who found her from some voluntary group.

'And mmm, there's Tone. He'll come in his black ensemble, with his swept-back hair.'

'Oh yes,' Tamsin murmurs. 'In his sexy black Joy Division look. I do hope Tone will come.'

Once the jellies are in the fridge we help each other put on party hats and wait, shaking wrists achy from the sandwich preparation.

Tamsin wears her pink dress. It's cute with short sleeves, a bit Twenties, flapper style. Her hair is blonde, bleached especially for her birthday. I notice she looks especially thin.

I ditch the bondage dress for a new one, still a bit Kate Bush, but maybe Poly Styrene, where I've slashed the hem of a long deep-blue dress with a low-cut neck and fitted body. It suits my curves and my undeniable bust. With my long crimped hair I'm a bit Pre-Raph, a bit punk with silver chains, but always me.

We wait some more, as we wonder when to start fetching in stuff, and decide to go in slow relays, wheeling to and from the kitchen for food.

The door buzzes. We look at each other and give a little cheer. Freddie swans in, a plastic bag held tightly in his hand.

'Dearhearts!' he exclaims and kisses me on the lips, squeezes my bum. Tamsin gets a peck on the cheek, and he hands her the bag.

'You're the first one,' I say.

'Tone is on his way. And you know what The Boys are like. Owen is probably ironing his stripes straight – and Craig, he's got to get the mascara perfect. And there's a bit of shit kicking off. Just as I left Tottenham. The pigs out to play in the shitty Broadwater Farm estate. That will screw up transport.'

'Not a footie match?' I ask brightly. Freddie likes it when I feign interest in his beloved Tottenham Hotspur.

'No, doll, not today. Don't know what it is. The peasants revolting prob. Come on, Tamsin.' He orders in a daft Kraftwerk voice: 'Open. Gift. Now.'

Tamsin pulls hard at the wrapping paper with her stronger hand.

'Rubbish paper,' she teases, looking at the floral design. 'Am I really a roses type of girl?'

'Shut it. Open the thing.' Freddie goes towards her, an evil smirk on his face.

'Nooo, don't you dare.'

I laugh, bursting with love. Freddie is a champion tickler.

Tamsin tears the final scrap of paper, to reveal a notebook with an elegant Egyptian cat on the cover and a pencil tin with pyramid decorations all over it.

'Freddie, that's lovely, thanks,' Tamsin beams.

Freddie hunches bashfully. 'I know how much you two like stationery and stuff.'

We decide to get the crisps out and at that moment Tone arrives in his long, black coat.

'A crisp for you, Tony?' Tamsin is behind me, her hat askew as she gives him a wink.

'Leave him alone,' I laugh. 'Food can come later.'

Tamsin looks at me, an innuendo on her tongue, but she says nothing and starts eating the crisps herself.

Tone sits next to Freddie on the scabby green sofa – now devoid of yesterday's clothes, which I dragged off and kicked underneath.

'I like that dress, Pen,' Tone says, between swigs of his beer.

'Hey mate, keep your eyes off my bird,' Freddie pretends outrage and puts his fists up.

They start horsing about and the door goes again. Tamsin wheels out to answer it. Jean and Naomi come through.

Freddie pushes Tone down on the sofa then goes to the record player to DJ, throwing on an Einstürzende Neubauten album. Tone starts to dance, arms flying like Ian Curtis.

Naomi, our trusty volunteer helper, is tall with large specs; a hippy in a collection of floaty browns. She doesn't pass our free-thinking test, but she's great, especially when it's not a Sandra day.

I glow with appreciation as she comes into the lounge with plates of our roughly made sandwiches. The door buzzes again. The Boys bounce in. Owen wears a set of dandy stripes in white and red; Dan is in a pale, Bowie-style suit.

I take photos between each glass of booze, thrilled we have a true party vibe. Tone poses with my aged keyboard across his head, covering his face, jabbering on about The Residents. Freddie pushes in, cheeks sucked to demonstrate his perfect fish lips. In the corner, over her vodka, Tamsin is in intense conversation with Owen, who sits on the floor.

'Freddie, put on OMD. Or Depeche Mode?' suggests Dan.

'Play "Sex Dwarf"!' yells Tamsin from the corner. 'Let's make this a Non-Stop Erotic Cabaret.'

'Who's doing the cabaret dancing then?' Tone asks.

'I think you boys should do it,' I say airily. 'After all, it's Tamsin's birthday party and our flat-warming. You lot should entertain us.'

Freddie stands up and starts to undo his black jeans.

'I can start by mooning,' he offers.

'No, no, you'll scare the cats,' I laugh, but want him to, my excitement a rush as good as the alcohol.

'Shall I join in?' Tone starts flashing his coat open and shut, to the chorus of 'Sex Dwarf'.

Jean stands up. 'It's getting a bit late, I'd better go.'

'Have another drink first,' I say.

I've known Jean since I was eleven. She was in hospital with me and it always mattered that she was eighteen months older. She isn't a bohemian. In some ways she is sensible and works in an office, has learnt how to drive. But she is a dark horse and can always make me laugh. I can't remember her ever once being cross with me. Not once.

'Go on, just for ten minutes more,' I add, as she looks at me.

'Things are only just warming up, Jean,' says Tamsin from her corner.

'Well, I did say I'd only pop in for a bit.' Jean smiles in her soft, clear way. 'I've got to get up early tomorrow morning. Join the rat race again.'

'I should really go too,' Naomi says. 'I'll see you next Wednesday. Think about where you'd like to go.'

Tamsin and me look at each other. Presumably, it takes a few hours to warm up for an orgy, and losing two guests at this point is a shame.

'And I'll be back soon,' Jean says as she puts on her jacket. 'We're practically neighbours now, you won't keep me away.'

There's a brief lull as they leave, then we settle down into an hour of music and booze, helped along by the odd cheese sandwich and chocolate mini roll.

We are left with The Boys, Tone and my Freddie. I bounce on Freddie's lap, buzzing with alcohol, my inhibitions melting into the dirty carpet. Tone occasionally pulls my hair, the long crimped extensions hanging near to my waist.

Tamsin is talking to Owen and I know she's as drunk as I am, but his stripy trousers remain firmly ON.

I have another vodka and Freddie puts on the 12-inch of 'I Feel Love'.

I sway to the music, the punching beat, smoothing my hands over my breasts, eyes closed, my skin on fire, and lust rising in Freddie's direction.

I slip into a drunken time warp. My heart races. Blood pulses in my cheeks. I drink something else. The music spins on. I wave a bleary goodbye to Tone, sad that he's leaving. I see Tamsin's face as Owen waves, kissing her too quickly on the cheek, shiny Dan in tow.

Freddie kisses me. I bite his lip. I want him.

The phone rings and stops the atmosphere, dead.

Tamsin answers it. 'It's your mum,' she slurs, handing it to Freddie. She turns to me, furtively rolling her eyes.

Freddie's mum worries. And it seems like she worries a lot about him especially when he is with me.

Freddie mutters into the phone, monosyllabic.

We gaze at piles of half-eaten sandwiches and scattered crisps; squashed jelly and tipped-over glasses adding more defects to our carpet.

Freddie turns back to us, frowning.

'Something's happening in Tottenham. Riots,' he says. 'Trouble on that estate. There's swarms of police. Mum is scared. I have to go. She is on her own, after all.'

My face stiffens as my blood frosts up. I want him, I want to take him to bed or have him on the sofa. Now.

'Can't you have a tea or something first?' I stutter, pushing back my inebriation and the rising urge to puke, and cry.

Freddie's eyes are focused away from me, from the party, as he goes to get his mac. 'No, I should go,' he says. 'Mum sounds really upset. She said someone's been killed at Broadwater.'

Tamsin looks at me but says nothing.

'I'll be in touch, dearheart.' Freddie gives me a casual kiss on the head and walks to the door before I can say anything.

My eyes blink.

'Sorry. See you soon, Pen.' Freddie kisses me again, and heads off to pass through Broadwater Farm estate.

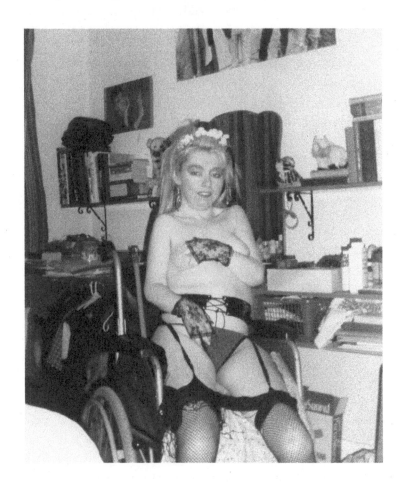

CHAPTER 7

*19 March 1986: Suddenly awaken to the fact that I really am
something of an anarchist. Freddie has always said as much.*

I'm in the lounge with every conceivable musical instrument I own
sprawled around every scrap of space. There's my Yamaha keyboard,
my favourite with the notes written on – for me and Tamsin at
our most nervous moments. A child-size tambourine with a pink,
bunny-decorated handle, Tamsin's Dr Rhythm drum machine
(on loan to me while she is at her parents' in Walthamstow), tatty
maracas, a miniature mouth organ, a cheap zither with a peeling
print of cute little boys in lederhosen.

Tone sits on the sofa with his bass guitar, fine, long fingers
strumming magic. Freddie bustles about making tea, and handing
out Pepsis.

True to his word, we're trying a new tack. Phase II after the
fuck-up with Bob. Freddie's brought along Tim Gane.

Tim is tall, softly spoken with short, black hair and a half smile.
He also knows how to operate the sacred machine that is the
Fostex 4-track, a mini recording studio no bigger than a typewriter,
with mysterious sliders, switchers and knobs. I want to learn. One
way or another this is my next target purchase, juggled alongside
my cravings for a word processor.

'It's best if we do drum machine, keyboard and vocal,' says Tim.
'Then Tone can add the bass. We'll see how that sounds before we
add another layer.'

I cough nervously. Tim is new and unknown, though he
carries much kudos with his band Stereolab. I realise I'm

breathless. I hate myself and my shyness. No one expects it from Kata Kolbert.

'Come on, drink this,' says Freddie, handing me a glass of water. 'No, there's no vodka. You'll get that if you're a good girl.'

I laugh and take a gulp.

'Good girl? Bloody cheek, I'll get you back later.'

Tone does a sudden, melodic riff on bass, accompanying my comments. 'You'll be fine,' he says. '"Truth Be Told" is a classic pop tune and completely yours.'

Tim nods, Freddie kisses my head. I count to three and start with the definitive chords of C and G.

> *I looked for love*
> *At least I think I did*
> *I need it too*
> *So don't be tough on me*
> *Please, just give.*

My voice lifts, my shyness dissolves. Tone nods his head to the rhythm, Freddie silly-dances boisterously, sending our cats – until that moment sleeping in ignorance – flying from the room.

The afternoon melts into night and we realise we're hungry. My innards gurgle, and I wonder if Freddie will let me have a Smirnoff, the bottle placed on the highest cupboard in the kitchen.

Tim packs away the magic box that is the 4-track.

'Three good songs there, Pen,' says Freddie. 'Top-notch stuff for a singles demo. If you can get the cover artwork done, I'll start by getting fifty copies with that guy at Enfield. He's always reasonable.'

'Let me know the cost though, Freddie, won't you?' I say. 'It was what we agreed.' Signing on, Freddie is as poor as I am on my paltry invalidity allowance.

Tam and me sing the Leonard Cohen track, 'Famous Blue Raincoat' swapping blue for black – and Tone is instantaneously the perfect romantic existentialist.

I thank Tim, who waves away my gratitude with another gentle smile. 'Fab tunes,' he says. 'Buy a 4-track as soon as you can.'

When Tim has left, Freddie sits beside me with a notepad, while Tone drinks his Pepsi. 'So, dearheart – titles. Single, A-side and two on the B.'

I grin. Freddie is always so sure, has infallible conviction.

'A-side: "Live Your Life". B-side?' he says.

'You decide,' I tell him.

'"The Deed is Done" and "The Truth Be Told", it is then. When the cassette's finished, we'll start on the record companies straight away. I'm going to blitz them, doll. I'll start big – EMI – RCA.'

'Yes,' I say, wanting to hug him. 'My big bouncy powerhouse. Will you take it to Creation though?'

Freddie turns serious. 'I haven't seen Alan for ages and I don't think it's the right label for you.'

'You're in charge,' I sigh. 'I'm just impatient.'

'Yep. In more ways than one. But don't forget, we have the Grant Showbiz link. I'll call him again tomorrow.'

'*The* Grant Showbiz?' says Tone. 'As in the guy who works with The Smiths?'

'That's him,' Freddie says. 'He's totally into Pen's music, said something really must be done with her songs.'

'Exciting, eh? Maybe I'll get to meet Morrissey at last,' I say.

'Grant's very busy, that's one problem. And I'm not sure if we could afford him,' Freddie says, zipping Tone's guitar into its case.

'Don't forget Gary,' says Tone, wavering at the door. 'He's a damn good producer and he loves your songs, Pen. Maybe even more than Grant Showbiz.'

I look at Tone, with his straight hair hanging in strands over his angular face. 'It's definitely an option.'

'Yeah, that's appreciated, mate. Let's see how far I get with this stuff,' Freddie says.

'Tamsin's been in touch with Gary for ages, buying his compilations. We should invite him around soon,' I add.

'I'll interview you for *Purple Twilight*, Gary's little music zine,' offers Tone, as he waves goodbye.

'Gorgeous stuff, Pen. Really spot on.' Freddie pulls on his big grey mac and kisses me. As always I don't want to let him go.

Maggie Thatcher is in denial about race riots and I'm writing to Harry Cohen. Harry is our MP and he always writes back.

There's always another letter to write and I do it by hand today as Tamsin uses her amazing graphic word processor, the latest thing in typewriters. She lets me borrow it when she's at her mum and dad's on Sundays. I envy the beast but have no money to get one.

I look outside at winter creeping up on us. I hate the biting wind that pushes into our draughty old flat.

Letter complete, we turn to our Open Uni books sprawled across the desk. Tamsin and me sit side by side wondering at the immensity of the task. The reading list terrifies me. I flick pages of Dickens's *Hard Times*, without much enthusiasm.

'You look tired, Pen,' Tamsin says. 'Too much screwing and not enough reading.'

'Don't, don't!'

'You, bashful? Shock horror probe! That would be a headline for the *News of the Screws*.'

'I don't know if I can do this now, do you?' I say, becoming serious.

'I know what you mean, but we have to get stuck in sooner or later.'

'You know what I'd rather be doing?' I narrow my eyes and look at her.

'No, not more nobbing. You'll wear it out. Besides, he's not due for another few days.'

Tamsin screws her eyes up, wrinkles her nose, pulls her lips in. Tamsin's cod-shocked face. It always makes me laugh.

'No! I mean let's work on *Pinch Me in the Pantry*. What about an hour before we let Dickens ruin our evening?'

'You know I'm not going to argue, and we'll squeeze tea in before *Hard* bloody *Times*.'

'As long as we avoid the Boil-in-the-Bag Cod,' I say. 'I don't think I could face that again yet.'

The last Boil-in-the-Bag Cod we tried to cook exploded, creating a buttery mess on the walls we had to live with until Naomi visited. Much to our embarrassment, she cleaned up for us. I now look on all Boil-in-the-Bag with fear and suspicion.

Eating only fish assuaged the guilt that weighed on me as a lapsed vegetarian. And food you boil – or microwave – is easier to cook. The reality of living without a mum as means of rescue was something we were still getting used to. When I fall asleep at night, Mum comes to my mind with her shaking wavy hair and warm, even temperament.

'No boiling bags,' Tamsin says. 'We'll have the leftover veggie sausage rolls instead.'

Pinch Me in the Pantry is our pride and joy, even if Life has stood in the way of its Destiny. We began it back in the time of my 5,000+ days of incarceration, and our fanzine is like no other, full of Crip Liberation and adoration of The Smiths and Morrissey. There's even an interview with old-timer jazz radical George Melly, who we met at a gig at the Theatre Royal Stratford East. An eventful night and one to relish because we could get in. (Rarity alert.)

I'm pasting up Freddie's piece for our fanzine using the cheapest glue I can find. It's about the TV Personalities and their cult single 'Where's Bill Grundy Now?', one of Ant's favourites. It's all cut-and-paste and photocopy, preferably for free as a favour from a friend of a friend. I've contributed to other fanzines – poems about the Brixton riots and one about Marilyn Monroe. We have a copy of *Sniffing Glue* and loads of Gary's *Purple Twilight*. *Pinch Me in the Pantry* will hopefully join this hallowed company and break new ground. Tamsin is cutting out pictures of toilets we've gathered from old magazines. Toilets feature largely in our lives due to the lack of them, in any shape or form, that we, in our wheelchairs, can get into.

Her piece is called 'Greatest Tales of Thwarted Craps'.

A familiar episode of insomnia. I'm not sleeping well and I'm plagued by dreams that make me jittery. Tooty sleeps by my feet, a bit of comfort. As I wake up I can smell the cold.

I hear a noise and blink, looking at the clock beside me. It's 5 a.m.

Following my usual methods of slow movement, I sit up with effort, creaky joints complaining.

The noise: a strange, tortured breathing.

'Tamsin?' I call out tentatively. 'Are you okay?'

The tortured breathing continues, and then I make out my name. I manage to swing into my wheelchair and foot-pedal to Tamsin's bedroom as fast as I can.

Her breath is squeezed and wheezing. I'm scared.

'What can I do, Tamsin?'

'Open window' – she pushes out the words with horrible, rattling effort.

I grab a six-foot length of wooden dowel, left by her dad as an experiment for such occasions – mostly for drawing curtains. Reaching up high, I swing the pole towards the small window, but my arm is not strong enough and I drop it over and over again. On the umpteenth time, I manage to knock up the latch and fresh air comes into the room.

'Shall I call an ambulance?' I whisper as her tight breath continues.

'It hurts, Pen, I'm frightened,' Tamsin says in a rush. 'Don't want a drama. Try the GP first.'

I call our GP, Dr Biggen, via a switchboard operator. He calls back within five minutes. I tremble, face sweating with anxiety. The phone is always an enemy. But I'm relieved. He is coming at once.

'Viral pneumonia,' he says, having listened to Tamsin's chest. 'Immediate hospital for you, young lady. You'll need intravenous antibiotics.'

I can't stop quivering. I'm terrified for Tamsin, and for myself – that I'll be alone for the first time in ages.

'Maybe I'm not very good at this independence lark,' Tamsin says to me through an oxygen mask, as the ambulance crew tend to her.

'It will be fine,' I say, 'it will get better.'

Tamsin coughs into the mask. 'Not so sure, Pen. I may need to go back to Mum and Dad's.'

Lightning shock jolts my body. I feel a bit sick.

'Don't worry about anything,' I say to her, as the ambulance men wheel the stretcher towards the front door. 'I'll come and see you as soon as they let me.'

'Let Mum and Dad know, Pen,' Tamsin says, her voice frail and fading.

I'm shaking, my chest heaving to deliver the first hateful sob.

'There, there.' Dr Biggen suddenly pats my shoulder. I jump as if I'd forgotten he was there. 'You'll be fine on your own for a day or two, won't you?'

He packs away his bag, not waiting for my answer.

I can't answer. I nod, the best response I can manage. And once he slams the door I sit in the lounge in the dark, shocked into silence, and not knowing what to do.

Maybe I'm not good at this independence lark either – but I have nowhere else to go.

By December, Tamsin is back, and a festive frenzy hijacks the world. It's decided we will go to her sister's in east London for Christmas Day.

Greta's house is warm and lively, filled with the racing of excited little children, hurtling up and down stairs, displaying new gifts opened that morning. There is drink, including mulled wine, a real fire and beside it the biggest Christmas tree, a real one, its needles shivering to the floor discretely. I've known Tamsin for seven years, so I know all the children, her family, and am touched by how they include me on such occasions.

Christmas dinner is at a huge, groaning table, but still too small for us all: crackers roll off edges, bottles tip over; there are accidents and laughing shrieks amid the sounds of pleasure and munching. Sat next to Tamsin, I feel transported to a dream world, where the family fun and games in their rough East End way are perfect – humour, filled with affection; affection filled with love.

Two days after Boxing Day we're back in our flat. Tamsin is better, though her face is drawn and very pale. She hasn't mentioned wanting to leave again and I'm too afraid to ask.

'God it's so boring, Pen. And you're looking too serious,' Tamsin announces. 'You know what, I think we should buy a vibrator as a personal present.'

I swivel my eyes, wordlessly.

'Nothing complicated,' she says. 'Something easy to use.'

'What, one we'll share?' I make myself turn to look at her, careful not to lose the granny blanket and expose myself to the flat's endless chill.

'We could, naturally we'll wash it between… uses.'

I start to giggle. Tamsin joins in.

'I read about it in *Cosmo*, so I really think we should.'

'I suppose we should,' I say. 'If *Cosmo* says so.'

'The thing is,' Tamsin continues, 'I'm finding it difficult to reach and maintain a good position. My right hand is so shit these days. Don't tell me you find it easy?'

I smile, revisiting the relief I have in always being able to talk to Tamsin about absolutely anything.

'Yeah, I can't really reach at all. I let Freddie's fingers do the walking. It would be another bohemian story, wouldn't it?'

'More sordid tales from the decadent lives of Kata K. and K. Oss,' Tamsin says, finishing with a hammy, devilish laugh.

We wait for our naughty New Year gift in anticipation and fear. We're both eager but I worry about our dodgy postman Dave. What if it falls out of its plain package? What if Dave guesses what it is and gets even more unsavoury?

My answer, as always – for now – is to ask Tamsin to check the door. A glimmer of new anxiety triggers as I try to imagine her not being here with me. Not having the rock of her friendship.

The vibrator arrives without fuss in exceptionally dull wrappings, not delivered by Dave, but a postman we've never seen before.

It's six inches and a creamy white plastic. Tamsin and me snigger. Masturbation is about to take a leap into a new and exciting phase.

It doesn't look or feel especially appealing, and after Tamsin's build-up I feel a bit let down. I put the batteries in with a bit of a struggle and flick the switch.

It jumps to life with a thrilling, buzzing promise. We laugh.

'You go first,' I stutter to Tamsin, handing it over.

She screws up her face. 'Oh scaredy-cat. Alright. I'll test drive the... Milky Bar Kid. But don't listen. Put the radio on loud.'

I grin as she scoots into her bedroom.

I turn up Patti Smith and make an effort to read the *Daily Mirror* with its picture of Neil Kinnock on the front.

Ten minutes later Tamsin appears, looking flushed and happy.

She shakes her head as I burst to ask a million questions. 'No, just have a go. I can't talk about it till you have. I'll wash it first. Of course.'

She raises her eyebrows and we both laugh, as she goes to the bathroom.

Clean vibe handed over, I go into the bedroom. There's the usual logistics of reaching. The stiffness in my arms means my fingers reach no lower than my belly button. I use my handystick to pull down my knickers and wriggle the thing around, not sure if I'm excited or terrified. I'm used to orgasms, Freddie always delivers; but this is something else, this is about having control over something disabled girls aren't expected to even know about.

Twelve minutes later I return to the lounge with matching flushed skin, in a haze of contentment. I didn't have to worry about my hands not moving well, my reach being limited, my fingers weak – the job was done by that unassuming length of buzzy-busy plastic.

Day one of the Milky Bar Kid. MBK. A glorious success.

Tamsin is struggling with Dickens. We're only on page twenty and I already hate Louisa. If the cold cow is going to do something bad I wish she'd get on with it.

Tamsin slams down the Penguin Classic and yawns.

I prefer reading about Bakunin, Kropotkin, Proudhon, and feel I was born to be an anarchist. For now, I try to ignore the gift from Tone tempting me from the edge of the desk – a copy of the erotic novel, *Story of O*.

'Take your eyes off that,' Tamsin says. 'You know you're not allowed any lewd thoughts while we're working.'

She goes to lift up *Hard Times* and looks at me. 'If I do decide to go, Pen, who's going to keep you on the straight and narrow?'

There's humour in her eyes as she looks at me and she says it so lightly. But inside, my stomach drops ten thousand feet and I can't think of anything I can say.

Me and Tim Gane having a cuppa after recording the demo.

CHAPTER 8

28 February 1987: Ill again. Bloody bastard ill. And I'm fed up with the flat being so bloody cold.

I think I am pregnant.

There's pain and there's pain. Freddie is frantic, Dr Biggen comes out and, before I can blink, I'm shunted into hospital for tests and antibiotics.

I find myself in Whipps Cross, in an old-style ward, beds laid out like barracks: endless rows of women of all ages, whispering about their gynae problems. I'm fed up. I don't belong and I'm impatient with their self-pity. 'My mother had a mastectomy and hysterectomy very close together,' I announce to Freddie, pulling up the shoulder strap on my slinky nightie. 'These women don't know they're born.'

Suddenly I want my mum and I'm feeling guilty because Freddie is with me.

'Concentrate on you, Pen,' Freddie says.

There's a bustle. I recognise it as the looming of doctors. My skin goes cold.

'Hello young lady, what's happened to you then? You're definitely not pregnant, thankfully. Penelope, isn't it?'

'She prefers Penny, actually,' mutters Freddie, holding my hand tightly.

'And who are you?' The doctor has a square head and flat black hair. His eyes flit around the bed but never fix on me. 'I'm not sure you should be in here, young man.'

'He's my boyfriend.' I tremble as my eyes prickle. 'I want him here.'

'Boyfriend?'

My tears brim up. I wish Freddie and me could start having sex on the bed in front of him. To show him. To take the stern, smug expression off his dull face.

'Nurse, can you show this young man to the visitors' room while I examine Penelope?'

Freddie stands rooted to the spot and I'm crying now but all I can do is shrug as the door is held open. The doctor leans close with his lizard hands.

As Freddie is ushered away through the curtain he turns back to me: 'They won't do this if we're married, Pen, will they?'

It's a drag into the new year. I write in my journals but what with all the stories, poems, lyrics and music – and the Open University – they've been a bit crowded out. Tamsin and me make our resolutions. Fixing our dates with Destiny like we do every year. Mine stay the same for now. Must try harder with everything.

I've written a long letter to Mum as I wait for Freddie to appear for his regular Saturday visit.

I can't wait to see him. I've told Mum how much I love him, how much he loves me, and as I flick through the pages of last year's journal it seems I had to make a note of it regularly. But I feel a pang that I've missed detailing many other things.

I know I love Freddie but as I look at the many empty pages of 1986 I realise that life comes before the recording of it.

Tamsin and me huddle underneath disgusting blankets, invalid granny wraps that we cling to. We've woken up to a land of cold, cold snow. The communal central heating isn't working. Naturally, the gas fire beside us is beyond our reach. There's no way we can turn it on.

Sandra wants us to leave it on full and promises it's safe. We are not sure, despite the temptation as we shiver and ache.

'Keep drinking warm tea,' says Sandra, folding sheets and heading for the kitchen.

There's a gentle tap at the door.

Tamsin and me tense up; we don't like strangers. Sandra looks through the spyhole – a privilege we don't have.

'It's your neighbour from upstairs,' she whispers. 'I'd better answer it.'

'Sorry, sorry – can I use the phone?' A thin woman with high bushy hair and a ragged miniskirt peers at us nervously. 'I'm Tracey, two floors up.'

'What's happened?' Tamsin is immediately alarmed.

'It's Albert,' Tracey whispers, nibbling grey fingernails. 'I take him a tea in. I think he's dead.'

Sandra gasps, hand over her mouth. Tamsin looks at me with a Tamsin scowl.

'How do you know?' she says to Tracey.

'Um, he's frozen. No fire on in there. I mean, there's no central heating yet, is there?'

I don't blurt that we have our own gas fire.

'The phone's in the lounge,' Tamsin says and in comes Tracey, trailing a cloud of bleach and Tweed perfume. Our cats, as always, scarper.

Sandra brings us in another round of tea before she leaves.

'Sleep in your clothes if you have to, it doesn't matter. Stay warm. Or I'll just keep saying "Albert" to you.'

I look at Tamsin and we both look at Sandra wishing we could hug her.

Later, as I immerse myself in my Open Uni reading list, we notice the police come and old Albert is taken away.

Freddie's managed to come through the snow and I've managed to put together some new songs ready for David. We found him through an *NME* advert. Freddie wants me to broaden my sound.

David arrives with his guitar, an accordion and a beautiful mandolin. His musical skills are daunting, but he soon puts me at ease.

'You keep writing and singing these songs, Pen,' he says, 'and I'll see if I can add stuff they deserve.'

I start writing a song with the words. And these words have a pattern and their own rhythm that tells me where to take the melody. Then I add a simple, underlying riff, a hook of two or three notes or chords. 'A Second Look' is inspired by the closing scenes of *Far From the Madding Crowd*:

> *When I look up, be there*
> *When you look up, I'm here*

Freddie sets off the Dr Rhythm drum machine. I play my riff with one finger and start to sing gently:

> *Blue lake eyes of calm*
> *Could I care to reach them?*
> *A smile deep as wide*
> *When you sighed*
> *I went through life*
> *Wanting everything.*

David begins a delicate accompaniment on the mandolin. We run through the song several times. Stopping, starting, tweaking – until a live demo is laid down on the cassette recorder.

'Your work is in a category all of its own,' David says over his can of beer. 'I can hear influences – The Smiths, naturally. A bit of Kate Bush. Glimmers of punk, and even a bit of good old English folk.'

'That's Tamsin's fault,' I laugh. 'As well as Leonard Cohen, she got me into The Dransfields and all that stuff.'

'We've delved into that together, haven't we, doll?' adds Freddie. 'Fairport Convention, Steeleye Span. All those folk compilations in Woolworths.'

'Oh I know the ones,' David nods his head. 'You might get fifty per cent crap, but the rest are gems.'

Freddie goes to speak, but we're distracted by Tamsin poking her head around the door from her bedroom. She looks pale, different somehow, and I can't quite work out why.

Sandra appears at the end of the cul-de-sac, defiantly cheerful and insistent she'll do our shopping, which always takes her hours. I make sure she clicks on the gas heater to full before she goes, leaving us warmer, if feeling guilty.

Tooty and Ollie sprawl in front of the bars within seconds, all secret cat conflicts suspended for the sake of warmth. I worry about Heathcliff, the large stripy tabby who we've half adopted, charmed by his crazy character and engaging vocalisations. I convince myself he's dead, frozen into the snow, lost and unwanted.

But as Sandra approaches, sometime later, I spot him winding his long scraggy tail around her legs. 'That's better, that's better. Lovely and warm,' says Sandra breathlessly, dragging our big tartan shopping trolley behind her. Heathcliff leaps into the kitchen, meowing and meowing.

I lean forward in my chair to scratch his wide, boy cat head. My Tooty is asleep on the bed so his nerves won't be frayed by the cheeky interloper.

Tamsin and me glance at each other and down at Heathcliff.

'Sandra,' I say slowly, 'I know it's not a good time and you're already running late, but could you quickly rustle up a shelter for Heathcliff? We've kept a box and Tamsin's got an old jumper.'

'Now girls, you know me. Five of me own, my son's got twelve and I can't see a puss-cat suffer. I'll make us a quick cuppa, check your dinner's ready to go in the oven and then I'll sort him out.'

Heathcliff looks at us with his big green eyes blinking, understanding he has pretty much just found home.

I'm on the last ten pages of *Hard Times*, waiting for Stephen to die, when the phone rings, a weary Freddie on the other end.

'Hi sweetness, the tape was rejected by EMI.' He sounds dull, his voice monotone.

I sigh and struggle to respond. Everything, absolutely everything, seems a fight. Rejection slices away my confidence in horrible repetition.

'I hate this,' I say, knowing I'm way too melodramatic.

'There's plenty more to go, don't worry just yet.' His voice warms up and I suddenly feel like crying. Again.

'You always make me feel better,' I whisper. 'I just feel like I'm always flying, then sinking. One extreme to the other.'

Freddie laughs softly. 'That's just you. Mad and scatty. Who I love. So no weeping like a dopey Dickens female.'

'Love you too,' I say, barely audible, always scared to say the words.

'Anyway, three days to go and I'll come and bonk all the misery out of you.'

I laugh out loud. We take five minutes of silliness to say goodbye.

Sandra goes. With the fire turned off, the room temperature drops fast. I settle down next to Tamsin, ready to watch a documentary about the Graeae Theatre Company, who are all disabled actors and writers. There's a woman in it being an unconvincing punk but Tamsin and me grin at each other. This is our brethren.

CHAPTER 9

31 May 1987: I respect Tam's decision to do this with her life but I'm sad and sorry and guilty. I will have Freddie but still I'll miss her liveliness, her fast indignation and many talents.

Sian Vasey from Artsline is chatting to me on the phone. It's interrupting Tam and me from fiddling around with our *Pinch Me in the Pantry* fanzine.

But I don't mind. Artsline is a group of disabled people wanting to poke the system in the bum, to shout for access for disabled artists and writers. I remember my excitement on seeing it mentioned in, of all places, *Woman's Own*, in some drab hospital waiting room. I wrote a quick letter to the group, pushing myself to say I'm disabled and a writer and a singer.

Sian is very proper Home Counties, but is easy to talk to. She says she's putting me on their new – if small – artists' register straight away. She works editing a magazine called *Disability Arts in London – DAIL –* which I sign up for immediately, especially as she says I could write something for them.

I'm impressed she is involved with the radical Graeae Theatre Company and I love her enthusiasm. She invites us to the next Artsline meeting in Camden and tells me about the new London Disability Arts Forum.

Tamsin is frowning and mouthing at me: who is it?

I put the phone down, astonished. I can't wait to join this fight.

'The revolution has begun,' I say to Tamsin, pinched with vague anxiety. If she goes, can I do these things alone? And will she really want to miss out?

We're dreading the election. Thatcher is a stubborn disease and it doesn't look like Labour can be the cure. I'm not sure about Neil Kinnock, but as I watch Ken Livingstone on the news I feel a familiar glow. Ken doesn't seem plastic and I like that.

'Where's the bloody revolution?' I say to Tam. 'Why isn't the rest of the country up in arms?'

Tam looks at me thoughtfully, scraping out strawberry mousse from a small carton. 'I don't know, Pen,' she says. 'All we can do is keep yelling. Keep our own revolution going.'

It strikes me that Tam is still looking very pale. She hasn't mentioned leaving again directly, but since her illness it's hovered there between us.

'Is Freddie coming on Saturday?' she says, putting the empty carton on the desk, not making eye contact.

'Oh yes,' I say. Thinking about my last conversation. How we want to try sex in a new position; it's a great game that I love to play.

'I'll get Ron to pick me up early then.' Tamsin fiddles with the spoon inside the carton. 'Best I'm out of the way.'

My stomach lurches as I don't know what to say. Down in my innards and down, down further, I'm glad when she goes to her mum and dad's. Glad I can sit on Freddie's lap in the lounge, tits pressed to his face.

'No,' I begin nervously, conflicts tripping up my tongue. 'You're not in the way.'

'Yes I do live here, don't I?' she says, and I can feel the undercurrent of her fast temper.

My face must look crushed as she adds, 'Oh I love going to see Mum and Dad, you know that. At least it gives me a rest from all the bloody struggling.'

I look at her, trying to laugh, then flick my eyes back to the TV. There's something on about the defunct Anti-Nazi League and I prickle with satisfaction that we got in there a while back and have posters proudly on the door.

'I'll have to join the Southampton Labour Party if I move there with my parents,' Tamsin says and looks at me.

And I know I cannot answer.

Still chilly, we raid our food money to get a taxi to the Artsline meeting in Camden, deciding not to take our wheelchairs. We regret this when the cab driver initially refuses to pull up right outside the offices in Crowndale Road, but after Tamsin sorts him out with a lash of her tongue we totter out directly by the door to Artsline. I'm hit by a recurring pang of how much I will miss her if she decides to go.

Shivering with nerves, I use my painted walking stick to get into the office while Tamsin is using her crutches. It's small but rammed with disabled people. Sian chats to us immediately, shows us to two chairs we can conveniently manage. Sian is charming, humorous, very posh, with straight, long hair held behind her ears. Allan wears a sharp trilby hat; Elspeth has waves of enviable deep brown wavy hair. We don't catch the name of everyone but we enjoy the rush of conversation. A northern man, with a white cane, speaks loudly:

'We have a right to be taken seriously! We have to get away from our art being patronised.'

'The big patriarchal charities still have such a grip,' Sian says, holding a pen between beautifully manicured nails. 'And it's all about fucking money.'

'And now no GLC,' says Elspeth mournfully. 'So if things are going to get moving, we've got to keep the dosh coming.'

'You know what it's like with Thatcher still in charge. It's not going to get better fast,' a short man in an oversized parka chips in.

I'm agreeing in my head, and nod.

'And we have to do something about public transport,' a small woman in a bright red wheelchair pipes up from the back of the room. 'Yeah, we want to make art but how about being able to go and see it?'

Everyone laughs in grim agreement.

'This all needs to be attacked,' says Allan, spreading calm into the room. 'But let's concentrate on making the London Disability Arts Forum something with clout.'

Sian looks at me and Tam. 'Allan's a great poet,' she whispers. 'One of our best.'

There's a bit of gentle shouting. Tamsin joins in with the odd comment while, as usual in my straitjacket of self-hatred, I'm too shy to say boo, even to a friendly goose.

'Okay, tea time,' says Sian. 'Do you want one, Pen?'

I manage to say 'yes, please', and promise myself that I will call Sian so I can talk to her on my own. Without anxiety mincing me to a gibbering wreck.

By the time we get home, I'm still excited and grab my journal:

There's poems to be written in protest.
There's songs to be sung and heard.
There's the buses to attack for access.
But we can do it. We can do Mutual Aid.
Kropotkin would be proud.
It must be time for our civil rights.
It must be time for our revolution.

Spring warmth makes an appearance, though the day is still dull across the east London skies. The slog of Dickens over, I'm back on track with work. My work. Words. Freddie calls it my work and I know he is right. Work that I love and the only thing I believe I'm good at, sometimes.

The phone keeps ringing. The washing-machine man. A man from Council Housing about our pathetic heating. More exciting is when Sian from Artsline rings to tell us about a big festival in a few months' time to celebrate disability art.

Halfway through the afternoon, I am lost inside another poem –

These bloody days of streets run red
The young must savour riots...

– when Freddie calls, his enthusiasm bursting like sunshine down the phone. 'Would you like to sing with Lol Coxhill?' he says.

'Yes, of course,' I reply.

I don't have the faintest idea who Lol Coxhill is. But I won't admit it.

'Fab, dearheart. I'll tell him.'

'News on the record label stuff?' I say, praying I don't sound like a ten-year-old waiting for a fluffy puppy. And to divert him away from the mysterious Coxhill.

Freddie is silent for a heartbeat.

'The thing is, Pen, I've been speaking to Gary at Color Tapes. We can record a single ourselves. He'll produce it. And we'll set up our own record label.'

'Wow,' I say, on a deep breath, struggling to calculate what that involves. 'And any news about Grant Showbiz?'

Freddie pauses again. 'To be honest, I don't think it's going to happen at the moment. He's busy and affording him will definitely be a concern.'

'Oh,' I say, wondering – suddenly – whether it's about It. The Lurgy. Me. My wheelchair.

'Look, let's go with Gary,' Freddie says. 'We'll hire a Portastudio, then he can mix at home.'

I'm getting emotional. My scars too easily raw and cut open by his belief in me, by all the love and desire.

'And by the way, Lol Coxhill is a free-form jazz saxophonist,' he says and laughs.

'Love you,' I whisper. Stopping myself from the stupid line: don't leave me, please, don't leave me. 'See you Saturday.'

Tamsin sits by the desk, coughing as she tidies piles of the *Daily Mirror*. She looks so tired since the pneumonia and stays with her mum and dad most weekends in Southampton, now they've managed to fulfil their dream to move from Walthamstow. I know she's worn down with the travel, and especially the tedium of our daily struggles.

Struggle, with stupid things. Having a shower, getting dressed – which takes all morning. Cooking dinner, which takes all evening. Then sleeping because we have minimal energy to do much more.

We're looking at our invites to the London Disability Arts Festival launch. I'm gobsmacked that Ian Dury is going to be the star guest. Freddie's really excited as well. He says I must flutter my eyelashes and give him a cassette tape of my songs.

'Do you know what you're wearing yet?' says Tamsin.

'Probably the old bondage dress,' I say. 'With a few layers. Don't want to be taken for a Nigel.'

Tamsin laughs softly. Nigel is our own secret term for normal. Not only people who aren't disabled, but anyone who's drab, dresses badly and has no politics.

'Pen, you're never going to look like a Nigel,' Tam says.

'Thanks,' I say, blushing a bit.

A stiff silence pushes between us.

'We have to be hopeful though,' Tam says, 'that things will change. Especially if we keep on it together.'

I glance around our lounge. The bespoke desk is buried under newspapers and notebooks and journals. A used wine glass rises through it like a strange bare tree. Rolled up tissues bury themselves in every crevice. The old green sofa slumps along the wall and I smile quickly to myself, remembering lying on it with Freddie. The walls are white and plain, though my signed Morrissey photo hangs in pride of place, and on the door so many art and history postcards, that space will run out soon.

I look back at Tam. 'Meanwhile, I suppose we should fight with dinner.'

Tamsin groans. 'I don't know if I can face it,' she says. 'What have we got we can just throw in the Baby Belling?'

'We were going to do fish fingers and mash – do you still want that?'

Tamsin groans again. She looks so ill and I hate it.

'We do make a marvellous mash, don't we?' she says. 'But I don't think I'm up to it, Pen.'

'Oh fuck it, we can do it,' I say, wanting her to eat, wanting to give her comfort. 'You peel and I'll mash. Or we'll do a bit each.'

'No, we can't.' Tam lets out a long sigh and closes her eyes. 'Well, I can't.' She lifts her right hand to show me her swollen wrist. 'This is totally fucked up.'

My own aren't that brilliant today, the Lurgy pushing creeks and aches along my fingers, but I find myself saying, 'I'll do it. I'll be fine.'

Tamsin sits upright. 'No, Pen,' she says, and the exasperation in her voice startles me. Or is it anger? 'It'll mean we eat far too late, and you know I hate that. I hate it. I don't want to eat that late.'

I fall silent, not believing she's upset with me. Not believing that's possible.

'Let's have soup,' she says tightly. 'There's some tins of Heinz tomato somewhere. At least that means only one struggle with the fucking electronic tin opener.'

She looks at me and smiles. All we can do is laugh, as the electronic tin opener is like a dangerous weapon, made for the lazy, not those with dodgy hands. We both bear the scars of our bloody battles with it.

But this time it cooperates and the soup is done in the microwave within minutes. We sit by the telly, sipping at it from small mugs, the telly volume low.

Tamsin looks up. 'I've not been myself since that Big Freeze, Pen,' she says, her voice hushed.

I nod, but dread wraps me in a shiver. I know there's more coming.

'I'm going to go, Pen,' she says, suddenly, carefully propping her mug on the desk on top of some envelopes. 'Especially as Mum and Dad have made it to Southampton at last, I want to go back to them. I need to.'

My cheeks flush and I feel sick. I don't know what to say.

I love my freedom. I love changing my mind a hundred times a day.

I have Freddie of course; that takes the edge off the struggle. He'll even help me shower now I've got over myself and it's no big deal.

'Well, I'm not very surprised,' I say at last. Swallowing. Swallowing hard. Must not cry. 'I know the struggling has got to you. And you don't have—'

'Yes I know. I don't have a Freddie.' She's shrill and I pull back. 'I have Mike,' she says bitterly, 'who never visits. Who lets me down. But Freddie doesn't let you down and now you can fuck whenever you like. And I won't have to listen to it.'

She wheels to her bedroom and closes the door. Soon I hear her cough, her deep hacking cough.

The lounge gets bigger and I can't hear the telly. I'm rooted in my wheelchair, my feet glued to our dirty brown carpet. My heart is split. I don't want Tam to need to get angry with me. She's never angry with me, not once. Until now.

I go to bed, eyes wide. Maybe I'm crying. I don't know. My head is spinning with endless prickly questions. Private times with Freddie are one thing, but how can I exist without Tamsin? What will it do to our Fates and Destiny?

One question keeps chasing me around all the others so that I can't sleep: can I live alone?

Me and Tamsin being me and Tamsin.

A bout of flu strikes me down on the day Open Uni work begins officially. Tamsin and me attack it in earnest. We can talk about our stuff, but the division is there. When Freddie visits she goes to her sister's, Ron coming to collect her like clockwork.

She's going and the date rushes closer. I shrivel with guilt that Freddie and me are part of it. That it's something I can't deny.

I can feel the fog descending, dark thoughts coming when I swallow down my painkillers. There's no one to talk to. Dr Biggen says, 'There, there. Be a strong girl, Penelope.' Sometimes Freddie cancels because his mum needs him. I get twitchy and the fog pushes closer. I haven't met his parents yet and he seems shy about introducing me to them properly. I try and push it to one side. After all, he's not met my family either.

Sometimes it's me alone while Tamsin's away. But unlike her, I now love these moments of my own company.

The day comes too soon. Tamsin packs with Sandra, the last few pieces. Our Leytonstone flat is forlorn now Tamsin has removed half of her things: most of the postcards on the door, her pretty bedroom curtains, the Indian candle holders. She's bright and jolly. I'm happy she looks less pale, but I can't say much. The knot inside me is the only thing tying back my tears.

'You'll be fine, Pen,' Tamsin says, as Sandra pushes the latches on her big suitcase. 'You've still got Sandra.'

'You're not getting rid of me anytime soon,' Sandra says firmly.

'And Freddie. He'll be around, won't he?' Tam says it lightly, but we're soul sisters and now we're broken I can sense the edge to her voice. I never wanted to be caught between them.

'Yeah,' I say, at last.

Suddenly, Ron is tooting the horn on his car as he pulls up. It's too soon. My eyes are hot and I curse myself for being weak.

I want Freddie. I want us to be alone. But I don't want Tam to go. I want to tell her I didn't mean to push her out.

But I can't say anything. As Ron comes in and grabs her case, Tamsin comes right up beside me in her wheelchair, laughing.

'Look what I packed,' she whispers, opening the top of her handbag. I peer in and see the MBK nestling at the bottom. I laugh out loud even though I know I'll have to cry.

'Tell you what,' says Tam. 'I'll order one for you.'

Ron is back, holding the handles of her wheelchair. 'You said your goodbyes, girls?'

'Call me when you're settled,' I say, the words coming out strangled and strange.

Tamsin looks at me, screws her face up into her little-old-lady mode. 'Yes, Pen my dear, of course I bloody will!'

CHAPTER 10

19 October 1987: Had a sodding nightmare about that knob Brian from Coldlane. I wondered, for about a second, if I should have called him back after all...

'Hey, let me in!'

A man's face presses suddenly against the pane. I jump and turn away. He bangs on the window. I don't know what to do.

'Let me in, I'm here about the gas,' he adds loudly, dark eyes trying to catch my gaze.

I scoot my wheelchair into the bedroom where the curtains thankfully remain closed. 'Freddie,' I say under my breath, shaking.

The banging on the window continues as darkness falls. No one is due about the gas; no one is due for anything. Feeling sick, I wheel myself to the kitchen.

Is the back door locked? Will he realise there's no side fence, that he can get in at the back?

I shake so badly I can hardly turn the key – a real struggle at the best of times.

There's a rap on the front door. I don't want to move, and swallow, swallow hard, again and again. The door bangs. I creep forward to the hall.

'Who is it?' I say, trying to sound in control, but wavering.

'Can you let me in? I'd like a drink of water. I'm from... Leytonstone House.'

'Go away please,' I say, feebly, touching the safety chain for reassurance.

Everyone knows Leytonstone House is the local loony bin. And I'm sure he's not come from there.

The man starts to kick the door. I know I have to get to the phone but I feel so sick I don't want to move. I want Freddie. But he's on holiday with his family and I don't know when he can call. I'm not even sure where he's gone. I miss him with every nervy beat of my heart and every inch of my flesh. I knew I should have drawn the curtains in the lounge, where the window looks directly into the street, but I couldn't face the six-foot pole and the painful fight with the rail to close them.

The kicking continues, the door jolting. My eyes begin to water and I'm split into pieces of a hundred different emotions.

Tooty appears by my feet and chirrups. This small reassurance spurs me on and I foot-pedal into the lounge, lift the phone with shaking hands and call the estate caretaker, Mr Cyril.

There's a lull as I hear the ringing tone − then I realise the man's trying the back-door handle.

Mr Cyril grunts at me down the line. 'There's a prowler,' I mutter. 'I don't know what to do.' In stuttered words I give him my flat number.

The prowler bangs on my bedroom window. I hear him shout: 'I know you're in there! I just want to be friendly.'

I wait forever for Mr Cyril, relieved that he is simply another human being. He mutters that he didn't see anyone but will keep a look out.

I cry that Freddie isn't with me.

But two weeks later, when he's back, he moves in.

June is ruined. Thatcher's elected − third bloody time.

As I look at the pages of my journal, humming along to 'Fiery Jack' by The Fall, I'm sad. So many pages are empty.

I wonder what Anaïs would say. But then she has shown me the way. I'm not compiling a calendar of events; I'm recording how I feel.

More fucking Thatcher.

I write this slowly and feel satisfied.

Freddie has put pies in the oven. The cats circle at the smell. Pies make me think of Tamsin. A pie was always her preferred back-up for an easy meal.

'I had an idea, Pen.' Freddie looks at me, pursing his lips. 'Creation.'

'Yes?' I say eagerly. Am I going to meet Alan?

'No, no, Creation Books.' He waves his hands to stop me. 'Could you rustle up an idea for them? Something really controversial.'

I chew the pen I'm clutching and think. 'Sex and crips?'

'Yes! Get thinking! There might be an opening there.'

'Oh no, matron!' I say, as we all enjoy a bit of cheap smut.

'Stop it…' He laughs and squeezes my left tit playfully. 'You never know.'

I nod and flip open a journal. This has to go down. I can't write fast enough, I'm so excited.

'And… we're going for setting up Nevermore Records,' I say, pen poised.

'We'll have Red Rhino peeps on distribution,' says Freddie. 'So I'm happy doing that.'

I scribble a few lines, ignoring the cramp in my shoulder joint for as long as I can.

'Just the money to get, then,' I say and look up at him. He is flicking through our ever-expanding collection of videos. I glow with sudden love. Optimism. Destiny kicks the door open a bit. Maybe.

I scribble some more. We're trying to raise £1,000. Then Freddie will be eligible for the Enterprise Allowance. Life might get easier.

'And then the single,' I say it as I write it in my journal.

'That's enough,' Freddie says from the kitchen. I wheel out to see him pop the pies on plates – cheese and onion for me, chicken and mushroom for him. 'That's the idea, doll. And indeed we make an amazing single by the very amazing Kata Kolbert.'

'Freddie,' I murmur, always bashful. 'Eat your pie.'

I'm basking in the summer sun. Tamsin's brother-in-law Ron changes my life.

It's five o'clock. I'm immersed in my new poetry fanzine *My Heart is Like a Singing Bird*, guilty, always guilty, that I should be doing something else. Especially OU. It's suffered a lot since Tamsin left. Studying on my own is twice as hard.

Ron waves at me as he comes down the path, holding a square box. I draw in a breath, making a fast move to the back door. Writing by hand has become a slow and often painful drag. The typewriter with the faulty 'e' went to typewriter heaven months back and all I could do was stare dreamily at Tamsin's wonderful word processor. Until now.

'Here we are then, Pen,' says Ron, presenting the box to me with a flourish. 'I bet you want it unwrapped and on the desk immediately.'

'Yes, yes! You know me – I can't wait.' I'm smiling stupidly as I follow him into the lounge.

Ron is a man who can get things. He knows people who know people in the East End, who circle and overlap. We don't ask where he gets all the stuff from. They are cheap and they work. I've already had a VCR and a replacement microwave. I'm also grateful that, while Tamsin is now happier in Southampton, Ron still pops in on me, especially on the days when Freddie goes out doing his thing, going to a record company and seeing his mum. Ron also drops off our bread and milk.

'Ron, you are a diamond,' I say, gazing at the cream-and-black creature plugged in on the desk. 'This is revolution.'

'You and Tamsin always talk of revolution,' Ron laughs.

'I've got to, Ron. Thatcher's back in! People are disillusioned,' I say. 'And well, I am studying Marxist-Leninist theories of Victorian class.'

'Of course you are, Pen. I'm glad the word processor will help.'

I hover before the keyboard. Then, with a pang of guilt, I turn to catch Ron before he leaves.

'Is Tamsin okay?' I ask. 'We do still speak on the phone for hours, but it feels odd sometimes.'

'We're going down to see them all next week,' says Ron. 'As far as I know, she's fine. Much healthier.'

I look back at the keyboard. All I want to do is type, type, type.

'Draw the curtains for me, Ron. I know it's early, but Freddie's not back until later.'

Ron laughs. 'Okay, but don't forget to eat and drink, will you? I can tell you're going to be attached to that thing for some hours.'

'Yeah, yeah. Of course,' I say, waving him away. 'I'll be good.'

But what I'm thinking is I can't drink too much because going to the loo gets harder and harder, as my knees stiffen up, my wrists get weaker.

And I don't know how late Freddie will be.

Brian is a record company executive, the first one I have ever met in my life. He sits on my drab green sofa sipping a coffee. His eyes swivel around the room, regularly resting on my cleavage. He has a terrible mullet and his leather jacket doesn't fit around his gut.

I've dressed to impress, in my beloved leather bondage dress, thick black socks, black kitten heels, my latest array of multicoloured hair extensions flying free. I wear studded wristbands and spent hours doing my best Siouxsie eyes.

'Great dress,' says Brian, gesturing towards me. 'Your whole look is fantastic.'

Freddie, who is fussing around to be the perfect host, fidgets in his chair. 'And the music?' he says.

'I love it,' says Brian, keeping his eyes firmly on my chest. He puts down his coffee, stretches his legs wide apart in horrible, flappy jeans. 'It all goes together really well. You've got my interest.'

He stares at me and I clench. Shyness is one thing, but I wish he'd stop ogling.

'Thanks,' I mumble and look at the pointy toe of my left shoe.

'We're thinking "Live Your Life" is a classic single and the turnaround on recording can be fast,' says Freddie.

I can tell he has noticed Brian sleazing over me.

I feel a bit sick and gaze at Freddie, a Bambi needing help.

'Tell me your dreams then. What you want, what you desire,' says Brian, ruffling the mullet and fixing his eyes to mine. 'I'm sure we can work something out.'

'Great,' I say, and look at Freddie.

'What would the next stage be?' Freddie asks, face hardening.

Brian nods, pushing his rough lips forward, ready to make a pronouncement: 'There is one key thing.'

Freddie and me hold our breath.

'You have to get rid of that,' says Brian, pointing at my wheelchair.

'What do you mean?' I blurt, shyness overcome by confusion.

'The wheelchair, baby, the wheelchair. It's not exactly sexy, is it?'

I stare at him, shaking, and have no words.

'Pen has to use it,' Freddie says in a low, controlled voice. 'She's not welded to it, Brian, I can assure you, but it's there and that's that.'

Brian shrugs, and spends a swift half second rearranging his testicles.

'Sorry babe, yeah, you are a cripple. You're damn sexy too, don't get me wrong!'

Freddie stands up and puts his tea on the desk, his back to Brian. I know he's angry. I know there will be words if Brian does not shut up.

'So you're saying the deal hinges on no wheelchair?' Freddie says without turning.

'I can't do that.' The words charge from my dry throat, the threat of tears as ever stinging under my lids.

Suddenly I'm frightened that everything will hinge on this.

'You're being unrealistic, babe. No one will touch you in that. It's all very well having handicapped kids singing on *Blue Peter* or something – but a handicapped pop star? I don't think so.'

Freddie turns sharply. 'Don't call Pen handicapped, she hates that word. And she's keeping the wheelchair, Brian.'

Brian finishes his coffee and stands up, oblivious to my distress. 'Sheesh. That's a damn shame. Are you sure?' He leans towards me, eyes drawn again to my tits.

Abruptly, he kneels beside my wheelchair. 'Here. You take my card, babe. Call me – you call me – if you change your mind.'

I tense myself away from him. He smells. Heavy man BO, layered with expensive aftershave.

Freddie's hand cuts between us and snatches the card. His other hand rests on my shoulder and I'm instantly calm.

'Okay, Brian, will do,' Freddie hustles Brian to the door at speed with perfunctory goodbyes.

Freddie comes back and hugs me.

'What a total knob,' he says. 'Call him if we change our minds? We're not changing anything.'

He kisses me and with a grin rips up the card, throwing the pieces in the air.

I laugh, but inside I am angry. Especially since I've found Artsline and the London Disability Arts Forum. Sian is helping me see I'm okay as I am. My wheelchair – the Lurgy – is part of me.

Why should I have to hide and pretend about who I am?

Freddie comes back, comes home, clutching fish and chips.

I've been sitting in the dark with the TV on, in between typing, typing and typing. I want to ask him how everything went, but the words won't come and stay locked away inside my fear. Don't rock the boat, don't rock the boat, I tell myself. I don't quite know what the boat is, but I do know Freddie has another life far from these shores.

'Getting chillier, dearheart. But let's hope for no more hurricanes.' He hugs me and I relax into his strength. I decide I don't need to ask him, that it doesn't really matter why he didn't ring and why he's so late.

The hurricane ripped down the aerial from the block roof and the power cut went on for forty-eight hours, weeks before Freddie moved in. I survived by huddling in bed with Tooty, paws against me, my heartbeat as fast and jittery as his. It felt like Doomsday, but we survived and here I am, Freddie one side, Tooty the other.

'Get the food out, honey,' I smile and let him go. 'I'll just nip to the loo.'

'Do you want a hand?' Freddie asks. I love him for being casual about it. It was the first thing he did when he dashed through the door, and part of me wants to say yes this time. But I can't – not every time, not yet.

Munching a chip, Freddie sighs. 'We've exhausted all the big boys now, Pen. I should have known they wouldn't pay any interest. It's all sewn up with A & R men. A shitty closed shop.'

I chew on a piece of coley thoughtfully. 'Disappointing,' I say. 'On with our Nevermore plan?'

'We'll do the recording with Gary, get Tone into play and I'll focus on sorting distribution.'

'As long as I don't have to meet anyone like that fucker Brian,' I say, with a shiver.

'Don't worry, Pen,' Freddie's face is grim. 'No tosspot will treat you like that again.'

We kiss and Freddie goes to the VCR, selecting Doris Wishman's *Nude on the Moon* for our evening's entertainment.

I make an effort to shove Brian and his handicapped ranting to the back of my mind. There's other things coming up. Better things.

There's the festival in Brentford – 'Our Arts Our Culture'. Disability culture. I know I want to be part of that.

CHAPTER 11

25 January 1989: My friends have to count as the most precious things in my life. To be able to speak freely, unafraid of any topic, is a wonderful thing.

I'm pleased it's warm enough to once more wear my black leather bondage dress, this time with a satin kimono-style blouse. Thick black tights – helpfully pulled into place by Freddie. I have swapped around my money envelopes: taken a bit from gas, a bit from food and, with Freddie's help, managed to come up with enough for the cab to Brentford.

I stare out of the window. The roads of the city never lose their grimy magic. I clutch my silky blouse closer. It's a bit too big as it flaps around my knees. It makes me think of Owen and Dan, who have faded from our lives, off to university and girlfriends. I lean into Freddie and close my eyes like a satisfied cat.

The Watermans Arts Centre is a big glass box. I'm nervous as Freddie wheels me through to the festival. But excited too.

Disabled people are everywhere, crips of all kinds. There is chatting in corners, there is waving and greeting. Sian Vasey appears on cue, a friendly face, slim hands open in welcome. My eyes fix on her electric wheelchair.

'You've made it, Penelope,' she says. 'I believe all the action is in the main hall.'

I introduce her to Freddie.

'Go mingle! Meet people,' she says. 'I've got to dash and sort out Heather. Total mess, Penny, with community transport. And she so desperately wants to come.' She rolls her eyes and whizzes off in her wheelchair. I have a deep throb of envy, wondering how on earth I can get one. Another precious to dream of, letting me do more things I dream of.

'Let's go and meet Ian Dury,' says Freddie and we set off in the opposite direction.

The hall is rammed. I have never seen anything like it. Not even at special school. I detect the buzz, the animation, and feel it lift my spirits. A blind woman is playing the piano. Clare Graydon-James sings as her deft fingers dance over the keys. I spot Elspeth and others I've seen at the Artsline meetings.

We applaud loudly when Clare finishes. There is a hush and from the entrance Ian Dury swaggers in leaning on a walking stick. Ian Dury, the disabled pop star with the flash brash of a cockney pirate, the Blockheads' frontman and lyricist. He had polio as a kid, walks with a limp, wears a calliper. He's one of us. As my excitement grows, all I can think is: he broke the mould, he broke down barriers.

Ian is handsome and his keen eyes sweep across us all. I'm struck speechless but wriggle in my chair to straighten my back and look my best. Ian launches into 'The Bus Driver's Prayer'.

I'm whispering to myself, following his words that I love so much.

Freddie fumbles around in the bag hanging on my chair, retrieving a demo cassette tape. 'Are you ready, Pen? As soon as he's finished, we'll nab him,' he says and edges me forward.

Ian goes through his hits and I stare at him, soaking up every piece he does, almost tasting his charisma. We applaud and cheer and show our approval in any way we can. My hands don't clap, but I stamp my boots on the floor.

Freddie pushes me closer and I'm sure I can smell the sweat of Ian Dury. His curious intelligent eyes catch me quickly. My mouth is dry and my hands quiver.

'Hello, my dear, and how are you?' says Ian with a big, sexy grin.

I smile and swallow, swimming in such shyness I think I might drown.

'Fine, thanks,' I croak as my face blasts hot, as my mind blanks.

Freddie looks at me with a sidewards gaze and a hint of a frown. Ian is entranced by my dress. The bust area especially.

'Fab to meet you, mate,' says Freddie and they shake hands. 'I wonder whether you'd take this demo tape. Pen writes and sings all her own work. It would be great to hear what you think.'

'Of course, darlings, of course. Can't promise to be quick though, everything is very full on.'

'Thanks,' I whisper, praying for Freddie to wheel me back and far, far away from this gut-churning embarrassment.

A blond man on crutches saves me with an interruption: 'Ian. Ian – sorry, can you come over and meet someone?' he says. Ian winks at me and he is gone.

Freddie wheels me to a table and gets us some tea.

'What was that about, Pen?' he says. 'We agreed you'd give him a good spiel, sell yourself and all that.'

I can hear a violin playing and laughter. I pull my kimono tighter, hiding under it.

'I couldn't, Freddie. I'm sorry. I sort of got tongue-tied.'

I can feel it might be a moment to cry, but I fight it and I win because there is so much else to see, to listen to: Ian is fabulous and famous and disabled; the others at the event feel like my friends already.

When Sian Vasey announces that we have officially launched the London Disability Arts Forum, there is no fear inside me.

I know I'm coming home, that I want to learn to be happy to be me. And whatever else, I'm not alone in knowing it's okay to be who I am, to want to write and sing, and to fight back.

Freddie leaves early to see his mum and I'm waiting for community transport to go to the clinic appointment at Wanstead Hospital.

I don't want to go, but know that I must and know the Lurgy demands attention in my life every so often. I submit like a good little guinea pig, so they don't get bigger ideas with their scalpels.

Today it's Dr Brown who will test my joints. He is elegant and friendly. Because I'm under fifty, unlike most of his patients, he makes me feel like a treasured pet.

The transport arrives. I swallow. It's Hughie, a flesh-creeping, greasy man in his fifties in a dirty grey Renault 5. Inside it smells acrid and used tissues lay in balls by my feet. He always wants to talk about porn movies and offers to lend me some of his collection. I'm wearing the plainest dress I own, and Sandra dug out a rare cardigan that buttons up to my neck. Hughie squeezes my thigh occasionally, making me jolt away.

I grit my teeth for the twenty-minute journey, muttering a few 'yeses' and 'nos'. Mostly 'nos'.

Doctors. I hate them and love them. What a varied lot they are, every appointment a chore and a contradiction.

'Hello Penny, how are we?' says Dr Brown.

'We're fine,' I say, without any connection to how I feel in reality. A timer clicks in my head as to when he will mention knee operations.

'How are you managing in the flat?' he asks. He has a pleasant grin with gappy teeth and short, greying hair. I'm pleased his bedside manner is up to scratch.

'My boyfriend Freddie has moved in now.'

'Oh, a boyfriend, goodness!' exclaims Dr Brown. 'How nice.'

The knee-op timer ticks on and I find myself thinking about the night before, when Freddie and me had hot dirty sex on the sofa and how, if I was grateful for anything from these doctors, I was grateful for my hip replacements aged thirteen.

'Yes,' I say brightly. 'I'm happy.'

'I've had a report from your GP. He tells me you have had ups and downs. There was the gynae problem and you are prone to being mentally ill.'

'Dr Biggen usually blames everything on my arthritis,' I announce, the words coming from somewhere, 'but it's not about that. I'm not... fed up.'

'I know you've been seeing the psychiatric community nurse. Has that helped?'

I think of Mr McAuliffe – Barry – and I want to be sick. Always telling me Freddie will leave me, that I will be a burden.

That it is inevitable. And Barry is the one who will help me come to terms with all these things, with the ways of the world.

'And we still have those knees to think about.' Dr Brown's statement comes in, bang on my prediction.

'No,' I say. 'I'm managing quite well as I am.'

'But no work at the moment?' he responds, as if the two are somehow irretrievably connected, when I know they're not.

'I work all the time,' I say. 'I'm doing the OU degree, I'm writing. And I'm recording a single.'

I want to say: *so there*.

Dr Brown shakes his head and pulls a woeful face. 'Oh, Penny,' he says. 'It's lovely you keep busy, but it doesn't pay, does it? Those things are all a bit of a pipe dream.'

I don't answer but stare at the floor with its grubby NHS tiling. I want to rage about Thatcher. That there is nothing for us, only endless idiot people going through the motions, not really understanding, endless specialists and experts. I grit my teeth at a sudden memory of a distant job interview set up by the Disability Employment Advisor. Working in a typing pool. Arriving at the building for the interview to discover a flight of steps.

'Okay then, keep trying and don't get lazy. I'll see you in four months,' says Dr Brown, scribbling on a form and grinning.

'I'm getting married,' I say, lifting my gaze, looking forward to when Freddie can join me in these sessions without any aggravation.

Freddie, Gary and Tone are in my living room. Gary has plugged in wires, slid controls and turned knobs for most of the day in front of a huge black slab of recording machinery.

I'm tired and my throat is dry. But I'm pleased and ache with contentment that only comes when a day ends with loads of good things completed. And this time, it's a single.

'It's done, Pen.' Freddie hugs me, his strong arms wrapping me towards him.

'I'll get it mixed within the week,' says Gary, his calm face framed by fair floppy hair.

'I can't believe it,' I say, wanting to laugh.

'Live Your Life' is the single. Recorded, polished, professional. I ignore the barbs of guilt at what they've done because they believe in me. And I'm learning that it's better to keep quiet when I'm frightened and can't share their belief because I know it upsets them. It upsets Freddie.

Freddie lets me out of his arms. 'It's all systems go with Nevermore Records.'

'Isn't that going to cost a lot?' Tone looks concerned.

'Don't ask.' Freddie raises his eyebrows. 'But at least we've got Red Rhino on distribution.'

'I hate the money stuff,' I say quietly. It gives me a pain somewhere near my bowels. So much for enterprise and Thatcher's words of helping new business. It's still all a class war. 'I'm doing my best with the shiniest begging bowls,' I grimace. 'It has to be done.'

'We'll do a fab video,' says Freddie. 'I've got a mate, a young kid from Ilford, who has just started film studies.'

'What's the location?' asks Tone.

'We're working on it,' says Freddie.

I say nothing and watch Gary winding the large tape off the spool with great care.

'Great work,' says Gary, his blond hair swaying as he nods. 'We'll get it ready as soon as possible, Pen. Come and meet Kaye. She's dying to meet you. We'll do dinner.'

'We will,' I say. I turn to look to Freddie: the word LOGISTICS burns at the front of my thoughts.

'It will be a wheel and walk,' Freddie says, slipping into a silly accent. 'No problemo, baby!'

I've never been invited to dinner before and I flush with a sense of suddenly being very grown up.

But I'm tired, very tired, and a sad thought creeps in about Tamsin, who's ill again. I make a note to myself to call her later, Freddie or no Freddie.

The weather's on our side as Freddie and me scoot across the Baker's Arms into Hoe Street, towards the house where Gary and Kaye live. Nerves are bubbling in my veins but I'm excited to see what kind of girlfriend Gary has.

The house is a small Victorian terrace in a quiet back road of Walthamstow, hiding Gary's indie empire, Color Tapes, and his latest venture in the planning, Acme Records. Kaye opens the door, three cats winding around her feet. She's tall and slim, with a blonde bob. The epitome of bohemian elegance in tight leopard-print trousers and a plain blouse. Long, jewel-heavy earrings and a blue ethnic pendant complete her look.

'Hello, come on in,' she says in a low, unhurried voice. 'It's lovely to meet you at last.'

She bends down to kiss me on the cheek and my nerves settle down. We move into the small lounge and I'm exhilarated by the decor, which is like nothing I've seen. Andy Warhol posters and other art prints on the walls, Marilyn Monroe books piled on the floor by the fireplace, a pack of tarot cards beside them. There are lit candles everywhere, Indian sofa throws and glorious scents. Gary comes in and offers us drinks. I go for a glass of red.

'I'd love to photograph you, Pen,' Kaye says. 'You'll need some photos anyway for publicity shots.'

I know Kaye has a passion for photography and shyly accept her offer.

'Dinner won't be long,' Gary says from the corner of the lounge, where he has floor-to-ceiling shelves of vinyl which Freddie has made a beeline for.

The cats are friendly, two plump black, and one black-and-white; Ruby comes and rubs round me for attention, but the youngest, the black-and-white cat, Deva, is timid and very much a boy cat, tilting his head and looking at me with big, round eyes.

Kaye Sayer-Mayers

Kaye creates the mysterious Pen.

We soon move into the dining space at the back of the house. I try and stop grinning like an overawed schoolgirl as I take in the light, civilised atmosphere and chic surroundings, pleased to note that the high, wide window has no net curtains but a panel of lilac voile.

The poll-tax riots come up for discussion and I love that I can get into a meaty chat of hatred for Thatcher. I wish with all my heart to protest out there.

'I refuse to pay that bollocks,' says Gary, with a hint of a smile. 'I'm planning to write a cheque out for the amount on my underpants. Take them to the council.'

We sit at a round table and behold a feast. Jacket potatoes with several fillings – not just the standard tuna or beans, which is the extent of my repertoire.

There's salad in bowls with tasteful blue salad servers. In the middle of this array, there's a jar of mayonnaise.

Kaye helps me put food onto my plate.

'Mayonnaise, Pen?' she says, bringing the jar over.

I look at it, wondering if I dare – I've never tasted it before.

Mum was strictly salad cream and even Tamsin and me didn't make it that far in our journey towards sophistication.

'Yes, please,' I say, determined not to show myself up.

Kaye puts a large spoonful on my plate and I tentatively push some on a fork with the salad – an intriguing mixture of dark leaves and unknown crispy things.

'Would you like me to do a tarot reading after dinner?' Kaye asks me as I munch. 'The boys usually go off to chat music and get all anoraky about it.'

She laughs and I swallow down the mayonnaise, relishing its creamy, savoury taste.

I know that Kaye is a new friend I will cherish getting to know.

CHAPTER 12

22 March 1990: Wrote to Evie Edworthy, local councillor, detailing my hatred of Maggie and asking for ideas of what Labour will do for the disabled voter.

I look at the thick, embossed paper, the letter from the Victoria and Albert Museum.

Freddie, on a usual wave of cheek and confidence, asked if my video could be filmed there, in the William Morris Room. I'd been once with Tamsin, Naomi driving all the way to South Kensington in the rain, to marvel at the Pre-Raphaelite treasures. Freddie likes to call me a Pre-Raphaelite stunner, even in a black, zip miniskirt, especially now my hair is my own – long waves dressed with flowers. But the letter delivers a big no.

£1,000 per day.

I write it in the journal slowly: '£1,000 per day!!!'

This is a barrier we can't get around. I write a few more lines, glancing at Freddie who is using my word processor, writing a comedy script.

Another day I go to write, and the Lurgy in my shoulder starts complaining and I wonder whether I should resort to typing my journal, pasting it in afterwards.

'Is it okay if I ring Tam?' I say.

Freddie looks up, distant. Then he nods, silently grabs the word processor and goes into the bedroom.

I hate that I feel awkward for the first minute or so when I call her. My phone phobia never used to be an issue speaking to Tamsin and I can't work out why I'm uneasy.

She sounds good, healthy, and I'm pleased she is feeling better.

'I'm going to move into my own flat soon,' she says. 'But things are very different down here, Pen. There's much better support for disabled people.'

I draw in my breath and don't answer immediately. There's a deep ache in my belly as I realise how I miss her.

'Be careful,' I say.

She brushes it away, telling me how much she's enjoying life in Southampton, moving on to grill me in her typical, humorous way about what's happening. I moan about the Victoria and Albert situation.

'Pen, there's a simple answer,' she says. 'You tell that Freddie of yours it's right under his nose. Do the video at the William Morris Gallery.'

'Bloody hell, yes!'

I remember the beautiful house – another afternoon out with Naomi. And another time within the shadow of the house with Freddie, sitting on his lap on a bench in a corner of the shabby, downtrodden Lloyd Park, a sad background of persistent chirping from the cramped aviary rammed full of tiny captured birds.

'Tam,' I say, 'you're a genius.'

'I know,' she laughs. 'But meanwhile, Ms Kata Show-Off Kolbert, I read your piece in *Feminist Art News*. Smart cow, aren't you? No, it's great stuff. Right on the bloody money.'

As we say our goodbyes, I'm flushed with happiness of a kind only Tam can create in me.

The William Morris Gallery on Forest Road, Walthamstow.

Charlie the curator meets us around the back of the large Georgian building. Apart from allowing us to film for free, he has also organised the date to coincide with the day that they are closed to the public. I'm grateful and I'm jittery.

Paul is seventeen with short, black, spiky hair – a typical indie kid. He holds a Super 8 camera and trots around, his face intense, staring at the lights.

I foot-pedal around the rooms slowly, in awe of the tapestries, gazing at the De Morgan tiles and first editions of William Morris's socialist writings. The carpets smell of clean, pleasant age.

My hair has been bleached all over and hangs free, pinned with more flowers by Sandra, who's helped me into a suitable ensemble.

'Are you ready, Pre-Raphaelite lady?' teases Freddie. 'Where do you want Pen to be first, Paul?'

Paul scratches his chin. 'The light's not so good, wasn't quite ready for that.'

'It can be moody,' Freddie says and I laugh, ignoring the fingers pinching in my belly as nerves build up.

'Are you going for a live record of the music?' Freddie continues, as he helps me move to a large black-and-white photo of Will.

'Oh no,' says Paul, 'that can be added later. There's no mic on this camera.'

Freddie grunts. 'But Pen should try to lip-sync to a track, shouldn't she?'

Paul chews his lip as if asked a question about advanced physics. Freddie and me hold our breath for an answer.

'Yeah, yeah. That'll be fine,' Paul shrugs, lifting the camera.

All of a sudden, I'm horribly self-conscious, and sag. 'Let me do a warm-up to the track?' I plead to Freddie. 'Then Paul can start filming.'

I do it a few times and start to feel better. Paul lifts the camera again.

'Can you say start or even action?' I ask, wanting to get it over with.

'Of course. But just one thing. Freddie, do you want me to try and avoid getting the wheelchair in?'

Freddie sits by the portable cassette player ready to press play and blast out 'Live Your Life'. He frowns. 'No, Paul, that's not really necessary. Use your skills. That's what we want. You can be all artistic.'

My shaking continues. I am not hiding my wheelchair. The thought runs furiously in my head but I can't spit out the statement.

Paul smiles nervously, lifts the camera and counts me in.

A few weeks later, after some effort, Freddie collects the finished version transferred to video.

'I do need to tell you, Pen' – he pulls an exaggerated sad face – 'unfortunately it turned out Paul didn't know how to lip-sync, so we've got something but it might need more work.'

He presses play and there I am, filmed from the waist up, mouth moving, body swaying. Without any connection to the words of 'Live Your Life'.

Tooty creeps out from the bedroom. He does this when he hears a new female voice. Freddie's asked over his friend Tanya, a punky Hackney girl. She is calm, has a warm voice, enviable dark hair, cut short, and perfectly shaped eyebrows.

Tooty jumps on her lap, which is like a blessing.

'Oh!' she says. 'I wasn't expecting that.'

Tooty starts to purr at volume ten.

'He's friendly,' I say. 'Are you a cat person?'

'I've never had one, but it looks like Tooty likes me.'

She strokes his head and exclaims when he pushes forward into her hand, before getting used to it.

I think it's love at first sight for us both.

We chat for some time. I give Tanya a copy of *Singing Bird*. She tells me she is starting piano lessons. I immediately love her calm aura, the way she moves her hands. She is dressed plainly, all in black, her delicate mouth highlighted with red lipstick. She's impressively a bit Patti Smith.

'Fuck off!' she yells at Freddie when he pulls his notorious fish face. 'I hate that.'

Freddie teases her a lot and she retorts with firm 'fuck offs' and smiling eyes.

Her voice is all her own, not much London twang.

'Tell me about Hagar the Womb,' I say. 'You know what Freddie's like – I've only had titbits.'

'I'm not with that band any more but I'll try and get you a copy of the last single. It's all Crass's fault. Me, I'm a bit of a hermit these days. All work, not much play.'

'Come and play with me then,' I say.

'Bloody hell, give us a chance. I've got to buy a keyboard yet.'

Her face is stern, but her eyes tell me she's teasing.

By this time, we've almost forgotten Freddie is there, typing in the background, knowing when to retreat from girl chat.

'Thanks for the tape,' I say, looking at the cassette she's brought me. Crass, The Slits, The Raincoats, Marvin Gaye, Joni Mitchell. A lovely mix, just how I like my music.

'Time for a surprise!' Freddie jumps up and leaves the room.

'Oo-er missus,' I say.

Tanya rolls her eyes. 'Fuck's sake, what you up to?'

Freddie swans in with something behind his back. He does a vocal drum roll and then presents the single.

The single!

The 'Live Your Life' 12-inch. With its chalk-on-black drawing by an artist I met through *Jamming!* magazine.

'I said to Pen, Tanya – it was a moment of pure magic hearing it boom out of the warehouse speakers.'

'That's fantastic.' Tanya smiles at me and I feel a delicious welling up from guts to eyes. I am happy. Very happy.

Freddie puts the record into my hands. I stroke it and then I sniff it.

There's nothing quite like the smell of newly pressed vinyl.

Our wedding day in June, and it's raining. A horrible, drizzly mist that I don't really want to go out into.

Sandra helps me get ready, putting on my heavy, cotton dress with its Bardot shoulderline. It's actually curtain material with a Morrisesque pattern of garlands and rosebuds in pinks and greens, handmade by Tamsin's sister. My regular hairdresser, Tracey, ringlets my hair. I feel good, despite the rain. But I still want to get it over with – Freddie and me getting legal to make life easier in a world where I simply don't fit.

My old friend Jean fusses over me. Jean, my angel from Romford. A calming presence, always indulgent and never judgemental. Her soft ginger hair frames her kind and tranquil face. She soothes me with a hand on my bare shoulder.

Dear Sandra at my wedding to Freddie.

There's a handful of my family milling around us. We make our way to Walthamstow Registry Office in two cars, Freddie and me in a minicab. I clutch his hand for the whole of the short drive.

'Do we really want to do this?' I whisper.

'We could just run away and leave them to it,' Freddie whispers back and I wonder for a moment if he is serious and whether we should. After all, we only want the bit of paper. And not one of his family is coming anyway.

As we pull up outside the registry office on a quiet backstreet, the rain picks up. I worry – always – about my hair going flat. But we are here and it is time.

Mum and Auntie Mary sit side by side in the annexe to the registrar's office. They both wear hats and you can tell they are sisters. They kiss my cheeks in turn and I sense their nerves are as bad as mine, but for vastly different reasons.

The registrar invites everyone in. The theme from *The Deer Hunter* shudders from small speakers. My ringlets stay pert as I clutch at the small, lucky black cat and flower posy that Sandra has brought me. Jean gives me an encouraging smile.

Freddie and me look at each other. My belly somersaults in disbelief that this is really happening. The music stops and the registrar starts the spiel. Everyone is grinning at us. Auntie Mary dabs her eyes.

I feel like a fraud, thoughts dragged back to Nurse Brandy and bra-burning. Did I really want to get married, after all my feminist proclaiming? Yet for me, it's different and I know it. I know I don't have as many choices.

Freddie puts the gold band on my finger. It's the ring from my mum and dad's wedding. We sign on the dotted line. Jean gets out her posh camera and we shuffle into different groupings, different combinations for a few minutes.

We only want the bit of paper. We don't want the fuss.

But my relatives have other ideas and back at the flat there is a small spread, a few bowlfuls of crisps and some presents. Tears burn my eyes when I open the ones from Tamsin. Sad she couldn't come and guilty in still feeling that somehow I drove her away.

Everyone leaves by five o'clock. Sandra – staying late and unpaid – helps me out of my wedding frock.

As she goes, Freddie kisses me. 'Fancy ordering in a pizza, Mrs Dearheart?' he says. 'And then *Pink Flamingos* vid?'

'Sounds good to me,' I say and click on the word processor. 'Just going to tinker while it comes.'

I go straight to my list of songs selected to go on the Spiral Sky LP. Spiral Sky, my new band, and the next push with Destiny.

Freddie springs a gig on me at St Margaret's church, next to the Houses of Parliament. It's on the back of 'Live Your Life' coming out and I'm not sure whether to be pleased – or terrified.

It's my first performance – since the drunken disaster that was The Ugly Pygmies. To Freddie it's a natural progression; to me, it's unnatural hell and we have our first tentative row over it.

He also surprises me with the revelation that I'm to be Guest of the Day on LBC's Steve Jones lunchtime show. This is not so scary, and as we set off into the grey day, I decide radio will be easier than performing.

Zed, my *Jamming!* friend, has come up from Sussex to be a roadie and helps Freddie shove speakers into the back of another rusty cab. One of Kaye's photographs has been used on our homemade poster in black and white. I look thoughtful, a bit Twenties, with hair tied to one side in lace. It puts a doubtful pang in my innards.

The church is vast with high vaulted ceilings. My voice seems to float into its upper reaches. There's three people in the audience, plus Zed. I sing the songs, quivering, but I get through.

A fast journey and we're at the LBC studio in some back alley near what was once Dr Johnson's house. The receptionist takes my name and I'm ushered through, nerves jittery but curiosity keeping them at bay.

Pete Murray, the DJ, walks by and says hello. I mumble something back, furious with myself – my shyness – for not getting his autograph for Mum.

Steve Jones is very friendly as I'm set up in front of a microphone.

Freddie kisses me on the lips. 'I'll just be outside listening,' he says. 'Do your bit, Kata Kolbert.'

Steve Jones makes the process easy. I talk about the single, almost forgetting I'm on a radio show. Steve mentions that there have been very few disabled pop stars.

'There's Robert Wyatt, of course,' he says. 'He did manage to get on *Top of the Pops*, but I believe the BBC didn't really like it that he was in a wheelchair.'

I think back to my John Peel session of Robert Wyatt and the killer track 'Shipbuilding' delivered in Robert's beautiful plaintive voice. Steve is introducing my single to the listeners and chitchats to me as a short burst is played.

As the song fades out he turns to look at me, white teeth showing as he smiles: 'Well, Kata, we have a surprise for you. Robert Wyatt is listening to the show! He's left his details and wants you to call him. Isn't that great?'

'Yes,' I say, knowing that I sound squeaky.

Robert Wyatt...

Steve Jones takes pity on me. 'What a great way to end talking to our Guest of the Day! Good luck with that, Kata, and we hope you'll be back here to talk to us soon.'

The next day I ring Robert. It takes me until 4.23 p.m. – after five attempts and hang-ups – my fear so present I am chewing on it.

But I get there. And Robert is nice and chatty and wants to hear more of my music as soon as possible. He gives me his address and I start by sending him a postcard: a photograph by Man Ray.

I'm crying. I'm laughing. I've got the telly on with the volume down but it's hard to not be glued to what unfolds.

Nelson Mandela is free. Naturally I'm playing 'Free Nelson Mandela' so loud my ears hurt.

I know it's history – out there, global. But it feels personal, and as I look at this elderly black man surrounded by the cheers of thousands I shake with a strange optimism for myself.

When I can pull myself away I reread the letter in my hands. From an agent. Yet another rejection, but at least I can say it's a nice one: you're too good and your beautiful prose and allusive style is sadly not what publishers want these days.

I'm trying to build up to a novel. Ideas pound around my head threatening to come out through my eardrums like manic ticker tape. Above all else there's the eponymous album. *Spiral Sky* by Spiral Sky. Tanya, with her calm soul, sharp humour and fast loyalty, is in the line-up on keyboards. She gives me a chance to develop melody without cursing my stiff fingers.

I'm working on the lyrics to 'Lady of the Chaise Lounge' when Tamsin calls. I'm relieved because Freddie is out all day and now, left with half a glass of water and a sandwich made by the new home help, Iris, at the end of her two hours, I am increasingly nervous of being alone, as practicalities get tougher, my body not cooperative.

Speaking to Tamsin always cheers me up, even if guilt still pinches me. The feeling that me and Freddie made her go hangs like a ghost hovering over our conversations.

We share a few tears over Nelson, recalling the petitions we signed, the letters we wrote as bitch Maggie held out against sanctions and lunched with the likes of General Pinochet.

'How's the new flat?' I ask, relieved she's now in a place of her own. 'Is this new support scheme working out okay?'

Disabled people in Southampton have a group, the Centre for Independent Living. CIL for short. They've helped Tamsin to get personal assistants – PAs as she calls them. A big part of the crip revolution.

'I'm loving it, Pen,' she says. 'It's what we needed in our flat. PAs. People that help out with the basics, and so much more. Who facilitate. Not take over.'

I laugh. 'I can't imagine the new home help facilitating. I have Iris now. She's a sweetie, a big Jamaican granny. But she just wants to care all the time. Granny knows best, that kind of thing.'

'Anyway, one reason I rang is to offer you a gig. The CIL are organising an event. I'd love it if you could do something. We're launching our own disability arts forum, like LDAF. You know you're good enough.'

I hesitate and look at the TV for a few seconds. I'm instantly overwhelmed, torn in two. Of course I want to gig. But how will we get there? Can I get the band together to perform live? Will they want to come? Will I keep well enough?

'I want to,' I say in a quiet voice. 'If I can work it out.'

'You can meet Simon Brisenden,' Tamsin says. 'He's such a great poet and I know he'll love your work.'

'I wish I could drive!' I say it abruptly, vehemently. I look at the TV again, lifted with the sense that anything is possible.

'Do it,' laughs Tamsin. 'Get the begging bowl out. Write letters.'

I look across the room to my latest precious, a shiny Amstrad PC, the monumental effort of begging to every charity it had taken to get it, the horror of demeaning myself, of exaggerating my attributes to squeeze out the cheques. Was I ready to do it again? Could I even learn to drive?

I think about a gig in Southampton. I think about *Spiral Sky* by Spiral Sky, and I know I'm ready to have a go.

Tanya and me are drooling over Leonard Cohen. We've devised our own version of 'Suzanne'. It might not make it onto the album but there's been a rush of gig offers.

The London Disability Arts Forum is in full swing, running an event called the Workhouse. Johnny Crescendo, singer-songwriter and disability arts activist, has booked Spiral Sky for a slot at Chatsworth Palace in Hackney. For once I'm excited as well as terrified.

'How long is the set meant to be?' asks Tanya, gulping her coffee, raising a perfect eyebrow.

'Twenty-five minutes, I think. It's not that I don't have the songs, but we're not exactly well rehearsed on them all.' I look around the lounge at the spread of random instruments, my very own Fostex 4-track perched on the desk.

'And I'm moving,' says Tanya. 'That's going to be an arse.'

'Noooo! It'll be great. You're coming into the fold of Waltham Forest! I can't wait. It's Fate and Destiny.'

Tanya is a new soul sister, and although no one replaces Tamsin, I'm pleased I have her around to talk girlie stuff. Not to mention that Tanya and me have a shared love of the Pre-Raphaelites and Thomas Hardy, as well as all the punk stuff.

Coffee finished, we return to 'Suzanne', trying to do it proud.

Coaxing Tooty off the lyric sheet, I wonder how Freddie is doing in his new job. It's nice to be with Tanya and not on my own. Especially after interminable bouts of ill health.

Soul sisters.

Women's problems. That's what my mum calls them. Periods. Thrush. All those things that are a bit embarrassing and not to be talked about, even to Dr Biggen. He's better than many but still too posh, and I'm not used to hearing anyone rabbit on about 'the vagina'.

Half the battle is reminding people I actually have genitals. And on the back of all that crap, here we are at a well woman clinic in downtown scabby Leyton.

It's a post-war building, a bit like a school with peeling grey doors and badly scuffed wooden floors. Freddie sits beside me on a long bench under the window which has a few half-dead spider plants on the sill, patterned with dead flies. It smells of antiseptic, wee and a sickly wave of competing perfumes. One of them is mine, too much Opium in the eternal battle to counteract the conditioned fear of being smelly.

Dr Biggen has taken me off the pill. Says I need a rest from it, that it's the cause of my period trouble. That's what he calls it. To me, it's like my insides fall out, painfully, with lots of blood and excruciating cramps. Dr Biggen suggests this clinic is where I can look at 'other options'.

A woman in her sixties with flat, slate hair appears and surveys us all until her eyes rest on me.

'You're Penelope?' Her glance is bored, working on automatic, weighing me up. 'I'm Dr Hainault. Follow me, please.'

I acknowledge myself with a mumble as Freddie wheels me behind her.

At the door to her room she turns, brow furrowed. 'And this man is?'

'My husband,' I respond, words firm for once.

It's a typical dull room with a high wooden couch that I only get onto with Freddie's help. I note the silver tray with the silver instruments – including a silver speculum for the vagina. My guts tremble.

'We don't usually allow anyone in, even husbands,' is her continuing gambit. 'I'll make an allowance as you're a special case.'

'Pen won't get on the couch without my help,' says Freddie drily.

'Indeed,' says Dr Hainault, staring at us in turn as if looking for hidden signals. She proceeds to read some notes, rustles some paper, head down. 'So you are having sexual intercourse?'

Sex-yoo-all inter-course. Syllables elongated with distaste, she doesn't look up and I squirm. She seems to strip away something human. Can't believe I fuck.

I scream inside. Not only my stubborn shyness, but in frustration that my anger never reaches my gob.

'We've been together a while now,' says Freddie. 'Of course we have sex.'

'I just want to sort out contraception,' I babble, angry, words bursting into the world.

She lifts her head and narrows her eyes. 'You might be a candidate for the cap, I suppose. I'll examine you in a minute and we'll see. Your, er, husband could help, I imagine?'

She says it in long words, as if ready to rinse her mouth out.

My stomach kicks off with a habitual churn at the thought of the cap. I have no idea what this thing looks like or how it is fitted. Freddie squeezes my hand gently, which seems to disturb Dr Hainault.

'Of course there is another answer,' she announces with sudden enthusiasm. 'You could have a hysterectomy. I know you're not thirty yet but in your situation it might be for the best. For multiple reasons.'

A charged silence smothers me. The buried voice somewhere in my scandalised head wonders how many women she says this to. How many women below thirty? I don't know about babies. Since my pregnancy scare I've pushed it from my mind, but I know I'm not ready to annihilate my chances altogether.

I don't know how she interprets my silence but I shiver when she gets up and moves towards the silver tray.

By the time I leave, shell-shocked, there's been no real answer and I'm clutching a small box with the latex cap and a tube of K-Y Jelly.

CHAPTER 13

28 January 1991: Must manage a brief note today on the news. This Gulf War is obscene, I'm totally sickened by it and go into a panic watching the awful blanket coverage. The war is obviously all about oil. Rehearsing for Chats meanwhile. A world away. Really worn out.

I'm shaking as we get into position on stage at Chatsworth Palace. It's a small low space, wheelchair-accessible from the side. I feel a bit dowdy, a bit council estate in my charity-shop clothes. I secretly wish I could ask someone else for help to get dressed up at gigs other than Freddie. He is a man, after all. He can't help it when he doesn't notice things out of place.

I'm wearing my big black hat, which covers a multitude of

Shaking on the Chatsworth stage.

horrors. Tanya, who is beside me on keyboard, calls them our Paddington hats – she's got one too.

Kaye photographs us in moody black and white. She flips around the front of the stage, crouching down to get good angles. I smile to myself – she's become Kata Kolbert's official photographer.

It feels very professional. There's a sound engineer, there's a microphone on a stand. The band's instruments are connected to a mixing desk. And there's a spotlight or two shining on my stage fright.

The lights drop and there's a hush. I look across at Tanya and we do a subtle counting in together. Her fingers dance on the keyboard, the opening riff of 'Career Girl', fresh and punky with a jagged pop tune inside it, poised for the album:

The man he shambles grey
Little words and even less to say
Said my life must go this way
Can't do this, can't do that
Fixed quite safely in the box
It's made for you, so take it.

Our sound is magnificent, chunky, solid, it chugs on with a punky attack. My voice floats between it – clear and on form. I can't see the audience and I'm glad. I can only hear my song and the sound we make together. I find the anger in my lyrics:

Oh no Mother, Mother no
Tell me now this can't be true
My world is held by limits
From another's point of view.

The applause is reasonable as we finish, even if I hate myself for not being able to banter. Tanya and me move straight into 'Suzanne', although I cringe a little as the keyboard is mixed too loud.

I sing and I sing into the darkness beyond the glare of the lights. I don't care that I can't see anyone as I lift into impossible euphoria.

Later that week we're offered more gigs.

Rehearsals chug on for a gig at the Hackney Empire. I write a new story a week. I squeeze in my Open Uni. It's tiring and crazy. And I love it.

There's even room for more. I take on being the local contact for Young Arthritis Care, who are part of the bigger charity, Arthritis Care. A visit from their new director, Kate Nash, convinces me further that I want to be involved.

Kate Nash has had the Lurgy – *roomertoyed* – since a child, and our bond starts here. Along with our shared belief in rights. Not endless do-gooding.

'I want to batter down their power structures,' she says in her clear, determined voice. 'Get the world away from all this tragedy stuff about disabled people. Society needs to change, first and foremost.'

I'm a bit in awe of Kate in her beautiful, tailored clothes, classy dress and long necklaces, but we speak the same language.

'Have you read *Pride Against Prejudice* by Jenny Morris?' she asks. 'It's revolutionary, Pen. It really deals with this new way of seeing disability.'

'I'll buy it straight away,' I say. 'Anything to push the crip revolution.'

'You could review it for the *Young Arthritis News*. "Every disabled person should read this book" – says our new writer Penny!'

I know there's no money in it, but I'm thinking sod the time, I'll find a way, somehow.

'I'd better go soon,' Kate says as she finishes her tea.

I want to stay chatting, to keep hold of the buzz our conversation creates in me.

'I've got one more rehearsal,' I sigh. 'I'm not sure I really like performing. But I suppose I have to.'

'You'll be great, Pen,' says Kate. 'And every time you do it, it changes something. Makes things better.'

Two days to go and I'll be on that stage. Kata Kolbert and her band Spiral Sky.

I listen to music through a slow breakfast. Pentangle first: 'Let No Man Steal Your Thyme'. Trojan Reggae Vol. 1, one side, and 'Jeane', the B-side of 'This Charming Man', with Johnny Marr's fabulous guitar and Morrissey's plaintive vocals.

Freddie leaves for work with a kiss on the head, my food and drink lined up by the kitchen sink. Only half a glass of water – my knees are too fucked for me to go to the toilet on my own.

I try to gather up stuff, ready for another evening of recording at Gary's. It's exciting but I'm tired. It's a graft, and there's loads of other graft. Life is busy.

Freddie is out until late, and Iris is meant to be coming but she is already half an hour overdue and I've not yet built up enough confidence to call her office.

I haven't seen Evil Shrink Nurse Barry McAuliffe for a while, despite some difficult mental moments, because I don't like him and it's easy to pretend I'm fine.

His last great comment about my phone phobia was to tell me to take ten breaths and then *make* myself do it. I'm seeing Dr Toby, occasionally, at Claybury, a gigantic old-style mental hospital, but I doubt if he can help. Especially as he wants me to have group therapy, which I hate.

A tentative tap on the back door interrupts my moment of staring at the phone and I realise it's the meals-on-wheels woman. This week, it's Monica.

'Pen, ducks,' she says, as I open the door. 'I can't find your lunch. You've been forgotten!'

I don't really know how to answer and have an immediate throb of anxiety. Monica reads my face and heads for the kettle.

'Now don't you worry, ducks. I'll make you a nice hot tea. We do have leftovers you can have. Mr Patel didn't want his curry and Nanny Cohen don't want her beef.'

I sip my tea, angry, always angry on the inside. Not with kindly Monica. But I know the system is wrong. It doesn't need to be this way.

I long for Freddie – but as always I wish I had a way over these obstacles that doesn't involve him. With an envious pang, I think of Tamsin with her new personal assistants.

'Is there meat in the curry?' I ask Monica. 'I don't eat meat.'

Monica looks at me with unnecessary concern. 'I'll have to check, ducks, don't think so. But the beef's kosher, is that okay?'

'I'll try the curry then,' I say, unenthusiastically, knowing the meals-on-wheels variety is likely to be tinned vegetables with a jar of sauce poured over. I sympathise with Mr Patel's rejection.

'There's a good girl,' smiles Monica and trots off to get it, returning with the little foil dish and a banana for good measure.

The awful meals-on-wheels curry is forgotten when Freddie prepares two big fat jacket potatoes for dinner, which we load with cheese and beans and French mayonnaise. I try to pull out a rejection letter from down the side of my chair, but Freddie whips it away.

'Nope. You're not looking at it again.' He puts it on a high shelf, on top of my collection of Klimt books. 'I know it's a pisser, but we always have to move on.'

I lean towards him for a kiss.

'But it's another brush-off, Freddie. And not a particularly nice one, saying my signature looks weird, that I'm handicapped?'

Freddie munches thoughtfully, lifts his fork towards me as he speaks: 'Put that letter out of your head. Think of the one you had last week, which said you are a good writer but you need to go in a direction that can find an outlet. We all have to do that, one way or another.'

I take a few mouthfuls of my own potato, as my mind ignites. I can almost write about anything and anyone, but must somewhere put disability in it – in new ways, in real ways. It's in the depths of my blood and fibre.

'Maybe sci-fi? I could have fun with that.' I look at Freddie, feeling the love – yet always, the lapping little red tongues of anxiety.

Freddie nods his head and swallows fast.

'Great idea. Do it by the numbers, bring everything in. It'll still be you.'

I look out at the evening sky. It's overcast and heavy with an orange glow. I'm so stretched for time. The band rehearses constantly, the songs are polished and polished again. There is the Open Uni – now a struggle as I take on Religious Pluralism.

I haven't got time for a big project, but it's there – the words start popping. By the time I'm sitting on the sofa with Freddie, for our regular evening of film, I've sniffed out a virgin notebook and started to write *Strangeness and Charm*. The heroine is K. C. Speares who is disabled, naturally. Speares, senior space crew member, an off-world expert in communication and languages, travels to the outer limits of the galaxy where the docile Lamerians wish for peaceful contact. But all is not what it seems, and KC must face up to her own past and prevent inter-galactic war.

I feel a pang of sadness as I pack away my Open Uni books for good. I can't quite face getting rid of them and I hope I can pick up where I left off when life is better, in a few years, after the album's released. I pat the arm-tatty wheelchair. At least tomorrow I get a better one, a little bit more freedom. Battery-powered. And remarkably, it's all down to Lord Snowdon.

I don't know how I got the award, scraping in under the criteria for an education grant from Action Research for the Crippled Child. Lord Snowdon is patron. This seems to be because he had polio as a kid – like Ian Dury.

Freddie and me edge into a sumptuous Guildhall, south of the river; my anxiety reaches into the high, ornate ceiling. There's lots of round tables laid out with napkins and cutlery. A delicate posy of flowers sits in the centre.

Disabled people are scattered throughout, some in wheelchairs, some on crutches. I'm glad I don't have to speak, although every so often a photographer appears and I'm immediately self-conscious. Always, always caught on the spikes of anxiety at odds with the boldness of my appearance, the inside me scared of the outside me. I'm wearing a white dress of muslin, the frilly wench design around the shoulders meaning my breasts look ginormous. The black cardigan and chunky jewellery can't hide them. I shrink into a small cave of embarrassment as people introduce themselves. Or are introduced by others. This is Lady Bloggs and this is Lord Blah. Fred Smith, OBE, Sir Loadsamoney who runs Botcthit & Co.

I sit next to Freddie at one of the round tables. The cutlery's too heavy for my small hands and I'm terrified of plopping food into my exposed cleavage. Somehow I get through lunch and then there are speeches, before we're lined up ready for the presentation to Lord Snowdon.

I'm suddenly angry. This isn't my natural habitat. I'm punk. I'm anti-capitalist. I'm anti the greedy rich. Yet here I am about to receive a cheque for which I'm not truly grateful. I find I don't want to call him sir or lord and I'm not going to bow – a difficult movement for me on many fronts, and also because I'm certain my tits will fall out.

Lord Snowdon is polite, on a walking stick. He shakes my hand and I don't move forward. I can't wait to get out of this place but as I look at the cheque I know a new sliver of independence is coming into my life. A good thing for Freddie, and for me.

I join the Labour Party. I still can't believe that Thatcher is out, but that we're stuck with the drab pronouncements of John Major.

Neither can Mr Katrinsky. He's the courteous elderly gentleman the local party have sent to sign me up. It's got to be done. Major might not be Thatcher, but he's still a Tory.

I'm at the old familiar desk, distracted by hints of summer in the outside world as blossom blows along the Leyton cul-de-sac like crazy confetti. I have got two big gigs coming up and I yearn for a car.

There's rumours that one day the government will change the buses, make them accessible to disabled people at last. But it's a rumour amongst my comrades and there's no sign of any changes any time soon. The tube remains an arcane mystery, an underground which may as well be the one ruled by Hades, who appears on the death card that comes up in Kaye's tarot pack. I'm fed up with relying on voluntary transport, on social workers rationing it. If I go on holiday to Dorset with Freddie, I want us to see it, lots of it. My mind is set on a car and somehow it will happen.

Mr Katrinsky doesn't have any idea about begging bowls and says Labour are always hard up. He advises me to write to posh people and celebrities. I want to rant about the capitalist system but instead, it's another letter:

> *Dear Blah*
> *I hope you don't mind me writing blah blah. I'm a disabled woman blah blah. Since childhood blah blah. I work hard blah blah. Doing an Open Uni degree blah blah...*

This is technically a lie, having now withdrawn from my course. My lead tutor, Belinda, is devastated and I am sad she is hurt. I tell her I might pick it up again. But I don't want to be an academic, I want to write and all the rest of it.

And for now, my skills are concerned with begging letters, if that is how it has to be to get a car:

> *My assessment in Surrey, blah blah and now I know it is possible, I'd love this opportunity blah blah blah...*

Begging bowls and donations are one thing but it takes over an hour to get to the driver assessment centre in Surrey, in murderously uncomfortable community transport, arranged by my social worker.

Tamsin reckons they send them on purpose – these awful rattling minibuses and rustbuckets with perverts or else God-squad drivers. They want to put us off.

Surrey is another country from Leytonstone, with leafy lanes and a quietness that hangs in the atmosphere, not unlike the well-to-do areas in my childhood home, the Chalfonts. I like it and fear it simultaneously.

I'm met by a tall woman, an occupational therapist called Amanda. She takes me quickly along to the testing rig, to try out my reflexes on braking and vision, along with arm strength on a steering wheel. Once this is done, there will be a final report on what adaptations are needed on my car.

As Freddie helps me into the rig, I shake. I know this is it. If the Lurgy plays up, if my knee goes crunch at the wrong moment, they'll fail me. And all the endless begging letters, full of the begging tragic blah blah, will be pointless.

Once I settle, the controls are explained.

'We want you to press hard on the brake pedal, Penny,' she says, 'whenever you see a light come up on the painting.'

In front of me, there is a large, roughly painted scene of a street. It's very Metroland, with women in scarves, one with an old-style pram. The kids look like Ladybird Peter and Janes. There is a zebra crossing and a dog.

'All ready then?' says Amanda. 'When the lights come on, brake hard.'

She leaves the room and I stare at the jolly scene. The light flashes on the dog, I ram my foot down. Seconds tick. The light comes on – woman with the pram, I thrust again. There is a longer time lapse. Then, a frantic flashing on Jane on the crossing.

'Fuck!' My foot hits the pedal, but my kitten heel skids off. I'm mortified. Freddie chuckles. Amanda is unfazed. I'm tense for her feedback. I want to drive, I must drive. I'm not the first disabled woman to do it, and I know there will be hundreds and thousands who will follow. But I want it now.

'Sorry about that last one,' I say, breathlessly, not wanting to ask if this was an automatic fail.

'You passed, Penny, it's fine. You're well within natural braking capability.' She looks down at my shoes and raises an eyebrow. 'We'd recommend different footwear, of course, and an extended pedal, but overall you've got no worries.'

I smile, a child with the best present ever.

'So I'll be able to drive? Once the changes are done on the car?'

'Yes,' Amanda says slowly, 'but let's check out your strength. You arthritics usually have very weak arms, so you probably need upgraded power-steering. Rather expensive, I'm afraid.'

The sun goes behind a stray cloud. I forgive her for 'you arthritics' but suddenly see the pile of begging letters multiplying.

By the end of the day, the conclusion is I should go for a Renault Clio and the adaptations will cost at least £10,000.

Freedom: girl racer at last.

It takes an age of begging and coaxing and scratching around. But, here I am, my hands on the small racing-style wheel in my slinky white Clio. There's max power-steering, there's an electric handbrake, there's endless mirrors to compensate for my neck not moving.

My driving instructor, Malcolm, comes from Loughton, near Epping. He's a small wiry man with lots of enthusiasm. He calls me his girl racer and loudly adores the range of multicoloured leggings I've taken to wearing.

'Loving the colour today, Pen,' he enthuses as we get into my Clio.

Today is the very big day of my driving test. After the long effort of begging and coaxing, I'm poised to launch into the world as free as a bird. At least I can say a happy goodbye to the endless money-grabbing array of minicab drivers, with their old bangers that smell of cigarettes and B.O.

'Are you ready, Pen?' Malcolm's keen face turns to me. 'I know you can do it.'

I feel like I can do it and I deserve it. My head and heart are crammed with touchable dreams. Going to the seaside, Walton-on-the-Naze. Driving to work. To Kaye and Gary's. Spiral Sky days. Socialising.

I drive to the test centre in Chingford, listening attentively to Malcolm's last instructions.

'Don't rush coming out onto the road,' he says as we pull into the centre. 'It's a tricky one for us all, where the road bends up the hill. Use your mirrors.'

I laugh at him, thankful this process has been made easy by his commitment and faith. A man with a clipboard approaches the car and introduces himself as my examiner.

'And what must we remember at all times, Pen?' says Malcolm, as he turns to wait in the office.

I laugh, pushing my nerves down as far as they will go.

'Mirror, signal, manoeuvre!'

Malcolm's face splits into a cheesy grin and I set off with the examiner.

I take my time at the exit as cars speed down the hill. But not too much time.

When I return to the centre, the sun is bright and, as I park the car, I'm splitting in two with elation. Malcolm rushes out and I hold up the pass certificate for him to see.

CHAPTER 14

24 February 1992: I am excited. I've given birth. Spiral Sky *is mixed and it sounds real. Like something proper. I say sod you lot, you disbelievers out there.*

Freddie is beside himself as he wheels me into the tiny back entrance of the Hackney Empire. There are a few steps but he manages. I crunch a little, torn as always between anger and anxiety. The question: why does it have to be so hard?

It's a chilly March day – International Women's Day. I see Tanya, her keyboard by her feet.

'This is seriously scary, Pen.' She's biting her lip, hugging her arms around her body.

'But you're going on the stage where Max Miller did his thing!' exclaims Freddie. 'This is history. Soak up those vibes.'

'Fuck off with that crap, you,' says Tanya, always fondly.

I'm soaking up nothing but nerves and hope my voice won't tremble. Apart from Tanya and me, there is no band because it's women only on stage. I have a backing tape, which isn't as good. We hope that the female sound engineer does her bit.

I suddenly need the toilet and know it's impossible. There is not enough time for Freddie to drag me around to find one. I'm fed up that he needs to drag me around at all. My nerves keep building and I pray I won't wet myself.

I'm pleased when I see Elspeth from London Disability Arts Forum, who is MC-ing the event. A woman in dungarees signals we are on next and with a smile coaxes us on stage, as we shake from head to toe.

I'm in a vast, cold cavern, yellow lights piercing my eyes. I feel the hum of a huge audience amid the glare. My throat is dry and I gaze at Tanya. She looks like she might shit herself and I'm sure I look the same. I grimace at her and she returns the look. I push my face towards the microphone, squeezing my bladder. The backing tape starts and, after four bars, Tanya comes in with the chunky riff. It is LOUD. Painfully loud. I wince and try to hear the drum underneath it, screaming inside for someone to sort the bloody sound out!

I start to sing and there is some kind whooping from the invisible crowd. I fear it is pity, an indulgent murmur for the brave handicapped girl. Somehow, we get through it but the sound person forgets to pause the backing tape. I imagine Freddie backstage, running around in furious circles.

I do another International Women's Day gig, on my own with a backing tape. In a draughty community centre in Hackney, the MP for the area, Diane Abbott, has the happy task of operating a large floor speaker. She's friendly and encouraging, and the small gathering clap in the right places.

The gig at the Tabernacle in Notting Hill is better. I feel a spark of confidence especially as I get a postcard that morning from Robert Wyatt telling me I sound like Poly Styrene from X-Ray Spex and my music has great verve.

The gig is another Workhouse event run by London Disability Arts Forum, and the whole of Spiral Sky are booked to do it.

On the night, Sian Vasey interviews me about the growing disability arts scene and what needs to happen to take it further. We know it's about access, it has to start with that. Getting in the venue, being able to go to the toilet.

I am Kata Kolbert in Spiral Sky, enjoying myself. The venue is accessible. There is a toilet!

The stage is small and I'm excited because everyone is here with me: Luke, guesting on drums, Tone on bass, Tanya on keyboard, Freddie on guitar.

I start with some punky pop which has a crip message – person-politics, about relationships:

Yes I've found I love
But once again, I'm told that's not enough
Don't I know it's different
For people such as us?

The crowd explode. Some are dancing; others clap to the hard, driving rhythm. Luke holds the beat, as Freddie and Tone play in counterpoint, Tanya's keyboard weaving between. My voice starts slow and soft and builds to the angry chorus as sweat gathers on my forehead.

Still two single rooms
How silly to assume
That once we found our freedom
Togetherness would lead on
A life to take us through.

We are on fire. We're tight, we're a unit and it sounds so good. I want to laugh out loud but I'm singing my heart out and I know the audience, my comrades, are there with me. I have created magic. Spiral Sky have created magic and I don't want it to stop.

My disabled friends and comrades have been protesting at the vile event that is the ITV Telethon. It makes us figures of pity, needy, begging, cripples. The famous put on posh clothes to swank about, pretending they care. Like fuck they care. Where's our liberty and our freedom? They can stuff it.

But the post does bring me a lovely – empowering – surprise. I've got a job as film reviewer for the disability magazine *Link*, edited by my friend Sian Vasey. Also, I'm to be the film columnist for *DAM* – the *Disability Arts Magazine* – a post sponsored by the British Film Institute. I write under the name of Kata Kolbert. Looking at the magazines, my copy there before me, I glow. Another kick in the arse for the cruel and the faithless.

I also like the money, which isn't vast but will help with running the car. And I'm halfway through a day of polishing another song that will go on the Spiral Sky album, 'Slime Pits'.

Days bounce by with loads of rehearsals.

We rarely expect visitors and I'm always wary when there is a knock on the door. We are presented with a short, elderly man who introduces himself as Eric, from the Housing Department.

'I'm here about your move,' he says. 'We really need to get on with it now as you're the last flat we need to refurbish.'

Freddie and me do cartoon double takes. We have no idea what he is talking about. I feel the slap of anxiety whack me in the guts.

'We're moving?' Freddie answers, uncertainty in his voice. 'Uh, since when?'

We show Eric to the lounge and he sits on the long, saggy sofa.

'Someone should have told you by now. It's a decant move – there's no choice, I'm afraid. But you've been left until last because of your special needs.'

He nods in my direction, as if to underline it's me he's talking about. Freddie sags down at the other end of the sofa and stares at him.

My head is a firmament, a mess of fear and maybe, just maybe, a whisper of excitement.

'The thing is,' Eric says, 'we'll simply rehome you. There's no point us doing your adaptations twice. We've got a really nice place lined up. It'll need a bit of work, mostly on the outside. My colleague Philip wonders if you'll go and see it tomorrow.'

'Where is it?' I say slowly, as if this is the most important question I have ever asked.

Eric looks at me with the expression of an antiquated politician.

'It's in Woodford. Not far from the green. A lovely Victorian house made into flats.'

I look at Freddie, who shrugs. The Leytonstone flat is wretched and worn out from years of neglect and patch-ups.

I know the area of Woodford from my driving-lesson days. It feels like a bizarre dream come true.

'We'll go,' I say.

All I can think of is the green, the trees, the proximity of Epping Forest, and yet still an inch from London as I love it.

The dark day suddenly shines.

The inaccessible Victorian haven.

Kaye brings in two mugs of camomile tea. She's wearing long, dangly gold earrings which I envy – but not as much as her slim face, which I know I can never have. No matter how many crash diets I do, or how skinny I get, the steroids I had as a girl give me the permanent 'moon face'.

Freddie gulps on his builder's-brew tea, in conversation with Gary and Tone. It's a sunny day and I'm holding my breath.

Gary's done the mixing on *Spiral Sky* and this is the first chance we've all had to hear the LP in its entire glory, after all the many days of recording. I'm excited and anxious, my standard condition which sometimes puts me into a state of complete mental paralysis. Evil Shrink Nurse Barry used to call it my overthinking – without saying anything else useful. Dr Toby at Claybury still insists I start with group therapy: it's that or nothing. But excitement drives me to be happy as Gary puts in the Spiral Sky cassette and plays it loud. 'Wanting Love' sways from the speakers, Tanya's orchestral keyboard framing the longing in my voice, as Tone's steady bassline grounds it, and Freddie's guitar echoes the melody. Hairs prickle up on my neck, a mixture of pride and childish glee.

'The whole album's a killer,' says Gary, 'and I really do believe it will sell out. The next phase is designing the cover.' He gets up, nodding. 'I've got this friend who does amazing line drawings, and I think something a bit art nouveau would work.'

Gary brings in a few samples and I fall in love with the idea immediately. As the album plays in the background I realise we've created something which is in a category of its own. There's punk tracks, like 'Career Girl' and 'Marriage of Inconvenience'. Then there's the folk covers, 'Reynardine' and 'Matty Groves', 'Kingdom for a Meaning', my own folky-influenced protest song. And the big pop tune of 'Wanting Love'. I know it's special, in the way that special should be.

The drive from Leytonstone to Woodford is ten minutes on a good day. And one I can manage in my sleep in the Clio. I turn into the road, as Freddie clutches the *A to Z*, and drive to the bottom. There's quite a few Victorian houses but none of them look suitable for me, all having five to seven steps at the front. We look at the number scribbled on a scrap of paper and edge our way back along the road, realising there's a huge sign over one of the windows which identifies the property as belonging to Waltham Forest Council.

'Philip's not here yet,' I say, as Freddie unpacks my power wheelchair slowly outside the house.

'Neither is Roz.' Roz is our allocated occupational therapist overseeing the adaptations to the new property. Freddie guides me down through the side door, which slopes past a coal bunker and into a vast wild garden. I hold my breath. It's beautiful. Fantasies form at once, a garden haven with honeysuckle, jasmine, bees dancing on the lavender as scents lift in the summer air, drifting through the French windows at the rear of the building.

Roz arrives and breaks into my reverie.

'It's a gorgeous place,' I say – 'once the access is sorted out.'

Roz nods. She's slim, in her twenties and seems to be very on the ball.

'Eric is confident we can put in a ramp in the front garden and a small one at the back door by the windows, so you can use the patio.'

'Any idea of timescale?' asks Freddie, taking the steps up to look inside.

'Not really,' says Roz, 'but Eric should have more information on that. If I help, do you reckon we can get Pen up to have a look?'

Freddie moves towards me. 'Of course, if we try the front steps. Pen first, then the chair. It's a heavy sod.'

Once through the door, my fantasies continue. Everything is untouched. Ceilings are high with centre roses. There are two vast rooms with elegant marble fireplaces and original Myott tiling. 'Look at that,' I squeal at Freddie, knowing that Tanya will be beside herself at such Victoriana. The doorways are wide, turning space is extravagant. The air smells cold but ripe with history, and outside I can hear birds. A blackbird in a tree. A swaying, many-branched, happy tree.

'Oh, Philip's here,' Roz says as she waves at him.

He comes in on a smile but it's soon lost. He doesn't make eye contact, screws up his face and announces: 'We don't know how long you'll have to wait. There's problems with planning permission.'

I look at Freddie.

Roz speaks for me. 'Surely there's some idea?'

Philip goes to the huge marble fireplace, tapping his finger into its dusty surface. 'The planning permission will take at least eight weeks, I do know that.'

He stares intently at the dust on his finger.

'But it will happen?' I say and my mouth goes dry, my throat feels tense. The problems with our Leytonstone flat are magnified by knowing we've been promised an escape.

Philip glances up at me and shrugs.

I clench up all the way down to my toes.

Waiting, why is there always so much waiting?

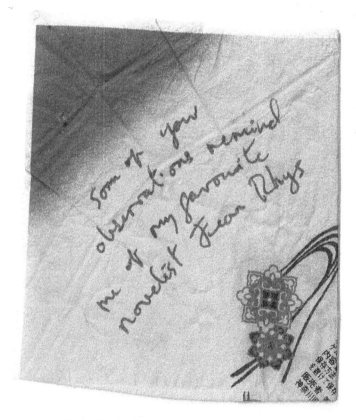

Treasured napkin featuring compliment from Robert Wyatt.

CHAPTER 15

10 December 1992: Tam wants me to understand about personal assistants. She loves the one she's recruited. They are not a carer! It will change everything, she says.

I don't want to admit it but I'm feeling like I've got a great big hole in me now *Spiral Sky* is finished. I'm back in the wilderness of struggle.

I sit in a small office in Euston talking to Kate Nash and Jim Pollard at Young Arthritis Care. I'm still obsessed with *Strangeness and Charm* and there's always a bundle of short stories on the go: *Cripples Fucking* for Creation Books – rude lewd stories of disabled people and sex. But then, the kickback. The publishers drop me because they run out of money.

But now it's the reality of the day job. The Young Arthritis Care plan is to do a project around sexuality in a way that's never been done. Kate Nash wants me to lead on it, to design a questionnaire to reach out to our membership.

She is wearing a beautiful longline blouse in a marvellous print of blues. She's always in a good humour. Jim is one hundred per cent behind the idea.

We're thrashing out the tricky issue of illustration.

'For a start,' I say, 'we can't have any beardy men as there was in *The Joy of Sex*.'

'What's wrong with beardy men?' laughs Jim, scratching his five-day stubble.

'It's not about beards,' Kate adds, 'it's about representation, eh Pen?'

'We need something almost diagrammatical,' I say. 'It's not

good to detail people with perfect bodies in sexual positions recommended for people with mobility impairments.'

'But we don't want literal representations,' Kate says, 'lurid depictions of swollen joints. But something that we can all relate to without feeling judged or put down by it.'

I love Kate when she talks like this. I'm flushed with a passion to get cracking, it's just what I need. If we don't break down a taboo, bring home to each other and the world that we do like a shag and that intercourse has many connotations, then no one else will.

'We'll have to take it up to the main committee,' sighs Jim. 'They might be a little nervous.'

'I'll bring them round,' says Kate. 'It'll be under the YAC umbrella. And after all, it won't be smutty, will it?'

'Well, not much,' I can't help teasing as I think about my notes for the doomed *Cripples Fucking*.

'Keep it clean,' says Jim, 'not lewd. Let's draw up the questionnaires as the first process. You do a draft, Pen; me and Kate will tweak them and we'll see what people have to say.'

I'm on the phone to Mum telling her the album is finished, and that I'm writing a booklet, a sex guide.

'I'll give it out to everyone.' I say, 'That should stop the curiosity about me and Freddie's sex life.'

'Pen! Jake's chucked his job in,' Mum says suddenly, the sentence coming out of nowhere. 'And we're going to move up past Cullumpton. A house all on its own.'

Immediately, I wonder where he is and if he is listening.

'How did that happen?' I ask.

'He said work wouldn't listen about the problems with his heart.'

I'm only half-listening, my thoughts racing into worried scenarios of Mum stuck at home with Jake and his dark, troubled moods. I want to rescue her, want to see her. I feel the familiar drag of past history, past hurts and traumas grabbing me by the throat.

'Will you have enough to live on?'

'I'll still be working at the factory,' Mum says, and I hate the tension in her voice. 'It's his heart, you see, he can't really put any strain on it.'

She'll be living in the wilds of Devon, not in a town. I don't know what to say to her, but I'm desperate to speak.

'I hope it goes okay,' I say.

'I get on with it, don't I?' she says, and I know that is what she will do. 'How's Tamsin?' she adds.

I'm relieved to talk about my own stuff, although I'm gloomy because Tamsin has been horribly unwell.

'You know she had that operation, Mum? I think it knocked her right out. Anyway, I'm going down to see her next week.'

I hear my mum sigh. 'Give her our love. And you drive carefully, there's a lot of maniacs in London.'

I laugh. 'I know, Mum, I know, along with the muggers and rapists. I'll come and see you soon, promise.'

'We had some old bloke exposing himself up by the canal,' Mum whispers. 'Dirty bugger.'

I laugh again without knowing why. It's so like my mum to end with a lurid local titbit of news.

We cruise along the M3, Freddie clutching a map, music pounding from the cassette, a mixtape. The Au Pairs. The Cocteau Twins. The Associates. The extended version of 'Say Hello, Wave Goodbye'. Two tracks from *Strangeways, Here We Come*, a chunk of deep visceral blues from John Lee Hooker and Bessie Smith. I like my music big, wide, varied when I'm on a long drive.

We get to Tamsin's flat in good time and I'm greeted by her personal assistant, Rona. She has a warm, welcoming face, short cropped hair. Probably not much older than Tamsin.

It's a nice flat with a pleasant open space at the rear. Tamsin looks frail and her voice is affected by recent surgery to stabilise her neck vertebrae. Yet within minutes I'm wrapped in the strength of our old magic, the soul sisters reunited.

We go into the garden and the awkwardness of our recent conversations blows away as we have a picnic on the lawn. I look askance at Freddie, as I wish, just for a moment, that he wasn't here.

'So I've met a personal assistant, at last,' I say to Tamsin. 'An actual, living, breathing model. Tell me everything.'

Tamsin grins and answers on a whisper. 'I'll do my best, Pen, but Rona might have to fill in the gaps because I get a bit breathless. She knows the stuff.'

Tamsin talks in short sentences and Rona chips in. I learn that only a few places support you to have personal assistants. I discover the idea comes from Berkeley, California, where disabled people protested for personal aides to support them to be independent at university. And now it's places like the Southampton Centre for Independent Living that have taken up the idea in England.

Tamsin tells me about independence, not care. About getting up when you want to, going to bed when you want to. Enabling you to live under your own control, not weighed down by outmoded ideas of care. Not stuck to a routine of someone coming in on Social Services' inflexible rota, the likes of lovely Sandra given no choice over who she saw at what time.

Sandra who left, leaving her job for a peaceful retirement in Norfolk. Who I could never, ever, hope to replace. Crying the last day I saw her, despite the promise to see me for a cuppa whenever she visited Leytonstone.

And now cheerful Iris, well-meaning but clumsy when she helps me shower. Both never really understanding for one moment the life I chose to lead – my music, my writing. And most of all, that the support I need is increasing. My arthritis was not a thing that relented. My joints were stiffer and often hurt. As a Juvenile RA I was adept at handling that. But one way or another it is all coming between Freddie and me.

I feel a tremendous surge of anticipation, imagining how much this might help us both. How much it might improve my confidence – from the simple things like combing my hair ten times a day if it needs it – to the crucial basics, like a drink when I need, a pee or poo when Freddie's out. I've known for a long time no one should have to be joined at the hip but could never see a way around it. My thoughts fizz with ideas of doing everyday things like meeting up with Tanya – on my own – leaving Freddie to one of his sulky moods. Moods that seem to be getting worse.

'So Rona lives here, with you?' I ask, relaxed in the summer breeze.

'Yes,' says Tamsin softly, 'and then you realise life is not just about that struggle, Pen. Like it was in the flat. It should never be like that. Of course Rona helps me shower, cook and with bedtime. All that stuff. But she also types for me. We go to art galleries. I do my voluntary work at S-CIL. Those things that give you a life. Especially as I felt a bit lost after Mum died.'

I look at Tam but don't say anything. We don't need to.

'Yes, and Rona pours vodka,' Rona adds, to break the sombre lull in the conversation, as Tamsin gathers her breath.

'Still vodka?' I laugh. I'm lucky to sip at a Babycham these days, what with my dodgy guts, dodgy kidneys and all the rest of it.

'Rona says we should go to France. We could all go together, Pen. Stay in a gîte.'

I smile and ache to say yes. But right now there's questions and logistics, the cost – and the compromise of being dependent on Freddie. Who says nothing, but continues to idly flick through a copy of *NME*.

As we prepare to leave and I look at Tamsin, I'm overwhelmed with the power of our friendship and feel the deep, deep bond healing over the subtle divisions. She looks very thin and tired. I can see the effort in every word she speaks. Later, I know I might cry but right now, over goodbyes, I touch her hand.

'Yes,' I say. 'Yes, let's do that holiday.'

I fall in love too easily and this time it's with the personal computer. It's another planet compared to the Amstrad I bought two years ago. There's windows and boxes and the screen can be white, the text black. Everything seems connected although there are separate components and floppy disks.

Once out of the box, it's on to another phase of me glued to keys until the Lurgy protests in my fingers and shoulders.

I'm pleased with the timing as I gaze at last at the publication proofs for my story 'Prue Shows Her Knickers', another breakthrough moment for disability art! I am chuffed to be part of it and can't wait to breathe in the smell of the published pages.

The PC is invaluable for the sex booklet, which we're now calling 'Our Relationships, Our Bodies'. I've written the first draft. Kate and Jim are pleased. The responses to the questionnaire are very honest. I cheer to myself at the participants' courage in revealing details of things so personal. I know we'll make our booklet groundbreaking.

I'm picking through the proofs while Freddie and me wait for the council surveyors, Eric and Philip. When they arrive, they look sombre.

'We've got to put in for planning permission again,' says Eric. 'So there'll be another delay.'

'We do hope you'll move this year,' adds Philip, 'and I understand this flat is really a struggle to live in now. But we can't do that much to it. Too much money.'

'We shouldn't start packing, then,' I say sarcastically. I want to move. They're making us go, but now they're making us wait.

They mutter on and on: there's confusion with the access because it's unlikely they'll get permission to put in ramps.

'We'll put in a nice lift by the front door,' says Philip and I force myself not to cry.

In consolation, I think of the lovely garden, the honeysuckle, the blackbird. They leave and I go back to the PC. It's quiet here in our Leytonstone flat. Freddie – weirdly subdued this week – is buried in work, the home help's been and gone and I should be getting back to the booklet.

If I'm going to write about sex, I'll have to talk about barriers and obstacles – negative attitudes that form the main reason for our exclusion from the world. I've read my feminist tracts: I know the personal is political and I know about the social model because it was explained to me by a woman with arthritis, older than me – a wise goddess who changed my life another little bit: Ann Macfarlane.

I'm in a room with twelve people. We've all had arthritis since childhood, but that's neither here nor there. Ann is going to explain why it's good to get away from feeling you are to blame for your limitations, when in fact those limitations are imposed on us from out there. It's about things we have no control over. How buildings are designed, how information is produced, how attitudes determine who we are. How others decide what we can do and who we can be.

Ann has an attentive face, her hair cut in a neat bob. She also has a personal assistant. I'm amazed as the PA helps her – and facilitates Ann's work. Handing out papers, writing on a flipchart, taking notes. Responding to Ann, but staying quietly in the background when not directly needed. I'm beside myself. I make a point in my head to ask Ann the crucial question. Even if I'm married to Freddie, can I get my own PA?

Ann tells us about the models of disability.

'What do we think is the overwhelming model, the way people see us?' she says in a clear, encouraging voice.

I'm still too shy to speak first, but I know a bit of this stuff from Tamsin and the Southampton CIL. And I know we both had the gut instinct this is right – even before we understood stuff about models and using the new language.

A young guy mumbles an answer. 'Medical?'

'Correct!' says Ann. 'And that means we're condemned to be seen in a very narrow way. By our medical labels. To them, we are nothing but our impairments, our medical conditions.' There's a murmur of agreement before Ann continues. 'But the reality is, for an overwhelming number of us, it won't matter what the medical profession do, they can give us pain relief and all that, but they can't cure us.'

She laughs gently. 'It's such an irony. A well-meaning doctor will always be devastated. He'll always fail.'

I absorb the excited murmur in the room as we process this radical idea. Someone in a red jumper speaks up: 'But I need a doctor to help me change things, don't I?'

'A doctor will help you with your impairment,' Ann says, nodding. 'But his power is very limited and he's only addressing the specifics with you. If we could rearrange the world, not only have stairs, but ramps as well, take out the barriers, it would transform the lives of many disabled people.'

A young woman with crazy ringleted black hair bursts into the conversation. 'And then it's not about us. It's about what is wrong with them, with society.' She has a humorous timbre in her Liverpudlian accent. I smile at her and she smiles back.

'That's right, Liz.' Ann agrees. 'It takes the emphasis away from us and puts it where it should be. Not what's wrong with us, what's wrong for us. We're going to break for lunch now, but this afternoon I want to look at other models. There's charity and religious, before we finish off with more on the social model.'

She smiles broadly at us all. 'Which is why you're all here this weekend.'

As we break up for food I make a fast exit to find Liz, as I know we have mutual friends.

'Hey,' she says, humour dancing in her dark eyes, 'you're Kata "Sexuality Booklet" Kolbert. I didn't think I could have sex till I read that.'

'And you're Liz Carr,' I say. 'Happy to have been of assistance.'

She laughs and we spend the rest of our first meeting laughing a lot more.

I put down the phone as Freddie rushes in with my red swing jacket. The vinyl pressing of *Spiral Sky* is at Gary's now.

'Fucking hell, let's get *Spiral Sky*!' I gasp as we leave the flat.

A quick zip in the Clio and we park outside Kaye and Gary's house.

I'm greeted by my proud producer Gary holding an LP. The

magic 12-inch object with its glorious sealed wraparound cover. I sniff it, remembering the single 'Live Your Life', and lifted as always by a sense of shock that I've arrived at this point.

That it's real.

Spiral Sky by Spiral Sky is an entity. It began with me. Within the next week those words that have taken shape over many years and grown into songs with the help of my fantastic mates will fly into the face of the world and let it know that I am here.

I. AM. HERE.

CHAPTER 16

15 March 1992: I only remember one other funeral, for Nanny. This is different. This can't be happening. But it is.

Tamsin is dead.

Tamsin.

Is dead.

I look at the daffodils in the vase on the desk made by her dad. Tamsin loves daffodils. I cry but I am numb. Freddie takes the phone from me and whispers comfort.

Somewhere, there is a knot in me. It's deep, dark, and furious red. I have been here before. Too many people have been taken from me before.

Daddy, so long ago.

My head squirms with the spiteful burden of memory, of things regretted. Guilt drags me into a battle I can't win. Because Tamsin is dead.

Tamsin cannot be dead.

We are going on holiday to France. We've grown up, we are reconnecting, catching up, healing the frayed endings.

Tamsin cannot be dead.

Daddy cannot be dead.

And I hate Jesus for wanting Daddy. Mummy tells me that is where he has gone. To Jesus. I'm in Candy's house across the road from mine. She is not here, only her mum Evie and lots of grown-ups, and Mummy whose eyes are very red with blobby bits from her eyeshadow, the one she let me play with last week.

Ant is being silly but he is only four. He came downstairs and told Mummy that Daddy's face was a funny colour. He keeps saying it and I want to smack him. There is a policeman and other men talking and talking, who want to put Daddy in a box. Mummy keeps crying and I start screaming: 'I hate Jesus. I hate him. I hate him!' But if he wakes Daddy up, I might forgive him.

Some woman I don't know squeezes me, tells me I have to be brave. But I wriggle away to find Ant. I want to cuddle him. I am seven, his big sister, after all.

Maybe if we're good Jesus will wake up Daddy very soon. I'm not sure what we've done and I don't know what to do to make it all better. I can't find Ant so I jump around on my bed till I hurt, till my knees swell up and up. I bang my head on the wall over and over, and that hurts me too, but I don't care, and I hate God and the angels and Baby Jesus.

Me with Daddy and baby brother Ant.

I decide not to cry as I remember Laura. Laura who was beautiful with long, blonde hair. Lovely lips that she kissed me with when my joints were hurting, in the kids' hospital with the nuns. When I missed Mummy and Daddy so much.

Laura sits next to me at the round table. Rodney is here too. He is small with a bad chest and is so shy he never speaks. Only three of us are allowed up out of bed for tea today.

Sister Mina wears big round glasses. She tries to make me wear mine. I won't because they are horrible and ugly. But I like her a lot. She gives me lots of gravy at teatime, especially like today when we have chicken.

'Penny likes it swimming in it, don't you?' Sister Mina says.

It makes me feel funny, the words tease me but I want to keep saying it. My food swimming in gravy. The words won't leave me alone and put patterns in my head.

Laura sits there in her nice green minidress. She is fourteen and almost a grown-up. I don't know why she's in hospital but it's not arther-rite-us.

'I think we should do a poem about it, Penny,' she says and holds my hand. 'Penny and her pool of gravy.'

'Pool of gravy,' I laugh. 'A swimming pool of gravy.'

Laura chuckles. 'That's a lot of gravy.'

Sister Mina is laughing too but Sister Drapse comes into the room and looks very cross. I hate her. She smacks the babies every single day.

'Don't be foolish, Sister,' she says.

Sister Mina looks right down into the stew pot and I'm scared her glasses will fall in.

'Get these children finished and into bed. Laura is due her insulin as well.' Sister Drapse always screws her eyes up tight when she's in a mood.

'Don't worry, Sister,' Laura says. 'I'm almost done eating and I'll help Penny get into bed.'

I look at Sister Drapse as Laura speaks with her pretty voice, a magical princess who puts a spell on all the moody people in all the world. Even Sister Drapse always smiles when Laura speaks.

'Oh you're an angel from God himself,' she says. 'Young Penelope cooperates with you, at least. The devil gets in her head and she is impossible.'

I don't know why Sister Drapse says these things. I asked for the Fuzzy Felt Farm from the toy cupboard and she says I don't deserve any toys because I have too much cheek. I never know what she means.

Laura walks me to the bathroom and helps me wash. It's good because she isn't rough when my joints hurt. It's cold and dark in there too and there's a funny smell of bad things. Laura says it's the old pipes, the ones that make noises at night and scare me. I tell her they speak but she teases me it's in my head, it's my imagination. But I mustn't worry about it. I can be happy I have such a good imagination.

She reads me some of *Mary Poppins* when I'm in bed. I love it a lot, especially since Daddy took me to see the film. I love that too.

I fall asleep just after Laura kisses me on the cheek. My eyes are almost shut but I can see her blonde hair on my face. Smell it, the nice smell of shampoo. And her, Laura's smell. It's almost as good as Mummy's.

I wake up because it's noisy. The nurses have drawn a curtain so we can't see into the corridor. I can hear men. I think one is Dr Prentice, he's nice.

I sit up when I realise the noises are from Laura's room. It's a bit outside the kids' ward, a room for her because she's an older girl.

The other kids are sleeping but I'm not. I'm all awake and wondering what is going on in Laura's room. I can hear the Sisters whispering but not all the time. Their voices get loud with long words and Dr Prentice sounds bossy.

Then I hear a funny sound. I can't work it out till I realise it's Sister Drapse. She is crying. It's a horrible coughing sound. But it's worse when everything goes still and quiet.

I want to get up, want to go and cuddle Laura, get them out of her room, tell them to leave her alone.

Dr Prentice walks into the corridor with another man. I don't hear all his words, or understand them. Even though Daddy tells me I'm very good at learning new ones.

But I do hear the doctor say in a strange low voice 'note time of death' and 'diabetic coma'.

I drive in a trance to Tamsin's sister's in Walthamstow. I know it's sunny, a sharp spring day building up to Easter. Daffodils flounce everywhere. But nothing can quite reach into me.

I'm welcomed into the family home with the usual affection. I mutter pleasantries, a robot, mouthing nothings. The house is full of people. Some of Tamsin's friends from Southampton. Others I know, including my old friend Jean, who comes to sit by Freddie and me.

'You never expect your child to go before you,' Tamsin's dad is saying. He looks old and his face is tense, anger fighting sorrow.

I drink two mouthfuls of tea and can't swallow any more. Hiding inside the trance, I'm awash in a storm of guilt.

Guilt that things cannot be said, that I wish had been said.

Regret that we cannot be as we once were. That there will be no new chapters for Kata Kolbert and K. Oss, The Ugly Pygmies.

No soul sisters living the bohemian life with lots of vodka. No adventures in the East End. No holiday in a French gîte.

No Tamsin wearing a beret and reading Simone de Beauvoir.

No sharing of the Milky Bar Kid.

I am cleaved open with torment and hopeless speculation. Did I push you out? Did I give you up too fast? Too selfish in my needs to lay in my bed with Freddie?

My eyes are hot but stay dry.

'The hearse has arrived,' says Ron, who squeezes my shoulder as he walks by.

No one says much as we leave the room, mostly dressed in black – apart from us, her friends, who know how much she loves colour.

Freddie helps me into the Clio and we wait for the cortège to gather. Jean joins us in the back of my car and we talk in soft, staccato bursts.

'I'm glad you didn't go to see her in the chapel of rest,' Jean says, catching my eye in the rear-view mirror. 'I don't think it would have helped, Pen. You can say goodbye at the funeral in whatever way you wish. Or do it after. Light a candle. Do it when you're alone.'

Ron is walking along the pavement, waving us on for the slow journey to the cemetery in Manor Park. We move for less than a minute when everyone including me slams on the brakes.

Ron appears, red in the face. 'Someone's crashed into the hearse, Pen!' he yells. 'Can you bloody well believe it?'

'Is everyone okay?' I ask. But something has happened – my guts, rolled as tight as steel coil, relax. The trance is shaken and I can feel something else seeping in from a distance.

'It's Tamsin,' says Jean softly. 'She's having a laugh with us.'

I nod and smile, relaxing into the sudden uplift of that thought.

'You're right,' I say as we finally move off. 'Tamsin would find this hilarious.'

I love this cemetery, with its Victorian gothic gateway, the democratic rows of graveyards old and new. The squirrels flying up the trees and perching as if for photographs on the broken angels.

Tamsin likes this place too and as we all make our way to the crematorium, we stop to look at her flowers. I spot the one which says 'From Mum, Jake and Penny's family', startled that Jake of all people was keen this was sent.

I smile broadly as I remember how she had a way with him, charming but fierce when she needed to be. I'm pleased they have remembered her.

I brought daffodils, plain and simple. We both love flowers, always had them in the flat. An indulgence we didn't care about when we had to raid the gas money.

As the sun streams down on the mourners and the happy floral tributes, I feel glad we did those things. Things that were not necessary, useful or productive, but things that reminded us what it is all about.

Inside the chapel, I am shaking. I see Tamsin's white coffin, which is too small. And a thing that cannot, no cannot, be connected to her.

Sitting between Freddie and Jean, when she passes me a tissue, I realise I am crying. There is a vicar who says some words. A friend plays a flute. I am quiet but at last I cry.

Into the silence, into the words, into the haunting melody.

I cry. I cry when the music begins and the small coffin goes behind the curtain. I cry going back to the car. I cry into Freddie's shoulder and into Jean's stream of volunteered tissues.

But the sun stays brilliant.

The daffodils still dance and the squirrels run to and fro, choosing the brightest spot to pose.

CHAPTER 17

9 July 1992: Nothing is easy. They. Them. Always have a problem with you. More double life. One minute, Spiral Sky. The next it's you get back to the sodding cripples' ghetto.

The season for daffodils is long past. But my eyes are caught by the vase of pink roses, their delicate scent stirring memory into the air. It's not such a jolt when I look at the desk, when I think of Tam sitting there, scrunching up her features, pursing her lips to mimic an old woman. Or when I look at the door to our lounge covered in postcards we collected together and ones she sent to me.

Sometimes I have to cry. Mostly, when Freddie is visiting his mother, those times when I don't know if he'll be back on time. When I'm sad. When thoughts tangle into a big lumpy confusion.

I miss Tam more than ever. And I'm angry that I can't seem to talk to Freddie. I hold back on asking him things I know I should. Things I can hardly think about.

I pull my concentration back to Philip, who sits on the long sofa, while Tooty perches suspiciously on the other end. Papers are strewn along the space between them: plans, lists, contracts.

'The thing is, planning permission is still an issue.' Philip raises his eyebrows. 'They're not going to have it. The residents are complaining so it's got to be a chair lift. I think one has been ordered, but I'll get back to you on that. Meanwhile, I need to take some measurements of your wheelchair.'

'Okay,' I say. 'But we can still go ahead with packing?'

From the kitchen, there comes a very loud 'fucking thing!' Philip looks quizzical.

'Nothing works here, Philip,' I say. 'You know Housing won't mend anything. The pipes are buggered up. Freddie's trying to fix the washing machine. It leaked all over the kitchen floor this morning. So it would be good to know a move date, even a very rough one.'

Philip shrugs. 'Probably another three to four months. Sorry. I'll get on to them about the plumbing. The delay is all about this planning permission.'

He gathers up the papers and piles them neatly into his leather-bound folder.

'The residents have a big bee in their bonnet about the changes needed in the front garden. But we'll get there, don't you worry.'

When he is gone, Freddie makes us a cup of tea and brings in the post.

'Don't look so pissed off, Pen,' he says. 'I think there's something nice for you in this delivery.' He passes me a package and I know at once it's a book.

'Oh, open it for me!' I'm a little girl in a sweet shop. Except the sweetie is the book *Mustn't Grumble*, by the Women's Press. I run my fingers over the pages, smell the freshness and... flick, flick – my story, 'Prue Shows Her Knickers', is on page 59! Lois has promised we will all be paid and I know it's not a lot but it doesn't matter. I'm going to frame the cheque, my first as a freelance writer.

As I gaze at the words smiling as though my face will split in two, I feel a new thrill that Kate and Jim want to talk about me doing more now that our sexuality booklet is done. Young Arthritis Care is flying high and on the back of my work with them, there could even be a proper job in it.

Freddie puts his arms around me, but today I feel tense. I'm not sure why. We had a bit of a row – as far as I can ever have a row – about going to Dorset. I love Dorset, but I want to go further. Abroad even. Why should I drive to the same place all the time?

'You're doing better than me, dearheart,' he says, looking at the book in my hands. And I wonder if I can feel a sharpness in his voice, whether I can trust that feeling.

I want Freddie to understand. He has his own work, after all, and responsibilities to his family.

'Where will I fit in?' Freddie says.

I put my hand over his but there's a feather of fear inside me. I want to do everything but there has to be space.

I can't stop doing these things that must be done. I gently ease away from his arms, clutching *Mustn't Grumble*. With a secret flush I decide I will sleep with it under my pillow.

It's the weirdest thing to be back at the cemetery, just Freddie and me, looking at where Tamsin's ashes are buried with her mum. I haven't brought daffodils but a small bunch of rich summer blooms that match the trees in full leaf, soaring around me, singing their soft whispering songs. The bold squirrels venture, very close, eyes upon me for treats.

Freddie has wandered off and I feel like I want to speak aloud.

'I wondered about the Milky Bar Kid the other day. Where did it end up? Did Rona get rid of it? I'm sad she burnt your diaries, but I've got your first Poetryzine safe. And *Pinch Me in the Pantry*.'

A slow breeze cools down the early autumn air and the squirrel moves to the other side of me.

'It's funny because it was Linda who taught me about masturbation. In Beechwood Hospital, on the same ward, a few years before our time. I didn't even know the word then. The way things are going with me and Freddie, I'll have to buy myself an MBK after all.'

I close my eyes and breathe in the warm air, the sad scent of flowers left on a thousand graves.

'And when Linda dared to die, I couldn't go to her funeral, wasn't even told about it for ages. It made me feel like a kid again when I was banned from going to my dad's. They thought it would be upsetting. Might flare up the old arther-rite-us.'

I swallow and see Freddie approaching from a distance. I don't care if I look silly and carry on.

'There's a lot happening. I've been offered a job. Can you believe it? I'm going to be a publications officer for Young Arthritis Care.

Only found out last week. There's quite a bit of writing. Kate and Jim will be my bosses. And it will be nice to have some money.'

Freddie comes up behind me, slides his hands around my shoulders and nestles into my hair.

'And before I go,' I add, gently moving forward from Freddie, 'I must tell you, I'm on track to get a personal assistant.'

I keep going, as much for Freddie as for my own need to say it.

'It will be a bit of a fight, they're behind the times with crip liberation up here. But some day soon, Freddie won't have to worry about helping me in the shower and all that other stuff.'

I pause in the silence to say my goodbyes in my head.

I'm thinking 'not long now'. I won't need to be stuck when Freddie's gone out and I don't know when he'll be back. Not stuck when I want to eat; drinking all I can and keeping my kidneys healthy like I'm supposed to. When I need the loo. All those things and a thousand tiny others.

And quite simply, doing what I want to do, by myself, under my own steam. Including work that I love.

My wrist aches and my fingers are stiff. I've signed over a hundred copies of the Spiral Sky album in gold pen and they are numbered 1–500 which adds to their rarity value. I'm bashful that everyone's here. Gary, smiling and urbane as ever, his long blond hippy hair hanging straight. Tanya sits beside me, eyebrows perfect, stroking one of the big black cats as Kaye brings in a camomile tea and lights the huge array of candles in the fireplace. Delicious scents quickly fill the air.

This is it. The official release. The day chosen by Gary – Mr Acme Records – when he fulfils the orders, sends the album far and wide. To Europe, America – even Japan.

Gary's put on an LP of classical Indian music with Ravi Shankar on sitar. Gary is the only person I've ever known who's got a sitar.

I keep signing and little stabs of sadness tug me whenever I realise this triumph cannot be shared with Tamsin. I often dream about her. She says to me, 'I'm only in another room. What's the matter with you?'

'How's the job?' asks Tanya. 'I hope you're not overdoing it. Even though I know you probably are.'

Freddie looks up and purses his lips in mock anger. I look away, detecting a hidden reality to his jokey expression.

'It is full on,' I say. 'Working to deadlines, learning desktop publishing. All that stuff.'

I haven't felt quite the same since Jim and Kate left but I'm holding on to the thought that the money is good and we'll need it when we move. I wince, sipping at my drink.

Tamsin and Zed grin at the camera for me.

'No, Pen, don't get caught in the rat race!' says Tanya. 'I always want to get out but it's never the right time.'

I put down my drink and stretch my creaky fingers a few times in preparation for the next batch of signatures. Kata Kolbert writ large and with a flourish, as I chatter to Kaye and Tanya about our favourite things. Books, movies, music and, for me and Kaye especially, clothes, Tanya preferring her sleek, black everything.

I'm touched that Kaye has brought me a new notebook, another friend I share my stationery obsession with. It's deep fuchsia pink with a peacock-tail feather proud in multicoloured sequins.

'It's gorgeous, thanks,' I say and pause with guilt. My journals cry out for fulfilment, starved of words, having to make do with random scribbled entries and occasional typed, pasted-in bits of paper.

The last entry was about *A Day with Sam*, a book project for kids with arthritis going to the hospital. Young Arthritis Care want me to edit and manage it. I keep getting stuck with everyone involved as I refuse to say things like 'I have bad legs'. Always stuck on the delicate problem of describing a test in a comforting way – but a test that I know will hurt.

Kaye deposits the black-and-white cat, Deva, onto my lap. 'You're looking too pensive, Pen,' Kaye says. 'We can't have that today.'

'I just want to read *Strangeness and Charm*,' laughs Tanya. 'I want to know who did it.'

It's Kaye's turn to laugh.

'Did what and where? I want to read it too, whatever it is.'

I sip some tea, enjoying the enthusiasm on their faces.

'It's my sci-fi epic, Kaye. Tanya's reading it chapter by chapter as I write it. It won't be long now before it's done.'

I glance at the boys, intense over a pile of vinyl and the packaging up of *Spiral Sky*.

'It's so tiring. And of course, I have to prioritise the paid job.'

'Yes, you certainly do,' says Tanya ruefully. 'Bread on the table and all that.'

'More like cable TV and thirty-three channels in my case,' I laugh. 'That's my consolation.'

'Well hurry up,' Tanya teases, giving me her beady stare. 'I want to read all of *Strangeness and Charm*.'

'You will, sweetie, you will.' I pause, weighed down by seriousness. 'Don't forget there's also this endless shit with our move.'

Kaye and Tanya nod sympathetically.

'When Gary's finished with your signing, I'll do you a tarot.' Kaye squeezes my arm. 'Let's see what that's got to say.'

I love Kaye's tarot readings. She's the real deal, no fairground fortune teller, but it's something like therapy, she picks out the psychology of the cards I choose.

Much better than a ward of Evil Shrink Nurse Barries.

'Is there one that's about moving house, with a date on it?' I say. 'We know we've got to go, but the waiting and uncertainty is complete shit.'

Philip is angry, though he hides it well, standing up, moving from one foot to the other in our cramped and shabby lounge.

'I've never heard anything like it. Your access needs, your wheelchair lift, described as an alien presence in the environment.'

I sag into my wheelchair.

'What does that even mean, Philip?'

In the background I can hear Freddie fighting with the lock on the front door, which catches due to the wood swelling. But of course, they won't change it. We're about to move, aren't we? Money can't be wasted.

Philip stamps his feet a little. 'It means they're all idiots,' he says, 'and they're going to put indefinite delays on the planning permission. Your name's been on that property for over a year. It's absolutely ridiculous.'

He doesn't stay long and I return wearily to editing the copy for the latest edition of *Young Arthritis News*.

Freddie and me are debating whether to order a pizza when Philip rings: 'Have you seen the paper? Some bastard has put a piece in the local *Guardian*. Did you know about this?'

'No,' I say, as tiredness sinks deep and heavy into my worn-out bones. I don't know if I want to move any more. I see the fantasy of the trees, the long wild garden, the butterflies and my best deco frames on the magnificent marble fireplaces. Is it a torment or a dream? I'm running out of energy against these people who seem determined to stop me having it.

Philip continues in fury. 'Some action group's been formed to stop you having any work done. I've got a nasty feeling it's your next-door neighbour. I'm definitely going to put in a complaint to the paper. There's even a quote from someone suggesting you got this flat because you work for the council. They say it's tokenism when it's an absolute outright lie.'

The phone is heavy and leaden against my ear. I mumble something and hand it to Freddie, who is listening beside me. After a series of grunts and 'okays' the call ends. Freddie sits on the sofa, running hands through his hair.

'I don't know what we're going to do about this, Pen. It's a fucking horrible limbo. Philip suggests the next planning meeting should be held on site and we should go there too. Do you think we should give up, Pen? See if there's somewhere else?'

'No,' I say, looking at the scraps of paper on my desk, hand-scribbles demanding I type them up at speed. 'It'll probably take just as long. And why shouldn't we have that lovely flat?'

'I know. I want us to have it too. It'll be good for us. A new start,' says Freddie. 'But there's so much going on, and you a terrible workaholic already.'

I smile and we kiss quickly, my eyes lured back to the notes.

Behind the piles, under a journal, inside another notebook, the siren call of *Strangeness and Charm*.

CHAPTER 18

4 September 1995: I should have recorded more about the events regarding the Disabled Persons' Civil Rights Bill. This was fucked out by the usual ploy of government amendment-sinking. We might get something later. Fine words from a mouth with no teeth. Surprise, surprise.

'Jake's dead. I just found out.'

My brother Ant is unemotional but I know we both feel a sense of shock. 'I'll try and get to the funeral, for Mum's sake. Do you think you can?'

'No, I doubt it. It's a long drive,' I say quietly, even though it's a lie. I drive to Dorset hundreds of times. To Birmingham, to Minehead. But I know I can't go. All I can feel is relief and I wonder if my old terrors have gone with him.

'I'm sad for Mum,' Ant says. 'In some ways, anyway. She's a widow again.'

'I hope she moves. Comes back to civilisation.'

'Feels weird, doesn't it?'

'It does, Ant. Almost unbelievable.'

'He was a funny old bastard.'

'Yeah,' I say as my thoughts run in circles.

Jake was troubled. I think he hated me, and then maybe didn't. Sometimes he seemed proud of me. Sometimes he seemed to hate himself as much as he hated the rest of the world. But in his own crazy way I knew that he loved Mum.

'I'll call Mum at the weekend,' I say to Ant. 'But let me know what's happening.'

I put the phone down and cast my eyes around our lounge, a few packing boxes here and there filled with junk. The final proofs of *A Day with Sam* are in front of me on the desk. Next to them is a letter from a new social worker who is coming to see me soon as the council sort themselves out. At last I can get the money directly. And get my own personal assistants.

I click on my wheelchair power and wheel into the kitchen. Freddie won't be back for a few hours and I juggle the idea of making a cup of tea against needing to go to the loo. I decide on a sip of water. As I return to my work, I know a strange cold fracture, a disconnection, has gone through my world.

Jake is dead. I can't quite believe it and I don't feel anything.

Woodford is green and pretty, although I've realised it is also shot with touches of revolting snobbery that are now colliding with me full on.

I'm jittery and tired. My anxiety demands attention with everything I do. And it's right here, flushing through my face, trembling on my skin as I park up the car and make my way with Freddie to the front garden of our promised flat.

It's a bleak day but not too cold. As we go through the gate I'm shocked to see how many people are here. Philip stands alone and smiles when he sees us.

'I'm so glad you've made it. They won't be expecting you. They need shaming. Let's see if they'll say these awful things to your face.'

'Who are they all?' I say, hoping he can't see that I am trembling.

'Members of the planning committee mostly, the conservation lot.'

'Why are they all here again?' says Freddie.

'The road is a conservation area. Winston Churchill stayed in a house down here. Or something.'

'So Winnie scratches his bum and the street becomes enshrined?' I say, trying to hide my terror.

Philip shrugs and looks grim. A few of the huddled group notice me and slowly make their way along the path. An elderly man with crazy white hair inspects me and I feel immediately like a beetle on a pin.

'Well now, my dear,' he says in a gruff, patronising tone. 'Why would you want to live here? Surely it would be better to go somewhere for... for people like you?'

I battle my old enemy, tears that rise before rage. I can't find any words.

'What does that mean, "people like you"?' Freddie is steely, and the gruff man shuffles away.

Philip comes over and points to a thin balding man who is playing with bricks. I look on in disbelief as he starts marking out an area, the farce reaching its height when a chubby blonde woman appears with a decrepit old-style wheelchair – twice the size of mine. She wheels it, badly, between the brick pathway that the bald man has created and looks up, beaming.

'See? Look at this, everyone,' she says loudly. 'There's no room for a wheelchair. Especially that electric thing.'

By everyone I know she doesn't include me. I'm merely the unwanted wheelchair.

I'm tired. Behind with deadlines on *Young Arthritis News*. And I want to finish *Strangeness and Charm*. I want to look forward to going back to Kaye and Gary's, seeing Tone, seeing Tanya. Hearing news about *Spiral Sky* by Spiral Sky and what the world thinks about it. If it thinks anything at all.

But I'm surrounded by drab bigots in polite skin. By people who don't want to understand, who see me as something alien, upsetting their fragile suburban lives. I manage not to cry, but imagine I must look close to it, as Philip takes sudden action.

'Okay, that's enough,' he says firmly. 'This is private council property and I think we're done here.'

There's some murmurs of resistance. Philip starts moving the bricks and the small crowd shuffle off reluctantly.

He comes over, his face tight with anger. 'You are going to live in this flat, Penny. I'm telling you. This NIMBYism is an outrage.

We've chosen this flat for you as appropriate, and you're going to get in it.'

I'm proud of myself for not crying.

For driving home. Not crying.

Finishing my workload. And not crying.

Philip rings a few days later.

'We've got planning permission,' he says, tersely. 'But there'll be a delay. All they'll accept is two lifts through the back garden, one up to the patio then one into the back room.'

'How long?' I ask him, desperate to simply know, to get on with life.

'Eight weeks, minimum,' says Philip.

I put the phone down. I'm glad I'm alone as I cry.

Freddie has a book deal and I'm excited for him but pine as my proper job zaps my energy and limits my time writing *Strangeness and Charm*. There is too much to do but I can't give up anything. And as usual, I always want more.

It doesn't help that I'm in an argument with the hospital as I sink yet again into a phase of women's problems, which they are ignoring.

While naturally, there are fresh ideas in my head. Another novel. A crazy, ridiculous adventure.

Fancy Nancy, the time traveller, the disabled outlaw, the queen of Victorian freaks. She wants to live, and fuck and sing and yell her rebellion to all who are ready to hear it. Tempt others into her life. Break down taboos.

I sigh, reining my thoughts right back in.

My new social worker – I call her Twiglet – is coming to do a Community Care assessment. The council have finally caught up with crip liberation. And thanks to Ann Macfarlane giving me advice and Liz Carr holding my hand, the money is coming for personal assistants, on the criteria of respite for Freddie and a begrudging little bit of independence for me.

Twiglet arrives on time. She is a nervy creature, full of 'wow' and 'fab'. I imagine her parents to be original, stoned, patchoulied hippies.

'It's all a bit exciting, isn't it?' she beams at me. 'We're not just getting our act together now, we're ahead of the pack.'

I don't spoil her enthusiasm by pointing out, firstly, others outside of London were much more ahead of this pack. And that there's not really a 'we' so much as an 'us' – the disabled people who fought for these changes.

For an hour, I go through the plod of my day, disgruntled in repeating what I can't do on my own when Freddie is out. Over and over again. Also, what I don't think he should have to do. I know we're too joined at the hip and it worries me, pushes in questions I'm not ready to answer. I want to go to the shops without him. I want to catch up with Liz without him. Sometimes, just sometimes, I want to be without him.

Twiglet asks a lot of how long does that take and sometimes I'm cross.

The frustration bursts out: 'How long do you take to have a dump?' I say sharply. 'How long does it take you to dry your hair?'

Twiglet always looks hurt. 'I'm on your side,' she says, widening her big grey eyes. 'This is just a form.'

I know about the form. I have challenged the form. I have challenged many forms.

I don't have a fast answer. But it doesn't stop me hating this process.

An hour later and Twiglet has almost finished exhausting me. I hear Freddie come in and put the kettle on.

'Wow, perfect timing,' says Twiglet. 'I'll get back to you with a result as soon as I can. There's a few logistics that haven't been ironed out. The money for your personal assistants has to go into another account at the moment before it can then come to you.'

I mumble a reply, acknowledging my women's pain, low and heavy in my womb. I feel that on my tombstone it should say: 'She was always waiting.' There is always a hold-up, or a catch.

I'm happier when I'm on the sofa watching films with Freddie.

It's one of my most favourite things in all the world.

'It will be weird having people come in every day,' he says. 'People we don't know.'

I am shocked at myself to feel irritated.

'But we will know them,' I say, ignoring the tearing cramps which show no mercy. 'That's the whole point. I get to choose them. I pay them and they support me in the way I need.'

Freddie nods and we sit quietly, watching *It Always Rains on Sunday*.

Philip catches me again as I'm about to drive to Kaye and Gary's. Some reviews have come in. It's exciting and scary. I can't wait to read them.

'More delays, I'm afraid,' says Philip. 'There's a long wait to order the right wheelchair lifts. And that neighbour is making a real nuisance of herself, bothering the workmen. I've told her I'll get a restraining order if she keeps on with it.'

'Thanks, Philip,' I say, listless, not wanting this joke, this mess to drag me away from *Spiral Sky*.

'I've told the tenancy department to draw up the papers. I hope that's reassuring.'

'Yes. Thanks,' I say flatly, expecting nothing. Grateful to him but hating the whole damn shitty mess.

My cramps flare up on the drive to Walthamstow, but I manage to push them aside once I'm at Kaye and Gary's. We're all here again. Kaye with her blonde hair and glitzy jewellery, Tanya hugging me as Gary appears with a bundle of clippings. Tone sitting beside me and kissing my cheek.

'I knew they would love the album,' Gary says. 'Sales are going really well. Look at these reviews.'

Tone grabs a clipping. 'This one from Italy is a killer. Gary got them to send one translated.'

'They love your voice!' exclaims Kaye. 'And so they should. It's about time, it really is, Pen. You deserve it.'

I know my cramps are demanding attention as a sensation of knives moving in my nether regions reaches a pinnacle. But I smile, and bask as happy as Kaye's cat sunbathing on the windowsill.

'Oh, there's another thing,' says Gary, as pleased as I am. 'The album's Number 2 in the Italian indie charts.'

I laugh, embarrassed, amazed and very satisfied. 'What does that mean? A big sale?'

'You know what the indie charts are like, Pen,' says Gary. 'The consignment I sent to Italy has sold out and I wouldn't be surprised if you make it to Number 1 in Greece. They really went for the signed copies.'

We're all smiling and I'm almost crying, but it makes a change that it's not from anxiety or pain or frustration. It's because I'm so damned pleased and lost in delicious gratitude towards my lovely friends.

'Well there's something,' I say. 'Looks like I might be first in the world somewhere.'

CHAPTER 19

9 August 1995: The Disabled Persons' Civil Rights Bill was fucked right out of Parliament. We might get a Disability Discrimination Bill later. This amounts to a lot of fine words from a mouth with no teeth.

Philip fights the good fight, and after a dull period of waiting, we move. As the late summer sun streams into our bedroom through the French windows – which form my only entrance – I feel home, at last. I stare at the garden for hours, through the long grass that stretches back into a little wilderness of brambles. Freddie finds treasure, a half-buried air-raid shelter keeping its secrets.

It's a wildlife haven. There are foxes sunbathing, who ignore Tooty as he makes elderly majestic tours of his new territory.

We don't have any hot water or any heating, and the two lifts they have put in at the rear of the property are not reliable. But the flat possesses magic and demands love for its Victorian features. I hear the lifting violin from *The Lark Ascending* coming from our front room. I close my eyes, a moment of bliss.

And yet, there is pain. The everyday Lurgy chugs on, my normality. But my thoughts turn on me too quickly and I lapse into battle mode. There is no more Evil Shrink Nurse Barry, and I gave up going to Claybury. I cry for no reason, or too many reasons. I convince myself I can see on Freddie's face that something is changing.

There are my women's problems. Ignored and brushed aside for months on end, I cling to the hope that my new GP, Dr Guinness, a committed, pleasant Irishman, will do something.

I'm waiting to interview a woman called Debbie. I'm hopeful

she will be my personal assistant, as I become one of the first to get funding in my borough. I know Freddie is wary, but his family pressures remain. I'm not happy struggling alone, when this radical option is finally mine. Gritting my teeth, drinking a sneaky vodka, I kick my phone phobia in the nuts for an hour and talk to Debbie at length.

Freddie comes into the room as my thoughts meander.

'Hey Pen, are you ready? Do you want me to stay with you?'

'I'll be okay, just lurk.'

He hovers in the doorway, leaning onto the frame.

'This is going to be a bit weird, Pen.'

'I know,' I say, not making eye contact. 'We've both got to get used to it. See it as a step on from having Sandra.'

'Sandra was different,' Freddie says quickly, coming back into the room and crossing his arms. 'We were comfortable with her.'

I chew the edge of my lip, hating that words stay trapped in my mouth. I want to tell him this is for me. I'm not going to struggle any more when you're out. Instead I sigh and put on my best conciliatory face.

'Hopefully we'll get to know Debbie just as well. And I'll be safe whenever you go out.'

I smile, thinking: when your family drags you away from me and I don't understand what's going on, or how long you're going to be.

I look up at him again and click on my chair, moving closer. He sinks down to hug me. The old swell of love floods contentment through my jittery nerves.

'This is good for us,' I whisper, nuzzling into him.

I don't want him to be wary. I hope he gets used to it soon. Because it's not just a radical choice – it's survival.

There is a firm rap on the door. Debbie is right on time.

She has short blonde hair and a lively, intelligent face. Her infectious laugh and sharp humour seduce me in seconds, and I know this is a woman who will never be shocked by my work in disability sex, or anything else I can throw at her.

I can never shake off my unease at working for a charity – especially as the radical powerhouse of Kate Nash has left. Charities remain so damn patrician. We discuss it at length at LDAF meetings and now there's DAN – Direct Action Network – Liz and other friends chaining themselves to inaccessible buses. There's PISS ON PITY and RIGHTS NOT CHARITY. We want autonomy. Not money raised through pity. With scarcely a disabled worker in sight.

But as Debbie drives me to the cobbled back street near Euston and the offices of Arthritis Care, I console myself that we don't do too bad, thanks largely to Kate and Young Arthritis Care.

I'm working with Joe, a sturdy bluff man from the Midlands. I like Joe as my boss. But he doesn't have the spark to change the world in a way that I want.

Debbie seems perfect and I marvel to myself at every moment of support. I think of Tamsin with gratitude and the ever-present whisper of sadness.

Debbie takes off my coat in the way that I have trained her. She brings my coffee – the way I like it. She sits quietly reading until I need her assistance. Perhaps for the loo or another drink. She holds my papers.

I go through my appointments seamlessly, doing the same tasks as my colleagues around the table as Debbie facilitates every action.

'So *A Day with Sam* is all done,' announces Joe. 'We're really pleased. I think we've done it again, Pen. Taken the lead on something special.'

'I hope so, Joe. It was quite a tough job. Not everyone gets where I'm coming from. You know I always want to rewrite the old-fashioned rules. Put in a bit of subversion.'

'And you do it very well,' says Joe. 'But you know I have to talk to you about *Young Arthritis News.*'

I glance over at Debbie and her presence reassures me. It is different and much more appropriate than if it was Freddie's.

'I know... I'm about two weeks behind. It's been a full-on summer, what with the move, getting a PA, learning all about that,' I say. 'Not to mention being a bit under the weather.'

'We know it's been tough,' says Joe, 'and we'll be as flexible as we can. But we do need the copy within two weeks. As long as I know you'll get us something, I'm happy. If you really need to, you can hand it over.'

I've got used to meeting the deadlines and rustling up something for *Young Arthritis News*. But a pang of guilt tightens my cheeks. I know the main reason I'm so late. I picked up a little job and one that I relish, writing essays and a chapter for *The Sexual Politics of Disability: Untold Desires*, commissioned by one of the co-editors, Tom Shakespeare. He's a bit famous as a pioneering disability academic. I'm very proud of my contribution. Proud of writing the most explicit chapter on sex, when many others had declined.

'You know I'll do it, Joe,' I say, as I gesture to Debbie to come over to gather up the newspaper, post and various stuff needed to finish the task. A sudden rush of satisfaction makes me smile. I know this is how it's meant to be and I already know that I never want to lose this independent living support that we, crip activists, and the many who came before us, fought so hard to have.

I have an hour left of Debbie's shift with me.

'Before I get home, let's have a quick look in Body Shop,' I say. 'We'll park up by the market.'

I'm getting used to training Deb to support me without challenging my choices. My exhilaration grows as she helps me out of the car into my zippy power wheelchair. Passes down the White Musk from the very top shelf.

I scrape back in just as Debbie's shift is ending. Freddie is already home and on the computer as I arrive, laughing and happy. But when he looks at me, my mood evaporates.

'Good day?' I say in a neutral tone.

He looks up at me with sad eyes. 'Not bad,' he says. Then carries on typing.

I want to yell at him. I want to go up and throw my arms around him, ask him to be happy for me. Instead I don't move and try to ignore the fog threatening at the back of my head.

'What shall we have for dinner?' I say, diverting my emotion to a very skinny Tooty, who makes his sedate way towards me.

Freddie looks up. There's a peculiar silence. I carry on stroking Tooty's head.

'You choose,' says Freddie at last.

I tighten up with hurt. I want him to ask me how it went. I want him to hold me, knowing I'm tired. I don't want to cry.

And sometimes, just sometimes, Freddie reads my mind.

'Hey,' he says, stretching away from the computer, arms in the air, 'how was it?'

The fog retreats. Anxiety backs off. Suddenly I love him again for trying.

I can't think about food: I've still got knives poking around my womb. But I look at him and I'm happy.

'Let's do jacket potatoes,' I say. 'We're on safe ground with those.'

Debbie works out a method of taking apart my motorised chair, which she fits into the boot of the Clio with skill. This means I am like a caged animal released, although for me, the rush is straight to the shops – shops that I choose. Shops I dash in and out of.

I explain to Debbie with a giggle, 'I'm like a big kid. It's freedom, Deb, freedom. And now it's Christmas I'm definitely in overdrive. Even though I claim to hate the damn season.'

Freddie and me have always shopped together, with him wheeling me. It's not a thing I've relished. For him it's something to get over with and I can never quite explain that I need more than a fast whizz around the big Co-op. Even our trips to Walthamstow Market are limited, and my eternal layers of guilt will not break open to challenge Freddie's choices. With him, I'm obliged and – until Debbie – that is how it's stayed.

'I'm happy if you are, Pen. I get it,' Debbie says, as I drive my chair past Iceland's freezer cabinet for the tenth time. Entranced by the packets of vegetables as much as I am by the market stall outside that sells only tinsel.

I get to the end of the aisle and an intense hissing rises in my head. I draw in my breath. I feel myself falling forwards. Debbie catches me, stops me slipping from my wheelchair, as I'm out for a few seconds.

'You've got to get this bloody period crap sorted out,' she says. 'I know, I'm not telling you what to do. But I help you when it's your period so I know that this amount of blood loss isn't normal.'

I know she's right. I've loved the first months in my Victorian haven, maybe sidelining my health as I fall in love with its beauty. The marble mantelpiece in the lounge is decorated with handmade gold stars. In the hearth there are piles of presents, including loads for my mum who's coming up for Christmas Day.

I've talked to Dr Guinness, who simply gives me painkillers. I've tried to be assertive at Dr Brown's clinic, so obsessed are they after all with blood tests for everything. I bleed and I bleed, and I'm told it's normal. Various medics persist with their habit of assuming it's all about the Lurgy, the rumer-toyed arther-rit-us. I can't have anything else, as much as I can never be anything else to them. That's my category. I don't have a womb, I don't have sex, I don't have women's problems.

Except all too soon, it's the day before Christmas Eve and I am in hospital.

I lay on the bed, staring at the grotesque grey ceiling of the barrack-like ward as I wait for a blood transfusion. So anaemic I'm near complete collapse.

I cry for my postponed visit from Mum as much as I cry for Freddie. I know I'm submerging into the fog of anxiety and frustration. If I submerge too deeply it's harder each time to come back to the everyday.

My blood pressure is through the roof but I have to have treatment. They put tablets under my tongue and attach me to endless wires. I think about Deb, about personal assistance. I think about all the fighting, the flat and the car. As the blood seeps into my veins, I think about the last holiday me and Freddie had in Dorset.

I've visited Dorset hundreds of times since passing my driving test. It's beautiful, but I remain gritty in trying to coax Freddie into broadening our travel horizons.

We stay at the same place, in a small village on the coast near Poole, with its unexpected curves, Jurassic cliffs and ancient secrets. This time, we have come with Tanya and Janis.

Tanya is eager to visit Wareham, to see the memorial to T. E. Lawrence, who she worships. We will also try and squeeze in some Thomas Hardy sights to indulge our mutual passion.

I've known Janis since I was nine, on the kids' ward in Beechwood Hospital. We connected quickly through our love of animals and our obsession with Tutankhamun. She is very impressed that I went to see the original exhibition at the British Museum on a school trip. Our lives took us in different directions and then we found each other again and, with Tanya, friendship reaffirmed itself in many shared interests. I'm beyond happy that they are with me in Dorset. It seems the most natural thing in the world to be hanging out with my best mates.

Janis drives her car with Tanya as the passenger, while I'm in the Clio with Freddie.

'A day out with three girls, what about that then?' I tease him as we drive towards Dorchester along the smooth, clear A roads.

Freddie frowns. 'They're going to make you overdo it,' he says. 'That's what I worry about.'

As always, always, I feel the cramp of guilt and the mess of feeling. Always wanting to please Freddie, always grateful, always feeling the core of my world pivots through him. And yet – especially now I have Debbie – I want time with my friends too and know I shouldn't feel guilty about this.

We head for the Tutankhamun tomb, recreated just off Dorchester High Street. Janis and me laugh in excitement at the thought.

I'm a bit sad that I don't have my motorised chair, but there's not enough room for that with our holiday luggage. I know Freddie will wheel me with his usual expertise, but I'm fretting. It's not about how well he does it, it's about not needing to rely on him, especially now I have a personal assistant.

We creep inside the tomb. Tanya, Janis and me laugh and enjoy being silly. At first I don't notice that Freddie stays back, his eyes cast down. I feel a poke of irritation and try my hardest to ignore him. To carry on enjoying the day with my friends. As usual, I'm tugged in two directions.

'Do you want to stay outside?' I say softly. 'I know this isn't really your thing.'

'God, what's the matter with you, you bastard?' Tanya speaks up, glaring at Freddie, never one to mince her words. 'We're on holiday, for fuck's sake.'

Freddie says nothing but shrugs and I feel rooted to the spot.

'No,' he says suddenly. 'You need me to wheel you round.'

I glance at Tanya, who rolls her eyes.

He grabs the handles of my chair and we go round the rest of the exhibition, our playful mood dampened.

By the time we arrive back at our holiday cottage, he stops talking altogether. Once we're inside, he whispers to me that we should go to the seafront without Tanya and Janis.

The sea is very blue in the late sunshine and sparkles with a million points of light. I don't want to be tired. I want Freddie to be happy. I want to be happy.

I draw in a breath. I'm never good at this stuff, rocking the emotional boat, scared I will tip it over but knowing in some distant, buried corner of me that I have to do it.

'What's wrong?' I say it nervously and fast, keeping my eye on the sea.

'Nothing,' he says and closes down.

'You're not happy. Tanya and Janis know it too. We've got half the holiday...' I trail off as I feel sick. As if I have spoken forbidden words that should not be aired to the world.

'They make you overdo it,' says Freddie, 'and you'll get ill.'

'No,' I say softly. But I'm thinking and thinking and thinking. Words trapped under that shell of self-reproach. I know Tanya and Janis love me as much as Freddie. I know it's different love. But I also fear that I don't understand what Freddie is feeling. And I don't know if I want to know.

We get back to the cottage before dusk. Janis offers to make us a cup of tea. Freddie ignores her.

'Do you have a problem with us?' she says to him calmly. I weep inside with embarrassment and envy that she speaks the words that I always fail to.

He continues to ignore them. Tanya erupts.

'We just don't understand what the problem is, so you need to tell us. What have we done? Do you want us to leave?'

'No,' I say spontaneously. I don't want them to leave.

'Pen's overdoing it and I know she'll get ill,' Freddie mutters.

'Are we making her overdo it?' says Janis.

'Do you think you're overdoing it because we're here, Pen?' Tanya asks me directly. 'We love Pen too, you know, and wouldn't do anything to hurt her.'

The waves of sickness gurgle inside me, aided by the humid heat of the day. This feels like a fight. I don't want to be in a fight. I didn't draw up the lines of battle. I squirm to know that Freddie wants to protect me, always, even when the threats he sees aren't really there.

'I'm okay,' I say tightly. And I can't say any more.

Freddie leaves the room. I spend the rest of the evening crying, then laughing with the girls.

'He can't have you all to himself,' says Janis. 'It's not healthy.'

'I know,' I say and think about Debbie and how things will be different. And I hope this will help Freddie and me, and not push us in a direction I don't want to think about.

The next morning we're up early. Off to a sheep farm near Piddlehinton. By the time we get there to feed some very large, late lambs with other tourists, Freddie is back to himself. Funny, warm and supportive.

I love him. I love Tanya and Janis. And I refuse to accept why one has to compete with the other.

CHAPTER 20

30 October 1996: Feel like I'm leading a double life through the internet. The new world of cyberspace creates excitement and freedom. But it can be a big headfuck.

Dr Guinness jokes with me. I trust him more than I have trusted many GPs. He sees me every six weeks, especially since the emergency admission for the blood transfusion. But as I speak to him today, I can't hide my trembling. I'm impossibly sad and I don't know why. I know I miss working with my mates, I miss singing and fucking around with them all. *Spiral Sky* has made its mark as a cult success and Gary is planning a deluxe reissue in purple and gold. But the sadness clings to me.

The Victorian haven, wheelchair lifts now working, remains an oasis. Still London but scarcely. Full of trees and green spaces that stretch all the way up to Epping Forest, where I drive most weeks.

Dr Guinness has small round eyes and a rosy bloom high on his cheeks. 'Getting proper help with this depression has been a bit patchy, hasn't it?'

Debbie brought me over to this appointment and sits in the waiting room. It's a new privilege to be seeing doctors on my own, and I'm still getting used to the liberation – of having that choice.

'Lots of places never have wheelchair access. Even places like Mind,' I say flatly. 'It never seems to get any better. And there's all this stuff where they always blame my—' I stop my words as I almost say Lurgy. Somewhere I hear Tamsin laughing. 'My arthritis,' I say on a small breath.

'Well,' Dr Guinness says with an avuncular smile, 'that must play a role in it.'

Not in the way you think. I shake, clutching a piece of paper in my strong hand: the name of Madelyn, a therapist who works at South Woodford. The only one I could find whose room is wheelchair accessible. The only one who replied to my enquiries with a kind encouraging word.

Dr Guinness is staring at me intently. 'Come now, Penny,' he says. 'Try and speak to me.'

I respond by handing him the piece of paper. I want him to refer me.

I don't want to go back on Temazepam. That's happened too many times in the past.

I think about the thoughts in my head that terrorise me. That tell me I should be dead. That tell me I'm a nothing. They have been growing louder every day, filling all the trembling gaps within me. They want to block the light. They scare Freddie. They scare me.

A week later Debbie helps me wash, put on my latest favourite dress – a mid-length crushed-velvet thing I can dress up with pearls and lace. I know I look presentable. I wonder if the results of these new freedoms with a personal assistant cover up the inner torment of my moods. But at least I'm not splattered in sick, left with tangled hair.

I'm in a small, terraced house, in front of Madelyn. She is Canadian. Elegantly dressed with a perfect brunette bob. I like her face and the warmth in her voice.

'We'll start with six weeks of cognitive analytical therapy,' she says. 'We work together on this, Penny. Is that okay?'

'Do I have to whine on about my past?' I wince.

Madelyn gives me a slight smile.

'Only if you need to. We'll unpick this anxiety together.'

I relax. This is no Evil Shrink Nurse Barry McAuliffe. Or Dr Toby and his obsession with group therapy.

I start to talk. I cry. And then I talk again.

I leave with some homework about the placation trap, already eager to see her again.

Debbie drives me home and Freddie returns from a day's visit to his mum.

He doesn't ask me how I got on with Madelyn.

Madelyn has an immediate effect. Her calm and empathetic presence eases my anxiety into retreat. She insists, gently, that I need to own the power of my own mind. Which in my case, she insists, is observant and funny.

My writing reaps the benefit as I plug in to my PC, re-energised to write some fiction about sex and disability. One way or another, to write *Cripples Fucking*.

Freddie is in a good mood and keeps up a supply of tea and biscuits. I know there's an end to the story I'm working on. I decide I will write until dawn if I have to.

'You go to bed, Freddie, if you want,' I say casually, not taking my eyes off the screen. My disabled couple are about to have sex and, as always, it has to be real and rude.

'Okay,' says Freddie and kisses my head. 'Just don't get ill.'

I feel a flush of love and surprise.

'Promise I won't,' I say, and as the words come out I realise they're meaningless.

'Do we have to have another row,' Freddie says as he moves away from me. 'This'll be the third late night in a row. It's unfair, Pen.'

I disguise my exasperation by staring at the screen.

'You know how it is,' I say, 'sometimes it has to be done.'

'Yeah,' says Freddie. 'I know.'

At least he's laughing now.

'You're just an obsessive.'

By 3 a.m., wrapped in the comforting background creaks of the Victorian haven, I've finished not one, but two short stories:

'Girls Wank Too' and 'The Summer is Free'. I go to turn off the PC but I can't help myself from the opening paragraph of another – 'Seven Days'.

I wheel into Freddie, sleeping peacefully, with Tooty on the end of the bed. My cat is old and – the thought shoots dread through my heart. I decide I won't wake either of them and I go back to the lounge to face East, to see the sun rise over the chestnut trees across the road.

Propped on the mantelpiece, behind my Egyptian cats, is the deluxe edition of *Spiral Sky*, a gorgeous regal object of purple and gold. I have written a few new songs. I miss working with the band and wonder when we can get together to at least do some jamming. But I know my regular days of gigging are over.

And it's hard to realise the world has not caught up with me. Access is shitty and outside of my precious bubble of friends and disabled comrades, I feel I'm still little more than a freak, an interesting anomaly. On my good days, still a big-mouthed punk down to my deepest soul. I close my eyes. There's so much more I need to do.

I cling on to my job with Young Arthritis Care. But it's arduous and now *Strangeness and Charm* has made its expensive way to DAW in New York – a sci-fi publisher – my heart for YAC fades.

For now, there is another advantage. And from today, another great plaything. Tech expert Pete is here to connect me to the internet.

After some deliberating, Freddie and me have swapped the rooms around: the lounge has become our bedroom, big enough for one end to be our work area and conveniently near the phone point where this modem thing will plug in and connect me to the world wide web.

Pete is young and wears an oversized suit. He bounces around the room with tremendous enthusiasm. He loves it that I'm playing Blur.

He quickly connects me to something called bogo.com, which means I can search for things using my connection. And I have an email address.

Pete explains with excited waving of his arms that this is a revolution.

'You're getting in early,' he says. 'And it will really help your work. Once people get used to it, everything will go by email. No more posting of big fat manuscripts to America, like you were telling me about.'

'Well, maybe.' I am unsure, but his enthusiasm quickly infects me with terms like private listing groups, Netscape, CompuServe.

'Think of something you're interested in, Penny,' Pete says. 'I don't know – music, gardening, cats. There'll be an email group that covers it. You join that and only you and the other members get to see what's being discussed. You'll have to learn words like flaming. Most of all, don't forget your passwords.'

Young Arthritis Care helped to set up the internet for me, hoping to make work and getting copy in to them a lot easier. And I'm grateful for my dad's genes, making me a fast learner.

Five minutes later, as Freddie comes in to ask me what we have for dinner, I'm already addicted.

I join three groups. One about dance – the progressive sounds coming out of the rave scene, such as Underworld and Orbital. One about disability, exhilarated by the revolutionary idea of disabled people talking to each other, no barriers on location or venue. For a while, through reading the *Face* magazine, I find myself in email correspondence with local Leytonstone boy Jonathan Ross, over a shared love of cult movies. And finally, urged on by the shared interest with Kaye, I join a Pagan and Wiccan email chat group.

Before I go to bed I notice, in my sparkly new inbox, that I already have a welcoming message from a music fan called Tim and someone describing himself as a big, hairy pagan called Kamesh.

I drive back with Freddie from West Bromwich. It's not a pretty place but the people at the hotel are friendly and my growing wanderlust relishes the chance to be somewhere new.

This was the venue for the Young Arthritis Care conference and I chose this time to resign as publications officer. It's been liberating, catching up with old friends, half the time meandering around the two-day event in gossip.

Freddie is relaxed, which makes me relax.

The M1 motorway seems to go on forever, but at least we can play some music – Trance Europe Express. It's loud, a drumming, a counterpoint to conversation between Freddie and me.

He turns the volume down as I fly by the Watford Gap.

'I'm glad you've given the job up,' he says.

I grunt. 'So am I,' I say. 'Apart from the money.'

'We'll manage, Pen. We're not doing too bad.'

He squeezes my thigh, which even now gives me a delicious thrill.

'But don't get overwhelmed by doing this YAC voluntary work.'

'Overwhelmed? Me?' I say. 'Never.'

Freddie gives my leg another squeeze. 'Come off it, Pen. You're already obsessing about this stall you're doing for YAC at Walthamstow Village Festival.'

'That's different,' I protest, shifting my position slightly. Driving is putting an increasing strain on my shoulder joints. 'I'm helping out Sharon. It won't just be me.'

'Yeah, yeah,' says Freddie, and we laugh together.

I feel love float me along all the way to Woodford Green.

Then Freddie says, as we get out the car, 'Oh you're going out tomorrow evening, aren't you? With Debbie. Again. To that bloody Disability Arts thing.'

I've been invited onto the editorial committee for *Disability Arts in London* magazine by the editor. Colin is a poet, an artist. A soft-spoken, attractive man with crazy hair and serious eyes.

We have a deep rapport and he is a great supporter of my writing. He commissions me on a regular basis to appear on the pages of the magazine – reviews, poetry and the occasional story. He gives me a space where my work is free to flourish, to a disability arts audience that understands. Allowing me to build a tentative writer's CV.

He lives in Tottenham and with Debbie driving the car to my sessions at the Camden office I've offered him many lifts home after the committee meetings. Through this I've discovered we have a shared interest in paganism and particularly goddess mythology.

'When did you feel drawn to it all?' I ask him. 'For me, I think something was always there.'

'We should do some work together, Pen. Cast a circle. Go skyclad,' he says from the back seat. 'When things are less busy.'

I hate that my neck will not turn to look at him as I sit beside Debbie quietly in the driver's seat. But at least he won't see me blushing. Skyclad means naked. Naked before the goddess.

'I'd love to do that,' I say in a breathless rush. 'Through the wonders of the internet I'm part of this Wiccan email chat group now. I've started having these get-togethers at the flat. I call them my pagan pizza parties. You should try and come to one, one day.'

'Maybe,' says Colin, but he sounds doubtful. 'I'm wary of posers. People saying they can see the goddess everywhere. In the wallpaper. On your shoulder.'

Debbie pulls up outside his flat. Colin comes round to the front to give me a peck goodbye, but on the lips.

'I know what you mean,' I say. 'I know one or two like that and I just tease them.'

'I'll be in touch soon.' Colin waves as he disappears into the block.

I'm tired and I wonder if Freddie is happy today. I shiver to realise that if I had the means to keep Debbie with me for longer I wouldn't have come home.

I'd have stayed with Colin. Maybe all night.

Every month, apart from being skyclad with Col, I lay my hands on a henry – an eighth – learning fast how to roll perfect spliffs on a rolling machine with minimal low-tar tobacco and a line of squidgy black.

In my Victorian haven with the sun shining low across my wild back garden, the cannabis lowers me into a different place of peace. My therapist Madelyn does not really approve. But at least she supports me to make choices and to understand why I make them.

I'm prepping for my pagan party, a few hours to go. I am generous with my spliffs and I enjoy a particular satisfaction, still new to me, of entertaining and creating a beautiful environment. Endless candles flickering in the lounge, on the massive marble fireplace. My art prints glimmering, and vases of beloved flowers release gentle scents.

I know the influence of Anaïs Nin is here, and Kaye – and at last, with Debbie's help, I'm starting to create this around me.

'I don't know what you see in that stuff,' Freddie says, doing a comedy frown, waving his hand through the pungent waft of weed.

'Are you going to stay tonight, Freddie?' I say, pulling my own face. 'Or are you giving the party a miss? Debbie's here after all.'

'I don't always like to be around listening to that loopy Wiccan rubbish,' Freddie replies sharply.

I drop my head, mouth closed.

'I'm only teasing, Pen,' Freddie says, stooping down to stroke Tooty's head. My aged cat opens a sleepy eye but doesn't move.

'It's fine. I can manage. Means you don't have to stay.'

'I know, I know that,' Freddie answers, but a familiar cramp of anxiety turns me inside out.

He goes over to the record player on his huge music centre and flips over the vinyl LP of Nirvana's *Smells Like Teen Spirit*.

'I'll stay,' he says. 'I can lurk somewhere. I like that older guy who can play bagpipes.'

I listen for a few seconds as Kurt Cobain's rage wraps around my heart.

'You should organise something, Freddie, get a bunch of vinyl junkies over. You know enough of them. It'd be fun.'

'I don't do groups, you know that.' His smile is half-hearted. I look away and say nothing.

When Debbie arrives the first thing she does is tidy the lounge to make space and put out a few fold-up chairs. Pizzas in the oven and lots of garlic bread. I'm lifted into the excitement – the freedom of doing this with her support. I'll use those plates. No, the green napkins, not the pink. And put the wine in the fridge please.

First to arrive is Nick with his partner Dawn. They are big, tall as giants to me. I am always pleased to see them, aware that this is what my connection to the internet has brought me. A widening of my horizons, the meeting of people in a way that isn't bogged down with the fuss and frustration of getting into a pub, a restaurant, a venue. I give them first choice on the pizzas and the door goes again.

I know Freddie is lurking as he said he would, doing stuff on the PC. I wheel into the bedroom quickly, unable to help a stab of regret.

'You sure you're not coming out?' I say.

He looks at me vacantly, then begins typing again.

'I'm fine,' he says. 'You're the one who wanted more friends, not to be joined at the hip.'

I say nothing and retreat, as Debbie brings Derek into the lounge. He's the oldest amongst our group, with long, greying hair pulled back in a tight ponytail. I'm fond of him already with his humour, his refusal to take anything seriously. He says he is very patchwork – a Wiccan, a Druid, a pagan, and – as he tells me – he is now a reverend, having chosen a perfectly legal ordination process via the wonders of the web.

Next to arrive is Wolf, all the way from Hastings. As always he comes through with a flourish, dressed in jeans and a T-shirt emblazoned with a Native American with full headdress.

'There's two troublesome entities at your front door,' is his opening line, followed with a wink. 'I'll get rid of them if you want. They're playful, but quite harmless.'

'Leave my entities alone then,' I say as he hugs me.

'Pen, I just felt your totem animal.' He stands back and beams. 'It's a slinky little fox.'

'Bugger, I hoped it would be a tiger,' I say and laugh loudly. 'Go and grab some pizza before the others eat it all.'

I go into the lounge and I'm pleased to find Freddie in conversation with Derek, picking out folk LPs from his vast collection. Within a few minutes, they are both singing along to the Martin Carthy track 'Sovay'. I join in now and again, loving the tricksy folk song about a highway woman.

When the track is over, Derek gets out his bagpipes and the group falls silent. I tingle at his exquisite playing.

I organise Debbie to offer more wine and, as she does, the doorbell goes again.

'Who's the latecomer?' laughs Wolf. 'Shall I curse him, Penny, for his bad manners?'

I know he is joking – mostly.

'No, don't be so mean,' I say. 'I know who it is. It's Kamesh. He has quite a journey, you know.'

Kamesh – big, tall, hairy and pagan – was the first person from the Pagan Wiccan emailing group to write to me. We've written most days ever since. We write about everything. I feel he knows me. And I want to know him. Not sure where this will take me. Uneasy but not for one moment thinking I will stop.

'Hello, Pen,' he says as he comes through the hallway, a large presence in every sense. 'Really glad I've made it.'

'So am I,' I say and he looks at me.

Looks at me with his deep, dark eyes like I'm the only person there. Looks at me until I am unnerved. Looks at me until the spell is broken – when Wolf bounds into the hallway with a yell of recognition, and into an instant man hug.

I have another party the evening that New Labour are voted in. I can't decide on Tony Blair. He's a bit like a wonky Thunderbirds puppet. But with Gary, Kaye, Tony and Zed we share some booze and put on Blur and Oasis. My favourites though are Pulp. Jarvis is a sex god and has an echo of Morrissey about him. 'Common People' is an anthem.

Kamesh emails me every day and I'm shocked when I realise I am sharing more with him than I am with Freddie. A muddle of thoughts burns across my mind – my funding and Debbie give me freedom. Safety. Often more choices than I know what to do with. I want to bite the world and taste it all. I envy Freddie, who seems happiest when we do what we always do – a film on the VCR, some music, jacket potato for dinner. Maybe a walk around the green opposite our flat.

I hope the thoughts won't fester but I know there's a space inside me that is quickly draining to empty.

Debbie drives me to Kaye's for the afternoon.

'We worry about you, my darling,' says Kaye. 'You don't seem happy.'

'I don't know if I'm unhappy. I don't think so.' I know I don't sound convincing. 'Everything seems in flux. I've run out of money from the YAC job and I face the horrible chore of going back on benefits.'

'But that's what they're there for, aren't they? To help when you need it?' Kaye smiles. 'You've explained that system to me often enough. How you're not exactly free to do any job out there. Because of all the barriers. The prejudice and stuff.'

'I wish I was just recording again.' I cry and smile all at once, and yet on the verge of a sob. 'Or just back into something solid. Creative.'

'I'm sure you'll do something else with Gary at some point. Ask him. We could at least organise a jamming session. Get Tone in, Tanya. And I take it Freddie would be up for this?'

I don't answer, not sure how I can.

'Did I tell you about this BBC film internship?' I say instead. 'I got shortlisted.'

'No you didn't!' Kaye exclaims. 'And you sit here, talking as if you're not doing anything.'

'I don't think I can take it up. It's too complicated.'

'You don't say that very often, Pen. You always find a way,' she sighs. 'I'll have to get Tanya to gang up on you as well.'

'Oh I'm scared now,' I laugh, as darling Tanya has very special skills in boosting me out of my melancholy.

'Are you still running the stall at Walthamstow Village? That should cheer you up a bit.'

'I don't know if I need cheering up,' I protest, but I'm grinning. 'I'm looking forward to it though. Tanya's going to wear a money belt. She's very excited about that. And most of the local YAC group should come along. Freddie, bless him, has even donated some vinyl.'

'So as usual, when we scratch away all these worries going around in your head, there's a lot, a huge lot in fact, going on to keep you occupied.' Kaye puts down her cup of herbal tea, crosses the room to fetch an orange, velvet-covered notebook. 'I remembered you told me that Madelyn said it would help for you to keep a different sort of diary. One to analyse your thoughts. I saw this and I just wanted you to have it.'

I take it from her and stroke it as I would my cat. 'Thank you so much, it's very me.'

'Yes, it is. So do your homework and get writing in it. I'll try and pop by for the Walthamstow Village Festival. I gather Deb is going to do some food for you to sell on the day.'

'She is and she's a very good cook. Now all we have to hope for is good weather.'

I look up and see Debbie approaching the front door. My time is almost up, I have to be home before her shift ends. This jolts me to remember to brave a phone call to my social worker. I've decided to ask for more funding, more hours.

The weather is warm and sunny and Debbie's cakes do not melt. There is a small gang of us behind the stall, along the path that leads to St Mary's church in Walthamstow Village. I'm surprised at how villagey it feels, considering how near we are to the noisy bustle of Hoe Street.

Freddie is happy when people browse his old vinyl and we both enjoy the moment when a local reporter comes to chat and asks me about *Spiral Sky*. I push away the little pang that makes me wish for a repeat of those intense and lively times.

Janis and Tanya are the boss ladies of the day. Tanya wears her money belt proudly and Janis organises the table – then reorganises it at regular intervals.

Sharon is a down-to-earth local who has had arthritis for as long as me. We share running the local YAC group together. She likes to say to me, 'I tell it like it is, Pen.'

Sharon tries to reorganise Janis's reorganising, back to an earlier version of the display. 'There's not enough room for all this shit,' she says plaintively. 'Get some off, please.'

'We need to keep the food out to try and sell it first,' I say, torn between competing loyalties to my friends.

'I know,' says Sharon, giving me a stern look. But I'm never scared, she just makes me laugh and I love her to bits.

'Sharon,' Janis pipes up. 'I had that arranged perfectly. It was a system. The food was safer in the centre.'

We all start laughing, stopping only when a sudden gaggle of old ladies descends and buy all Debbie's cakes in one swoop – for the old people, they say.

'They must be the old, old people,' I laugh when they've gone. 'Now we just need to sell out on the rolls.'

We are trying to raise enough money to go on a day trip. Maybe up the River Lea on a canal boat. And to keep us going with room-hire costs. I love doing this with Sharon, love that we can make a small difference here and there. Most of all by letting others know they are not alone.

'Have you made your mind up about that new freelance job?' Tanya asks me, nibbling a cheese and tomato roll from Debbie's pile.

'I'll probably do it, though I'm a bit scared. I'm not a trained researcher, am I? I know fuck all about statistics.'

'A bit too close to maths, I suppose,' laughs Tanya, used to rescuing me from many spreadsheet disasters.

'Pen, you know you could do it.' Janis grabs a roll and joins in the conversation.

'What job is this, Pen?' Sharon pipes up.

'It's a project about harassment of disabled people in Waltham Forest. I know I can do the writing bit but it's going to be grim.'

'Do it, Pen,' says Janis and Tanya nods. 'Think about the writing and ask for guidance on the other stuff if you need it. It will stop you worrying about the benefits trap.'

The next day, I'm on the phone to Sharon. We have raised £186.92.

'We can do that boat trip,' she says. 'I'll get on to that bloke tomorrow. He's a bit of a wanker but I'll sort it out.'

'Great,' I say. 'I'm really pleased. It was a good turnout, wasn't it?'

'Yes it was,' Sharon says in her plain voice. 'And you need to make that call about that job.'

Within the week, I've signed the contract and begun to think about questionnaires as I sit in the Victorian haven, occasionally distracted by new neighbours moving to the flat above us. Feeling selfish in wishing we always had the whole house to ourselves.

I'm going through my latest draft alone, as Freddie attends to family duty, when the phone rings. It's Janis.

'Did you hear the news, Pen?' Her voice is wavery. 'I'm not sure why, but it's really upset me. And that shocked me more than anything.'

'What news?' I say, a little absently, my mind swiftly into overdrive. I've been in the bubble of work with only music for company. Kate Bush's *The Sensual World* and chunks of the *Chants of BoaBoa and the Fiji Islands*.

'Princess Diana is dead. In a car crash. Put the telly on, Pen. The news has gone crazy. Maybe I'm upset because she was so young.'

I think about my dad. I think about Laura. And most of all, I think about Tamsin.

Sex our way: my groundbreaking booklet.

CHAPTER 21

27 March 1998: Look at me, here is another new life. It is tenuous, a wavering of extremes. The threat of submerging into depression. Or flying high through a wonderful fire.

The daffodils are out the day Freddie leaves.

I am numb. There is fighting and accusation: all the clichés of a break-up that naively, or in my arrogance, I never expected we would act out.

I look at the rejection, from DAW publishers. One of those nice ones. They say they love my writing. They want to see more, but *Strangeness and Charm* is too British.

I put the letter on top of a pile of questionnaires. Questionnaires I can hardly bear to read. Details of abuse. Name-calling, and even physical violence towards disabled people. The reports fold into my brain like an infection, despite my therapist Madelyn always being there, always able to pull me back from my fog. I've come to hate this work on the harassment project. It makes me hate myself as much as those that hate us.

I'm wretchedly tired, staying up late to work on my newest novel, *Fancy Nancy*, glued to the internet, wishing I could upload myself all the way to Kamesh.

He's soothed me over the weeks when Freddie wouldn't speak to me. When Freddie confronted me with my feelings for Kamesh. When he bitterly announced that personal assistants had invaded our space and ruined our relationship.

I ache with guilt and deep, long love for Freddie. For all he has done and all he has brought me.

It's Madelyn that reminds me that my own contributions are of equal worth to our relationship. That I have been patient and uncomplaining when the heavy family demands on him took him away.

And now he has gone.

Using my own money, I add to Debbie's hours, meaning she can work for four hours every day for my first week alone.

I'm scared. I'm excited. I'm split into a thousand arguing thoughts and feelings. They press into me like pins. Anxiety grabs me back and mocks me, trapping my words in my gullet. It's so bad it takes me almost the whole of my hour with Madelyn to speak a few words.

Debbie locks me in for the night and Tooty gets on the bed with me slowly. I think about Kamesh, how I want to be with him. But I also think about Freddie and wonder if my life can really move on without him.

At 1 a.m., I manage to get myself out of bed. It's a struggle but I do it because I can and because I feel as if I will never sleep again. Tooty meows, a small frail feline complaint. I pet him for a moment then go to the PC.

I stare at the monitor. I want to write to Kamesh, beg him to come and see me. I want to tell him what has happened.

Instead, I put on a CD, *Dubnobasswithmyheadman* by Underworld. The tight beat entrances me, the layers move with a sexy visceral power. It fires me up. I grab a tattered old notebook overflowing with notes and type: 'Nancy hears horses and the racket of screaming children as she slowly opens her eyes.'

Late next morning, Debbie makes me a cup of tea.

Debbie – who is leaving, returning, with the demands of her kids, to her roots in Nottingham.

Tooty moves slowly to his bowl, his creaky bones showing through his fur as Debbie puts down his food.

'I'm really sorry I've got to go,' she says, eyes sad. 'And I'm sorry it's come around a bit sooner than I'd hoped.'

I'm still in shock. Debbie has got me through so much. And now there is the anxiety of starting again with someone new. Somewhere, distantly, Tamsin is laughing: the responsibility of choice, Pen!

There's one person in the pipeline to interview as her replacement: Roxy, who lives about a mile away. She fits all the basic criteria.

'Roxy's ready to start, isn't she?' Debbie says gently. 'She was good watching me. Seemed to pick up what I do really fast.'

'Yeah, I know,' I mumble, always hating the fucking endless anxiety that puts shakes into my voice and my fingers, threatens to stop me dead, and yet clings to me like a soggy blanket. 'She seemed quite funny, that's a good thing.'

Debbie fetches her scarf and bag, then comes back to hug me and as she leaves I feel like the loneliest person alive.

I look down at Tooty. He is coming up to twenty. I know he won't be with me for much longer and I can't bear it. Go when you're ready, my little old man. Go when you're ready.

I swallow my disquiet, unenthusiastic to go through the harassment questionnaires piling up by my computer. Female, 41, verbal abuse at swimming pool over scars on leg. Male, 68, walking stick kicked from under him. Female, 23, touched inappropriately by visiting neighbour...

On my desk, the orange velvet notebook from Kaye lies tempting me to give it attention. Its sheets are lilac and I write randomly with a purple pen. I know I should resist it and plod on with the questionnaires. But I have opened a document, another chapter for *Fancy Nancy*.

Nancy is stuck in the Victorian freak show she has created, a twentieth-century time traveller, unable to find her way back, or track down her beloved William Copple... I want to make things happen for them, I want to push her adventure on. Maybe this is the one. This is the novel. I glance at *Spiral Sky*, a proud feature of my mantelpiece. I have to believe that one day there will be books alongside it.

I'm still shaking at the realisation that Debbie has gone. The world is fragmented. I pick up a questionnaire: female, mother of two disabled children, verbal abuse: 'they should be put down'.

I seemed to have so much of what I thought I wanted. Now I feel terrified.

Kamesh comes to see me, making the long drive into London. I feel we have a relationship from a fable. The Giant and the Cripple. I quite like this idea, as Kamesh embraces me, moves me, sits me on his lap – teaches me about tantric sex. He's serious but I know he enjoys me teasing him when he gets too intense. He is my solace and my new comfort. I battle my depressive moods with his company – and his food. He promises he will teach me how to cook. He also wants to take me on holiday – abroad.

'Tantric sex is not what you think, Penny,' he says, grave blue eyes upon me. 'It's about ecstatic connection.'

'You know me well enough by now, Kamesh, to know I'll give most things a try,' I laugh. 'But first, we've got to work out some basic stuff. You know, x into y. What with me and my dodgy joints and you…'

'A big fat bastard!' He grins and strokes my hair, folding his fingers into my newly home-grown dreadlocks.

'I was going to say giant. Like Brân the Blessed, stomping about pre-Roman London.'

'Penny, my clever clogs, reading up on your mythology again, hey?'

'Oh, I read the odd book or two,' I grin back at him. 'I even write them. Not that any bugger wants them.'

Massive Attack's 'Dark Angel' simmers from the speakers. Kamesh holds me gently and I feel like a changeling, small and slight against his large chest and deep sturdy heartbeat.

'Don't say that,' he says. 'Your time will come. I have asked the Goddess. I made offers to Lakshmi. I believe she is the archetype who most looks after you.'

Transglobal Underground plays around our conversation, the

rich swooping vocals of Natacha Atlas spinning a spell. I nod my head, still amazed to hear him speak like this. Loving it, biting the urge on my tongue to always be silly. I know he likes the ritual and he is keen to initiate me formally as a Wiccan. I will go along with it as I know it will please him.

Freddie is in my head and I still find it hard to think about having sex with Kamesh. Outside of the logistics, which I know are surmountable because I trust him.

But my heart is divided, bruised in disbelief that Freddie and me have not lasted, that our journeys were in opposing directions. That my journey took me elsewhere. Took me to the bed with Kamesh.

'I want to take you to Portugal,' Kamesh says suddenly. 'Would you like that?'

I hate the instant fear, the usual battering of anxious questions dampening my excitement. I know I can't take a personal assistant, there is no money. And Kamesh wouldn't like that anyway, even though he has taken on board how important they are to me. But I know he'll want me to himself and he will be expecting to help me.

'Well?' He tugs one of my stray, orange dreadlocks. 'Don't be so excited, Penny!'

I sigh. 'I am. But you know I've never travelled abroad. Never looked into it. Transport is still a nightmare for disabled people.'

My mind pulls back briefly to the holiday in Jersey that Tamsin and me shared in 1984 – a monumental effort of logistical organisation. Staying in a special hotel. Going on the special minibus. Getting on the aeroplane on a platform, attached to a wobbling forklift truck.

'I really need to encourage you to practise what you preach.' His laugh is a deep bear laugh. 'You've taught me so much, Penny. And I've got every faith we can do this. I've looked at some wheelchair-accessible villas in the Algarve. I've got my eye on one with a heated plunge pool, where we can bathe naked at midnight looking up at the stars.'

His blue eyes look into the distance. 'I'll hire a car because I'd love to take you up one of those mountains, above the cloud level.

And to one of the very neglected stone circles.' He narrows his eyes and licks his lips. 'I can put you on the altar stone, very gently. And slowly take off all your clothes.'

I laugh aloud. Pleased as my thoughts turn towards curiosity, thrilled that this could happen.

He helps me stand up and transfer back into my chair, then goes off to make chicken risotto for dinner. I go over to the CD player and put on Portishead's 'Strangers'. I immerse myself into the grinding fever of the track, eyes closed. Kamesh makes me feel like an angel, some dark, wonderful, wilful otherling.

Roxy's humour is always turned on to full. She's good at the work, learns the ropes fast. Adores driving my Clio. It's an easy decision to take her on, although I stay sad to see Debbie go. Leaving me, and leaving London.

I let Social Services know about Roxy. Trudging through the usual slow bureaucracy of the paperwork, the nagging that I must keep my monitoring up. Add up totals, the ins and the outs.

'Fucking numbnuts,' Roxy sneers with a wink. 'Numbies are everywhere. Fuck 'em, Pen, I say. I'm not bad with figures, so I can help later if you like.'

My social worker, Ranjit, is a mordant man always full of weak dramas from his own life when he visits. 'Penny, my wallet was lost in Ilford!' 'The kids broke the TV today, Penny.'

But I'm relieved he has done as he is meant to and I now have enough money in my account to have personal assistants for ten hours each and every day.

'You could go to the Bahamas on that,' Ranjit says during our next meeting.

I explode.

'If you want to just put me into a fucking home, say so!' I sob angrily. 'You just don't get it. Never. So I can sleep in my own piss, but whatever, I can go to the fucking Bahamas?'

I zip out of the room, power at full on my chair.

Roxy is in the kitchen putting away crockery.

'Come on, Pens,' she hisses. 'Total numbie. Save your energy.'

I dab my tears and gulp myself back to calm.

'Get what you're entitled to, then he can fuck off.' She lowers her eyes. 'After he's gone, I think you need to take Tooty to the vet. He's not really moving.'

I look at my aged feline asleep on his favourite cushion, his breathing scarcely detectable. But when I gently stroke his head, he opens his eyes and blinks slowly, a long cat kiss. The cat who would not last, the cat Stepdad Jake hated. The cat who has outlasted him, and everything else, as much as I have. Can I ever be ready to lose him?

I curse Ranjit. Tooty's frail body stirs me up. Everything is splintering into new spaces and I don't think I have the strength to manage.

Ranjit leaves after another half an hour, saying that when the time comes for me to have more funding for twenty-four-hour support, I can go on the Independent Living Fund.

The vet tells me Tooty is fine. Simply dying of old age.

I wake up vaguely anxious with thoughts of the neighbours upstairs. They've been a problem for some months, scratching my Clio and slashing my tyres. Jealous of my disabled parking space.

I stir when I hear Roxy put the key in the lock on the front door and wait to hear her greetings. Usually something like 'Wake up, tart face!', said with glee and gusto.

But there's nothing, just the noise of her feet, heavy on the carpet.

'Pen, Pen, wake up.' Her face leans over me, her eyes not quite on mine. 'I'll help you out of bed. It's Tooty.'

I don't register what she means and don't want to. I rise, bleary, silent, as Roxy helps me into a dressing gown.

Tooty is lying still on his favourite cushion, under his favourite chair. It was put there because he could no longer climb up onto anything.

His eyes are frozen slits. His tongue hangs to the side of his mouth.

He is a month away from his twentieth birthday.

'Get him up here!' I shriek and Roxy slides out the cushion and puts him onto the sofa.

I pet him over and over. He is cold. I know he is dead.

I close his eyes, gently move his legs into his body.

'Maybe a stroke?' Roxy whispers.

'My darling old boy,' I say and let myself cry. And cry. 'You did it, you chose your time, my lovely, lovely Tooty. Thank you.'

It is hard to bury him, but it's all I really want to do, quickly. Cats. I love them and their strong-willed ways. And they wreck me each and every time they die. They are never *just* cats.

I put Tooty in his favourite pink blanket, take off his collar. And stroke him.

Tooty, who made it despite Jake, who's travelled all the London years with me. A presence. A comfort.

A kind friend, Ryan, comes over to help with the burying as Roxy helps me prepare him. I smile for a heartbeat, that at least the sun is out.

I'm sobbing, on my patio, by the small flower bed as Ryan digs out the pathetic little hole. I don't want to put Tooty into it.

But I do. With his blanket, his old toy, some sprigs of the lavender he used to love to hide in.

I hear a noise. We all look up and see my trash neighbours throwing things down at me from the top floor.

'Fucking fucking bastards!' I scream. Sobs turn to anger, from somewhere, from stores of past hurts. 'Let me bury my cat in peace. You fucking dumb shit wankers!'

'Call the police. It's more harassment,' says Roxy quickly, scowling thunder up towards them. 'Fucking ignorant scum!'

'No, no,' is all I can say before weeping like it's the end of the world, as I slip into a pit of loss and pain.

Part of me wants to call Kamesh. Another part wants to call Freddie.

But another chamber inside my scattered mind doesn't want to call anyone.

Colin phones me to say we should start to do stuff around the full moon. Skyclad. Cast a circle. Call the corners. I'm a bit nervous and wonder if it will change how we work together. Most of my writing work comes through him now and I've told him about *Fancy Nancy*.

I've written a few more chapters now the disability harassment project has finished; I don't want to be that kind of writer ever again. But there is no one who will take things further; repeats about disability being 'depressing' still appear in loving rejection letters from publishers.

Work on *Nancy* almost fills the vast cavern in my heart that was Spiral Sky. Yet nothing new waves from future musical horizons, as the damage from my break-up with Freddie inevitably shakes friendships and sides are drawn. Quietly, Tone drifts out of my life, and Kaye and Gary leave London anyhow.

Tanya remains true, juggling both of us separately, and we sometimes dream about making music together. My *Jamming!* friend Zed visits me and we jam over Beatles tunes and folk. But the rift is there and my mind judders along in need of something to get my teeth into. Something with an end to it, that's complete. Another birth.

I am not sleeping well and the fog is at the window.

Madelyn pulls me back from the fog, although Dr Guinness insists I must go on Prozac as well. To take the edge off me, he says.

'You're just very super-sensitive,' Madelyn says, her calm eyes upon me. 'Let's resist any more labels than that. This sensitivity makes you who you are, Penny. Gives depths to your talents. I just want to help you ride the waves that buffer you so they don't drag you into the depths.'

'What about the Prozac? I'm a bit scared of it.' I say it in a whisper.

'Only you can say whether that will help,' she replies. Always kind, and always truthful.

I think it does. Soon the fog I'm in becomes more like a plate of glass between me and the outside world. I don't like it but I don't want to drown in that awful suffocation called anxiety.

I want to be myself again. I want to let Tooty go to join Goddess Freya on her cat-drawn chariot.

I want to go to the Algarve. And finish *Fancy Nancy*.

Roxy comes into work, as usual, key in the lock and an ebullient hello as she strides past my doorway.

I keep my eyes shut and pull the duvet higher. I am not ready for the day, not yet.

I hear Roxy bustle into my room. I don't care and bend my head into the bed. But I jump when she puts something by my chin.

It cries, a tiny little insistent noise.

The squeak of a kitten.

My eyes open as this small black fluffy thing nestles against me.

'You know you want one,' Roxy smiles. 'You're a born cat lady.'

I move so the tiny cat and me can gaze at each other. She squeals and rubs my nose before settling back down against my cheek. It's eternal love in an instant.

'Bessie,' I say, looking at Roxy. 'After Bessie Smith.'

'I told you mine was pregnant. And the amazing thing is that this is the only one who's made it.'

'We're meant to be then, aren't we?' I tickle new Bessie with a light touch on her ridiculously small nose. She blinks, mews a cute kitten mew.

'You'll look after her when I'm in the Algarve, won't you?' I say, wondering suddenly if I really want to go.

'Yes, yes, don't be silly, of course. Now let me help you up. You wanted me to iron your hair today. Fucking hell, Pen. Only you.'

A friend had told me that putting beeswax on my burgeoning dreads would help the process, along with the twisting. It hadn't worked and I want Roxy to iron them lightly onto greaseproof paper. Especially as they need to be pristine for my trip to Portugal.

I am in a great mood by the time I wake up properly. Bessie runs around my Victorian haven at a hundred miles an hour, a complete distraction from organising my day's work.

But *Fancy Nancy* grips me again. Handsome black street-fighter Gresham wants to sweep her away and protect her. But Nancy is torn, hates his bossy ways, and needs to talk to Ma Three Titties Morgan. There is a lot at stake. I have to write the scene.

I have also returned to *Cripples Fucking*. I know there's something in there waiting to get out. I begin with a new title: 'Desires'. Then – once Roxy has done her best to soak up the excess wax from my hair – I call Kamesh, pleased when he says he can visit the next day.

I settle down in front of the PC and fly back to Victorian London.

Within a few weeks the dreads recover. They are less sticky but I wonder how long I can manage them.

Roxy packs the last items in my orange suitcase, the biggest one I have owned ever. The case is new, a present from Kamesh for our trip. It's a nasty overcast day and I try to think of the warmth awaiting me within the next twenty-four hours.

I'm playing light Debussy tracks as I put in my personals. Make-up, cotton-wool balls – and gadgets, so many gadgets. For reaching, picking up – and even a rather useless one for wiping my bum. I know Kamesh has done this, I know he does not mind. But I do mind and I need a back-up.

And I love Kamesh for saying he will design a better one for us all one day.

As we cruise to the airport I let myself fall into excitement. My glee at travel flits like a butterfly over every stage of the journey.

'Don't be cross with me, Kamesh,' I say, out of nowhere. 'I've never had this life. Ever.'

'Cross about what?' He smiles at me. 'My wild little witch. Why would I be cross?'

'Because everything will excite me. The airport. The plane. I'll be pointing. A big kid.'

'I love that about you. Seeing, sharing the world through your eyes.'

I frown, but laugh. Sometimes, just sometimes he talks like a script and I don't want to be cruel. But it hangs on my tongue, ready to wind him up, in my eternal fear of being patronised. Hating a lifetime of pats on the head. There, there. That's nice for her, poor thing.

I manage to keep bouncy despite various cock-ups at the airport. We wind through the process slowly. I feel like an alien, and everyone treats me like one. A disabled woman, orange dreads and a bearded man, a giant, in hippy sandals, pushing through their rigid system.

Kamesh booked through a special disability company – at least it is owned by a disabled person – and the first concern is over fast when a man with a card is waiting for us at Faro airport, ready with a minibus.

We are driven quickly to the complex where our villa is located. I am happy to be an alien here. It's a different planet of sunny warmth and the heady smell of bougainvillaea pervasive in the air, tinged occasionally by olive oil and fish.

'I'll take you into town tomorrow,' says Kamesh. 'We'll have some *bacalhau*, salted fish. You'll love it.'

He helps me into my power chair – thankfully in one piece after the flight – and I drive into the large airy villa, floating into a sudden fairy tale. I can see the bougainvillaea as it trails around our large patio. I shriek in delight when I see a gecko on the wall.

Later we make a trip to the local supermarket. I drive around practising my *obrigado* and *obrigada*.

Kamesh buys a chicken. Freshly killed, feathers still on. He makes a huge delicious stew which settles us in. I'm pleased Kamesh has booked a maid to clean and prepare a meal occasionally, even if I'm unnerved by the idea. If nothing else, it eases my guilt about the support he has to give me every day.

Before bedtime we sit on the patio looking at the stars in the dazzling clear sky. With 'Brimful of Asha' lilting in the background from our villa.

'We'll go into the pool tomorrow,' says Kamesh, gesturing towards the hoist. 'Naked. And gaze at the sky on our backs. Before I have you in the water.'

I shiver, entranced and stirred. The cripple kid from nowhere, relishing the big adventure with the lovely giant.

'I want to enjoy every moment with you, Penny,' he continues in a low serious tone. 'Because every time I bring a woman on holiday, she always leaves me afterwards.'

I look at him and laugh, assuming this is his dry humour.

I have got my journals ready. There will be a lot to write about.

Living the naked life in the Algarve villa.

CHAPTER 22

27 April 1999: Gabriel, my eccentric, romantic, Jewish pixie boy. Muse and confidant, he has unlocked me from a self-imposed silence. He will love me into action – and into success?

Kamesh stays over at my flat on the day we return from Portugal to rest up before going to his place.

The spray from the Atlantic thundering on the beaches is still in my hair, the golden sand between my toes. I have gazed at a multitude of stars, lain naked in a plunge pool. I have been to a market, heard panpipes played by Colombians, seen an old woman crocheting on a stool – pretty woman she said, touching the eternal flower in my hair. I've been refused entry to a restaurant – not sure if it was my nippy power wheelchair, or whether it was because Kamesh and me were too scary to comprehend.

London welcomes us back heavy with fog, making even the Victorian haven seem dreary. We sit on the sofa eating takeaway pizza. Bessie hurtles around in over-excitement, climbing the curtains, balancing on the rail. I quickly nickname her 'Monkey Cat'.

'Will you marry me, Pen?' Kamesh asks suddenly. 'We could ask Roxy to go round the corner and get a bottle of champagne. If you don't mind.'

'No,' I say. 'I don't mind.'

'And?' says Kamesh, folding me into his giant arms. 'What's your answer?'

No answer will form into the white sheet of shock at the forefront of my thoughts. I don't know what to say but then I find my mouth moving. And before I know it, I say yes.

Kamesh hugs me tighter, rubs his beard over my nose that makes me sneeze and giggle.

Roxy comes back from the corner shop. I sense that she doesn't like Kamesh; she never does spell it out. As she leaves the flat in her big fur coat, clutching a rustling carrier bag, I'm distracted by a memory – that I need to ask her to help me look for some mislaid clothes.

Kamesh pulls me back to the moment, into his chest. 'We'll be happy, Penny. I promise.'

I try to relax into his love. We clink glasses and I gulp down the bubbles, shocked at myself.

'I feel it's only fair that I tell you about Demeter. She is my Basingstoke woman. I know I've explained a little, but this is most certainly the time for more.' He sits up straight and looks at me earnestly. 'I want you to see that this polyamorous relationship structure is no threat to me and you.'

I am not as shocked as I think I should be. Demeter is his older woman, a hedgewitch. He tells me she is an important presence in his life.

'Okay,' I say, keeping in neutral. 'What else is there to explain?'

'We've spoken about monogamy and polygamy. The term I prefer is polyamory. Loving the many.'

'What, biblically?' I say, stifling a laugh. 'That might be exhausting.'

After the sadness and pain of ending with Freddie, I'm not open to get bogged down in my own jealousies or the games of others. And yet, I have just agreed to marry Kamesh. The abrupt presence of my old familiar, the monster of guilt, bites me.

'Listen, I've told you, Penny.' Kamesh is serious and lifts my hand to kiss it. 'Keep the cage of love open and the bird won't fly away.'

I know when he says this he means it. He wants me to feel safe to challenge conventions. I don't really know why I'm annoyed when he talks of cages, but deep down in the dark edge of my gut I think it is because I don't believe he has really been in any.

'So I could have a man in London?' I half-joke. 'There's one or two pagans I could call up.'

I wait for him to laugh as I pose ready to pat his Buddha stomach, to tease him and scratch his deep, dark pirate beard.

But Kamesh looks at me as though I have chopped his heart in two.

'Oh, not yet, please,' he says. 'Please wait. Let us enjoy ourselves. Demeter is no threat.'

It is on my tongue to lash out: 'But you do fuck her, don't you?' Instead, I sip my champagne and wonder about a painless strategy for backtracking.

'I'm engaged,' I tell Bessie as I sleep alone the next day. 'How the fuck did that happen?'

It starts with Josh. He's a weird mixture, a posh boy from Manchester. An unlikely pagan type, in his Green Man T-shirt and old-fashioned spectacles, and very 1970s porn-star hairdo. He likes to show off about how rich he is and is very argumentative. But he is one of the most unprejudiced men I have ever met and doesn't put demands on me.

It is fun sex all the way and a shared eagerness for me to try everything. Endless positions. Nothing too vanilla. What is possible, without hurt or breaking me. No awkwardness. No hang-ups. I yearn to ride him but my knees don't bend, so we do the next best thing with me sitting on his lap, facing forward. Sometimes, just before I come, I give thanks to dreaded Dr A. My hip replacements, at least, still in reliable working order.

On one visit, he brings some bubbly, my new obsession. I manage to stand up leaning against my big high bed, between his open legs.

'Don't let me fall over,' I giggle. 'But I do want to try and give you a blowjob like this.'

We both laugh as I lean forward, my dreadlocks brushing his balls. The room spins and before I know it I am flat on my backside. Bessie bounces in, squeaks at me, then bolts over the bed. Josh looks down.

'I better help you up then, hadn't I?' he says. I'm relieved he is strong and I come out unscathed.

Dan is better looking than Josh, but not as relaxed.

He's obsessed with velvet bras. He puts his cock along my cleavage and yearns to come all over my breasts, but it never seems to happen. While I am lost in the rush of this adventure, I have a tiny qualm that his reluctance is over the old chestnut – the Lurgy. Pen, you're too fragile. I might hurt you. Oh, didn't realise you had a scar there... I need to get used to it...

But I go through a few others, almost start an affair with a woman who gets scared and I debate a swingers' party. I'm exhilarated and defiant. I've learnt a lot, caught up on lost time.

Kamesh for once seems unconcerned and I'm relieved. We have a lovely winter break on Exmoor in a B&B with an open fire, hawks flying high into the desolate landscapes that we peer at early in the morning.

There is a rupture in events when I tell him I'm still working with Colin. As in, Casting the Circle. Calling the Quarters.

'Can't you keep something back for me?' He is angry and, I fear, unreasonable. I have never judged him or questioned his views. Never questioned what he does with Demeter.

My old emotional scars throb from deep buried pasts. The ones labelled with fear. That my anger gives a permission for others to punish, an allowance to hurt.

The work I've done with Madelyn sends a breeze of cool reason through my thoughts. I try to find words. I really try.

For a while I stare at him and his anger increases, not helped by the whisky that sits by his side. I care about him, but I don't know that love has lasted.

He swept me up, the changeling cripple, taking me on marvellous capers, into the loving arms of giant Brân the Blessed.

But it is not a fairy tale; it is not love forever.

'We really shouldn't get married,' I say, quietly, and shut myself in the bedroom.

In front of the computer, *Fancy Nancy* takes my hand. We walk together through the Victorian landscape, fleeing along the ancient Ridgeway towards Avebury. With shire horses, aged lions, the conjoined twins, Binky and Bina. The sweet little twisted nightingale May Hammond. Somewhere Nancy's love awaits, within the ancient sacred circle...

It's 2 a.m. before I come back. Bessie, the clever monkey cat, has learnt how to jump on the arm of my chair and now nestles behind my bum, her careless little claws pricking me as she preens and stretches.

It is getting too near to Christmas but I've already decided the Morrissey Christmas card from 1984 will have to come out again. I am in a World Music phase and have already booked my tickets for the following year's WOMAD. I play Natacha Atlas, the *Gedida* LP, floating into the powerful Arabic sounds.

Kamesh and me are on and then off. Although, we have been off before and on again several times. I know I won't marry him. I'm sad and often think of his words about how women chuck him after he takes them on holiday.

I'm looking at my paltry bank statement when the phone rings. I shiver. Sometimes Roxy takes it but today I grab it without a second thought.

'Hello, is that Penny?' A clear, pleasant female voice. 'This is Rina from Channel 4. My director Paul Sapin and me wondered if we could talk to you about featuring in a unique documentary about sex and disabled women. We got your name from Tom Shakespeare.'

Within a few days, they have come to my flat. I am on a high from recent life-modelling and their ideas intrigue me. The project is called 'A Love Less Ordinary'. Paul is a tall, skinny man with George Clooney eyes and a marvellous New York drawl.

'We'd like to take you through your own story, Pen,' he says, and I love how relaxed he makes me feel.

'What we're wondering,' adds Rina, 'is whether your current partner would feature with you?' She laughs. 'Nothing pornographic, but we do want to make this groundbreaking. This is for the season about taboos, after all.'

I am not sure what mode Kamesh and me are in and I know there is an irony that his body image is much worse than mine. I feel doubtful that he will be interested.

'I'll ask him,' I say. 'But everything's a little tricky at the moment.'

'Don't worry,' says Rina and taps my arm. 'We can get in a lovely young actor to do some love-making sequences with you if necessary. Would you be up for that?'

I feel the world has changed – and a piercing awareness in this moment that I have too. 'I'll give it a go,' I say. 'It all sounds fun.'

I call Kamesh later but he does not answer his phone.

Christmas stumbles close and I don't know how I feel about being on my own. Tanya and Kaye say they will help as it is always a fight to get personal assistants in on holidays.

Roxy has left, suddenly – and, it appears, with lots of my wardrobe and a few other personal items. I am disturbed at this unexpected turn but Liz Carr assures me it's all good learning. It is never as clear as it seems, but next time, I must not be so trusting.

The next personal assistant I find is Looloo. A slim, energetic woman, with short hair and an amiable cockney twang. A tomboy with a clutch of kids, she has an obsession with knitting and is clever without quite knowing it. I know the lines must not blur. But she is impossibly likeable. And somehow I feel she's on my side – she's not another Roxy. At least, that's what I hope.

It's chilly on the road to Swiss Cottage and I am glad she is such a good driver. The Lurgy is pushing its presence forward in a new, if familiar, cycle that I can almost ignore. Take some more pills, maybe see Dr Brown. Have a bit of physio. Keep up with the Indica hash, though I am not able to use the bong Kamesh bought me.

'Christmas party then, Pen?' says Looloo as we coast onto the North Circular at Chingford, heading west.

'Yep, haven't been to one for ages. Any party. My friend Lesley is having it at her flat and I thought, why not?'

'As long as you know the way, I'm happy. Keep directing me though! That's not my thing.'

I laugh. Ever since hearing her say she took the A-ScoobyDoo road home, I have worked this out.

Lesley's flat is modern and not far from the busy Swiss Cottage triangle. She welcomes us in, and after Looloo helps me take off my faux fur she slips into background mode, as Liz calls it, and immerses herself in knitting.

In the lounge, music plays: the Best of Motown. I gulp back some rosé, let it lift my blood as I contemplate the other guests.

There are a few people in wheelchairs, others sit on the small sofa. Meandering about us all with a white cane is a young man in an oversized coat and Russian hat. I smile. He smiles back at me.

The rosé and the music make me happy. I start to dance, my own little hand jive, and shimmy my breasts.

'I'm Gabriel Pepper. I'm Jewish.'

He says it as if stating he is the king, as if not expecting an answer.

'I'm Penny. I'm a witch.' I carry on waving my hands, my blue velvet bra peeping over the top of my silver lurex dress.

Gabriel taps his cane to the music and contemplates my answer with the barest hint of a smile. But his eyes tell me something else.

'I've had two brain tumours. I live over in Woodford.'

I stop mid-hand jive and tug up the collar of my dress.

'No you don't. You're winding me up.' I look at him intensely, his irises the colour of tiger's eye.

And they move – fast – in multiple directions.

'Yes,' he says. 'My eyes. They wobble.'

I laugh.

'I do live in Woodford,' he goes on. 'I'll show you my Freedom Pass.'

He starts to rummage inside the pockets of his oversized jacket.

I'm curious and want to know more. 'Come and talk to me in

the kitchen, it's too noisy in here.'

I smile to myself when he takes hold of the handle of my wheelchair to steady his progress out of the room. Crips always help crips.

I've bought my glass of rosé with me. 'Don't you want anything?' I say as I sip it.

'I don't drink, Penny. I do other things. If you come on the patio with me, I'll show you.'

'That sounds very cheeky and forward, Gabriel,' I say. 'You're not going to pounce, are you?'

'I'm a gentleman, Penny.' He smiles and I like it. I like it even more when he takes off his anorak and poorly fitting hat.

'That's better. I can see Gabriel now.' I emphasise his name the way that he is emphasising mine. He is dressed in clothes that are either old-fashioned – shirt, trousers, braces, stripy tank top – or making an unknowing vintage-tinged fashion statement. His hair is short, shaved at the sides. A fading scar runs down the back of his head.

'Look at this, Penny.' He shows me his Freedom Pass with his name and address. A thrill of spooky shock makes me murmur. He lives about a hundred metres from my Victorian haven.

'That's weird,' is all I can say. 'An amazing coincidence. Especially to meet you here, in Swiss Cottage.'

'No, Penny.' Gabriel points his finger to emphasise his words, and his face takes on a cheeky determined look. 'It's not coincidence. It's Fate and Destiny. These things happen to me.'

'They happen to me too,' I say. 'Now, are we going out on the patio or not?'

Gabriel stands up, steadies himself with one hand, fiddles in the coat pocket with the other, and brings out a lighter.

'I hope you indulge, Penny,' he twinkles. 'I do like my 'biss. As in canna...'

I'm sleepy by the time I get home, stomach sluicing like a drain with too much rosé and not enough food. I think a little bit about Gabriel, who is twenty-six, an archaeologist, and who lives round the corner.

And when a card comes through my door the next morning, I'm flattered and a little bit perplexed.

Penny,
I think you are awesome.
Gabriel

Kamesh takes me for dinner but I know we have no future. I am sad and don't want to hurt him, but as always guilt sticks in my craw.

'You know I can't do this TV thing.' He looks at me, lowers his eyes to poke around in his duck breast. 'You mustn't be gullible. It's all about exploitation. People having a laugh over the big fat guy.'

I ache for him and how weird it is that I, as his changeling cripple, with the Lurgy and my supposedly odd body, have no worries.

'They're really great people, Kamesh. This isn't some awful fly-on-the-wall documentary. It's a genuine examination about disabled women and sex.' The words feel unsettling. I am not so strong that I don't need the flames of my own confidence to be fanned – a lot.

'I drive down to the hotel in Maidenhead tomorrow, with Looloo. Shooting starts at 8 a.m., at my old hospital, Beechwood. It's completely derelict now. That'll be unnerving.'

We are silent for a few minutes as if we have suddenly nothing else to say. I know I will always love him but the romance was brief, a magnificent catalyst that has taken me to places I never imagined.

Kamesh pays the bill, as always dismissing my offers to contribute.

As I prepare for bed with Looloo's help that evening, I decide to write him a goodbye letter.

A thank-you letter. A letter which I hope will release him – into a place where he is happier with himself.

I put Looloo on overtime so I can go to the location for the shoot. She handles my Clio smoothly as I navigate west along the A40, on a journey I haven't done in a very long time. I see the Paddington flyovers in reverse, pierced with memories of Stepdad Jake abusing the masses.

We coast along to the hotel where the crew are waiting. Rina takes me to one side and shows me the shooting schedule for the next day. It is suddenly very scary and I feel nerves nibbling around my insides.

Eight o'clock on a cold bright winter's morning. Somehow, I have made it. I am wearing my long velvet dress and over it my heavy Bet Lynch effort of fake leopard print. My dreadlocks feel cold and stiff in the chill air.

Paul comes out to greet me with a peck on the cheek. 'Hey Penny, all ready?' he says. 'The guys are setting up dolly tracks in the main corridor. We think there's enough space for you to do your piece to camera as you move along it.'

'Just tell me when to start.'

'Yeah, Pen.' Paul crouches down to be on my eye level. 'You were here for a long time when you were a kid. Good memories? Bad memories? Tell us the stories.'

I nod as a crew member hands me a coffee in a takeaway cup.

The old hospital falls down around me and ghosts scream from every corner, hiding under the debris. Built like a barracks with rows and rows of wards, it smells of decay and I'm disturbed as they film me along the corridor, where, aged eleven, I giggled with Janis on the way to physiotherapy. Or aged thirteen, pushed back in an antiquated chair, by a grey middle-aged porter with dirty hands he'd put where he shouldn't.

I am surprised when we are done and surprised, when I stop listening to the ghosts, that I have enjoyed myself.

'We'll be in touch,' says Rina. 'We'll let you know when we have a transmission date. And before then we'll need to do publicity shots. Preferably with your partner. Would he be okay with that?'

My thoughts, always contrary, are sad. But quickly pleased.

'I don't have a partner at the moment,' I say. 'But I think I know someone who might do it very soon.'

Gabriel courts me with cassette tapes, dropping them through my letterbox on a daily basis on his way out to University College London, where he attempts to complete his PhD in medieval archaeology.

He goes for brevity: three Bowie tracks, my favourite being 'Lady Grinning Soul'; four from William Orbit's *Strange Cargo*, with a two-word note – '*Penny, unnerving!*'

He outdoes this on Valentine's Day, arriving with two cassettes, one classical, the other about as mixtape as you can get. A card of a cat. And a single white rose. The more he visits, the more I lose my worry at the twelve-year age gap between us.

On his fourth appearance for dinner, I observe that he is picking over his pasta.

'Not hungry today?'

'It's not that, Penny.' He narrows his eyes and pulls a very particular face, followed by the finger in the air. 'I don't really like pasta.'

'Gabriel! Why didn't you tell me?' I laugh, having assumed his previous gusto meant the opposite.

'I'm a gentleman, Penny, I've told you.' He puts down his finger and beholds me with his deep brown eyes. 'Now are we going to have a kiss or what?'

We do kiss and I like it. He comes back two nights later and I do him a chicken stir-fry with Looloo's help. He eats every scrap and promises this is not only politeness. And then, after sharing a spliff, we go to bed. I hush him as he apologises for his terrible scars from his brain tumour treatment.

'None of that in this house, Gabriel,' I tease. 'You hook up with me and it's all pride against prejudice. The crip revolution.'

'Right dear,' he grins, an imp with naughty, eager fingers. 'If you say so, but let me take your knickers off.'

At first we struggle with sex and can't find our own way. His shitty balance makes him nervous and we almost fall off the bed a few times. But we manage, of course. I feel happy, emerging out of many months of chaos. We fit together well in the bed, and in our heads.

I get divorce papers from Freddie.

I do the necessary as quickly as I can. Not happy. Not sad. Relieved to have closure.

Fancy Nancy has languished but at last I have set her free. Three hundred and ten pages sit in front of me. I stare at the pile until Looloo comes in, asks me what I am planning for dinner.

'Gabriel's coming over,' I say. 'We might just do pizza.'

I fall silent. I am not sure if Nancy is ready for the world. I know I am doing something different but there are still not many disabled heroes and Nancy is someone who laughs and cries and fucks her way through two timelines. Working out where she belongs and who she is. I ache with tiredness and, even while I am proud, an instinct tells me there is a long way to go.

There is a knock on the door, Gabriel tapping a pattern with his white cane. Bessie shoots into the hall, meowing and jumping onto the arm of my chair for a ride. Gabriel comes in, showing off a new haircut, the shaved areas of his head maximising the areas of hair loss from his radiotherapy. We kiss and I detect the fresh sap of spring has come inside the Victorian haven with him. He visits so often, walking the hundred metres from his father's house, that he may as well be living here.

'Penny,' he says, with a smile and a raised finger, 'what are you doing tomorrow? If you've nothing planned, I thought we could go to Waltham Abbey and the water meadows.' He narrows his eyes. 'Pleasant spot. Decent archaeology.'

'Sounds like a lovely idea,' I say, 'but remember Looloo only works for me until 3 p.m.'

'Yes dear.' I know he is pleased and I'm eager that we settle down on the sofa with food and music. 'And by the way,' he adds, with no preamble, 'I think you should become a Penny Pepper.'

Rina from the production company tells me that *A Love Less Ordinary* will be broadcast soon and of course she will let me know. But she's caught me on the wrong day. I can't think about it; I am immersed in preparations.

Maggie, a friend of Looloo's, has cut off all my dreadlocks, which had turned into half-twisted scraggy nothings, although I keep one inside a journal. My hair is short, cerise, and Maggie has pinned the flower Baby's Breath throughout it. Looloo, as skilled with sewing as she is with knitting, has fashioned Gabriel and me complementary robes. I wear a fitted bodice in black with a raggedy handkerchief hem. The material is a deep pinkish-purple and, like Gabriel's, which is a blueish, mauve lurex, it comes from the best sari shops in East Ham.

I fly in a dream to the registry office at Redbridge, Gabriel beside me.

I am scared and hold his hand, calmed by his long, fine fingers which once played a violin.

A happy day: I become Penny Pepper.

The registry office is overflowing with the crazy mixture of our friends and Gabriel's archaeology colleagues. My mum meets Gabriel's mum.

There is a part of me, the familiar, doubting unhappy child that whispers in my ear. Madelyn has helped me soothe her, but as everyone crams into the main room for the ceremony, I allow myself a throb of nerves. Am I doing the right thing? I know Gabriel is extraordinary. I know we love each other. And I know his belief in me is absolute.

The words are being said. I say yes. Gabriel looks at me and I hear him say, 'Well, if I must.' He squeezes my hand and slips on the silver knotwork ring, a nod to Jewish tradition. The great gathering cheers. My mum cries.

We hurry back to my haven. Looloo does us proud. There is a banner of congratulations, the cards displayed on the fine mantelpiece, piles of sandwiches and a cake with white icing.

'Dance! Dance!' a friend shouts and, in his methodical way, Gabriel goes over to the CD player and returns as Bob Marley's 'One Love' lifts from the speakers like an embrace. We don't dance very well, we make up our own, with Gabriel leaning over me in my wheelchair, underlining the similarity in our height.

'Love you, Gabriel Pepper,' I whisper. He squeezes himself against me. 'Love you, Penny Pepper,' he whispers back. Then stands up, finds his white cane. 'You know we're going to travel the country, Pen,' he says, as the guests chat and eat and look at our cards.

'I know, we'll get our personal-assistant issue sorted and then we can fly.'

Gabriel looks at me and then around the room as if seeing it for the first time. 'Look at that,' he says, with his finger pointing, the *Spiral Sky* album, visible behind two cards and nestling beside the first, now framed, postcard from Morrissey. 'This is the beginning, Pen. You know what you are, don't you?' His face is serious and I feel like the guests are listening. I blush, but I look at him knowing that I love him, that I am going somewhere new, again. 'You, dear, are a catalyst and a conduit for change,' he says.

'If you say so,' I tease. 'I'd rather be Penny Pepper. Scribbler, Siren, Saucepot. Pioneer!'

I look around us. Our lounge is bursting with people.

Gabriel sits on my lap for a bit, then mingles. Laughter lights up the space.

There's my mum, Gabriel's parents, a room full of friends. So many true friends.

Tears well in my eyes.

I think of those who are not here – all the way back to Laura and Daddy.

Tamsin.

It's November. No daffodils.

But my sadness passes. The room is loved up – for me.

This is where – yes – I'm truly first in the world somewhere.

ACKNOWLEDGEMENTS

First in the World Somewhere has journeyed through a long gestation, just as my creative life has gone through twists and turns. My gratitude is big and wide and slushy. To my supporters – some I know, some I don't – who made this memoir happen, your loyalty will be appreciated always.

I thank the beautiful people at Unbound, who have been unfailing in their commitment to this book and a delight to work with. Also thanks to Kate Murray-Browne for the most stalwart and inspired editing, holding my hand to the end. There's my brother in words, friend and mentor Dr John O'Donoghue, whose involvement has ranged from soothing my wayward mental health to chewing the literary cud in the cheapest pub in town – love and thanks bro. Many thanks and love also to Bethany Pitts for surviving the hands-on task of typing but so much more – organising and managing me on a day to day basis – without Beth, no memoir!

Heartfelt thanks go to The Literary Consultancy – to Aki Schilz for being such a solid advocate, and to the late Becky Swift, in sadness and love, as the instigator of my relationship with Unbound. Becky championed me for over four years and believed passionately in bringing untold stories into the heart of literature. I hope that I've repaid her unflinching faith in my work with this memoir.

My close friends – Liz Carr, Tanya, Kaye, Jo Cox and Janet Raven (warhorse!) to name a few whose shoulders I've cried on, not forgetting my seaside beloved Kevin and good buddy and ex-husband Gabriel!

My family of course, some of whom are in the book, I thank for their understanding, especially my big brother Ant and my darling beautiful Mummy, Shirley. I'll end with thanks, gratitude and love for Tamsin who I hope every reader will grow to love too. She helped me on the path that set me free.

SUPPORTERS

Unbound is a new kind of publishing house. Our books are funded directly by readers. This was a very popular idea during the late eighteenth and early nineteenth centuries. Now we have revived it for the internet age. It allows authors to write the books they really want to write and readers to support the books they would most like to see published.

The names listed below are of readers who have pledged their support and made this book happen. If you'd like to join them, visit www.unbound.com.

Tim Abbott
Geoff Adams-Spink
Jez Aitchison
Mark Aldron
Helen Aveling
Michelle Baharier
charles@barraball.com Barraball
Xaverine Bates
Liz Bentley
Sue Bodkin
Emma Boyes
Phil Brachi
Andrew Bruce
Pauline Buck-Evans
Suzanne Bull
Geoff Burton

Dame Jane Campbell
Bernise Carolino
Liz Carr
Sophie Churchill
Ellen Clifford
Stephanie Cohen
Robin Coles
Mandy Colleran
Sheila Cook
Anne E Cooper
Sarah Corrie
Jo-anne Cox
Liz Crow
Janis Crowder
Claire Cunningham
Cornelia Daheim

DAiSY (Disability Arts
  in Surrey)
Paul Darke
Natalya Dell
Les Dodd
Edward Doegar
Peter Driver
Sebastiaan Eldritch-Böersen
Helen Evans
Richard Farhall
Jen Farrant
Julian Fiorentini
Aldo Framingo
Mat Fraser
Naomi Frisby
Richard Gerrell
Jennifer Goddard
Kevin Gostelow
Steve Graby
Elaine Green
Helen Hadden
Karen Halvey
Colin Hambrook
Lisa Hammond
Esther Harris
Bozena Harvey
HAVE (Hastings Access to
  Venues and Entertainment)
Tina Hawkes
Fran Healey
Tony Heaton
Enid Hedgehog
Maria Herbert-Liew
David Hevey
Graham Hodge

Jessica Hodge
Theresa Hodge
Martin Hodgson
Christopher Holt
John Hosken
Cherylee Houston
Kelly Humphreys
Pat Hynes
Sara Jai
Claire Jeffrey
Lara Jephson
Helen Johnson
Gwyneth Jones
Jess Mabel Jones
Tracy Jones
Caroline Juler
Lois Keith
Esther Kempson
Angela Kennedy
Laura Kenwright
Angela Kiely
Dan Kieran
Tash Kingston
Warren Kingston
Grace Kitto
June Knight
Christopher John Laudan
Rastko Lazic
Eleanor Lisney
Emma Love
Kate Lovell
Heather Mack
Carrie Mackinnon
Mike Mantin
Juliet Marlow

Tess Marsh
Rebecca Maskos
Janet Mason
Carol McGuigan
Stephanie Mchugh
Erol-antony McKenzie
Dave McQuirk
Maggie Mills
Mave Mills
Simon Minty
John Mitchinson
Stephanie Mole
Lieve Monnens
Melissa Moore
Antoinette Morris
Bill Morris
Rachel Morris
Melissa Mostyn
Kate Nash
Carlo Navato
New Writing South
John O'Donoghue
John Paul O'Neill
Anthony Oates
Ken Olisa
Corbett Joan OToole
Grace Over
Michael Paley
Richard Parker
Sophie Partridge
Carol Payne
Gabriel Pepper
Penny Pepper
Auntie Mary Peppiatt
Joanne Piper

Bethany Pitts
Sarah Playforth
Justin Pollard
Jennifer Porrett
Suzanne Porter
John Pring
Francis Pryor
Katharine Quarmby
Dennis Queen
Melance Radley
Janet Raven
Anna Ricciardi
Sylvie Richards
Cheryl Robson
Kate Rosie
Clair Ross
Jacquel Runnalls
Bernadette Russell
Laura Russell
S I
Kaye Sayer-Mayers
Aki Schilz
Marianne Scobie
Dolly Sen
Jan Sensier
Zarir Sethna
Tom Shakespeare
Richard Sheehan
Mum Shirley
Hazel Simmons
Marc Skeldon
Fiona Smith
Paula Smith
Shelley Smith
Deborah Soal

Mike Steel
Becky Swift
Nick Tapp
Lillian Taylor
Karen Thomas
Simone Toor
Catherine Towner
Kev Towner
Kevin and James Towner
Bertie Tweed
Nick Upson
Con van der Ham
Sian Vasey
Kristina Veasey
Jo Verrent
Sasha Vodnik

Mariz Voesenek
Regina Volkmer
Simon Waters
Sandra Watson
Simon Webb
George West
Sian Williams
Bob Williams-Findlay
Naomi Woddis
Jo Woolnough
Tony Wright
Robert Wyatt
Ros Wynne-Jones
Dr John Yeadon
Jane Young
Rob Young